The Japanese "New Woman"

The Japanese "New Woman"

IMAGES OF GENDER AND MODERNITY

DINA LOWY

Rutgers University Press
New Brunswick, New Jersey, and London

Library of Congress Cataloging-in-Publication Data

Lowy, Dina, 1966–
     The Japanese "new woman" : images of gender and modernity / Dina Lowy.
         p. cm.
     Includes bibliographical references and index.
     ISBN-13: 978-0-8135-4045-0 (hardcover : alk. paper)
     ISBN-13: 978-0-8135-4046-7 (pbk. : alk. paper)
   1. Feminism—Japan.   2. Women—Japan—History.   I. Title.
HQ1762.L68 2007
305.420952'09041—dc22   2006024862

A British Cataloging-in-Publication record for this book is available from the British Library.

Manufactured in the United States of America

To my "new men," Len Lowy and David Heinzelmann

CONTENTS

PREFACE

I learned of the existence of the women who form the backbone of this work—the Seitō women—during my first year in graduate school. Even though I was an Asian Studies major as an undergraduate, I began my graduate studies unaware that women were engaged in gender debates and feminist activity in early-twentieth-century Japan. I was fascinated to discover this alternative to the stereotype of the "submissive" Japanese woman. As I began to study the writings and activities of these women, I realized that they were part of a large picture. They were connected with the international phenomenon known as New Women, yet they were also distinctively Japanese. Like their international counterparts, these New Women were an intrinsic part of their nation's modernizing process. I wanted to understand them in this context, and my dissertation topic began to take shape.

Two graduate programs and three teaching positions later, I am still captivated by Japan's New Women. This book was a long time in the making. My aim was to produce an account of these women and their place in Japanese history that would be both of value to the Japan specialist and intelligible to a lay audience. In particular, I wanted to provide college undergraduates with an introduction to Japan's New Women, the gender debates surrounding them, and their importance in Japan's modern history, a story that was not available to me as an undergraduate. To facilitate exploration of these topics, I have chosen to rely mostly on secondary sources available in English. An extensive literature on these topics exists in Japanese, and I have cited those works that have most aided me in my research; but many fine sources have not made their way into this book. Most of the primary sources I use are available only in Japanese, but people are currently hard at work on translations to help remedy this situation. Throughout this book, translations from the Japanese are mine unless otherwise noted. When I give the English translation of a newspaper or magazine article title in the text, I provide the original Japanese in an endnote.

This book would never have been completed without a tremendous amount of support and encouragement. Jan Bardsley was there from the start and helped me formulate my dissertation topic. Her enthusiasm throughout the years has never waned and has helped to keep me going. The faculty, staff, and graduate students in the Rutgers University History Department provided a supportive and stimulating environment in which to pursue my research. I want to thank my advisor, Don Roden, for believing in me and my project. He, Bonnie Smith, Dorothy Ko, and Kathy Uno shared their extensive knowledge and guided me with patience and compassion through the trying process of completing a dissertation. Fellow graduate students Kim Brodkin, Karen Balcom, Serena Zabin, Dana Capell, Jennifer Brier, and Sidney Pash provided much appreciated friendship, inspiration, insights, criticism, and good food.

The friendship and intelligence of Pamela Abee-Taulli and Christienne Hinz helped me through a hard, but productive, year at the Inter-University Center for Japanese Language Studies in Yokohama, Japan. Sumiko Otsubo and Rumi Yasutake, as copanelists, made my first major conference presentation enjoyable and made me think about my topic in new ways. I have also benefited from the encouragement, enthusiasm, and expertise of Barbara Sato, Barbara Molony, and Sally Hastings.

My research would not have been possible without the wonderful collections and helpful assistance I had access to at Princeton University and Rutgers University in the United States, and at the National Diet Library, Tokyo University's Meiji Shinbun Zasshi Bunko, Tokyo Women's Plaza, Kansai University, Osaka University, and Wings Kyoto in Japan. I would also like to thank Otsuki Shoten Publishers, especially Kawakami Yūichi, and Fuji Publishing Company for allowing me to reproduce illustrations for this book.

Gettysburg College has provided a supportive atmosphere for me as both a teacher and a scholar. Start-up funds when I first arrived enabled me to purchase for Musselman Library the reprints of *Seitō* and Hiratsuka Raichō's *Chōsakushū,* sources vital to my research. The library's solid collection proved helpful, and the interlibrary-loan staff filled in the gaps with amazing speed. A Gettysburg College Research and Professional Development Grant allowed me to spend three weeks in Japan pursuing additional research. And a one-semester pretenure leave provided me with the time to work on revisions and to complete the manuscript. My History Department colleagues have made me feel welcome and valued. I am particularly grateful for the friendship and good advice I have received from Bill Bowman, Tim Shannon, Magdalena Sanchez, and Carla Pavlick. Work-study students helped with many of the little details. I especially thank Holly Hannema and Jonathan Lore. In Eleanor Hogan I have found an amazing colleague, a kindred spirit, a sister.

Rutgers University Press has made the process of completing a first book as painless as possible. I would like to thank Melanie Halkias for believing this project should see the light of day, Kendra Boileau for making sure it did, and Marilyn Campbell for guiding me through to publication.

My Japanese home-stay families have enriched my life and my studies by opening their homes and hearts to me. The Shimadas in Tokyo—Tomio, Yasuko, Seiko, Ayako, and Takako—took me in as a high school student and sparked my interest in Japan. The Obayashis in Osaka—Motohiko, Kimie, and Yukie—were the best part of my semester abroad in college. They have all been to the United States, and they continue to provide me with a home away from home in Japan. Seiko, her husband, Satō Hironori, and daughter, Yui, continued the tradition into the next generation by welcoming my son and me into their home during my most recent research trip. I cannot thank them all enough for their generosity and willingness to embrace me and mine as family.

I offer a general thank you to my wonderful friends. Those of you who listened to me whine and complain, who made me laugh, who provided much-needed distractions, who cheered me on, who provided meals and play dates for my family to tide them over while I was busy working—you have all made this possible.

I truly would never have finished this without the love, support, and encouragement I received from my family. They never stopped believing in me. My parents, Rita and Len Lowy, taught me I could do and be anything and always stood beside me as I pursued my dreams. My brother, Brett, sister-in-law, Rikki, and their children, Mark, Meri, and Mia, have provided a steady flow of love, support, and comic relief. My aunt and uncle, Lillian and Len Simon, provided me with financial support and my own personal cheering section. Cousin Debbie Simon has waited a long time to finally get to celebrate with me over some serious sushi. My in-laws, Lee and Fred Heinzelmann, helped me keep my sanity by teaching me to play bridge. I have asked my husband, David Heinzelmann, for patience, understanding, support, and love. He has given me everything I have needed, and so much more. Our children, Drew and Kim, are a source of wonder and delight. I thank you all for supporting my career and making my life so rich.

Chapter 2 is a slightly reworked version of my article "Nora and the New Woman: Visions of Gender and Modernity in Early Twentieth Century Japan," *U.S.-Japan Women's Journal* 26 (2004): 75–97.

The Japanese "New Woman"

CHAPTER 1

New Women, Gender, and Modernizing Japan

The day the mountains move has come.
Even though I say this, people don't believe me.
The mountains have been asleep for a long time,
But in days of old they all danced with fire.
It is fine if you don't believe this.
But, people, please believe:
All the sleeping women are now awake and moving.[1]

*T*his poem appeared on the first pages of the first issue of the Japanese women's magazine *Seitō* in September 1911. Yosano Akiko, the already-famous poet and writer, penned these lines to celebrate (and help legitimate) the groundbreaking new magazine, produced by women for women. Her choice of imagery was fitting and familiar but also fearsome in a land with much volcanic activity. She evoked a distant past, when women produced a great deal of Japan's classical literature, even as she announced a fresh eruption of female talent and activity. This image of newly awakened women was not only exciting and full of possibility but also ambiguous and potentially dangerous. In this brief but powerful poem, Yosano heralded the arrival of Japan's New Women, noted people's skepticism, and hinted at the controversy that would ensue.

As Japan entered the twentieth century, the government and various intellectuals worked actively to (re)define acceptable gender roles as part of a continuing effort to create a strong national identity. The resulting debate in the government, schools, and media over the proper role of women in the family and in society was referred to as the "Woman Problem." At first this reevaluation of gender was carried out by men, but women soon became actively involved as well. In the 1910s, a group of well-educated, upper-middle-class women gathered in Tokyo to create the feminist literary organization the Seitōsha and its journal *Seitō*.[2] These women used *Seitō* as a means of expressing themselves, testing new ideas about women, and challenging old assumptions. Their unconventional lives and writings made them pivotal in the Woman Problem debate as representatives of Japan's New Woman.

The New Woman was a widely used international term. Although the specific outlook and activities of the New Woman varied from country to country, a common characteristic was a heightened awareness of self and of gender distinctions, which led to changing views on such issues as marriage, sexuality, and fertility. The New Woman was also associated with a renewed sense of community for women through college, clubs, or reform or suffrage organizations, and an enhanced sense of worth stemming from women's active engagement in society.[3] Seitō women embodied many of these features but also exhibited variations specific to the Japanese context.

I draw on Seitō women and their writings as a window into a turbulent period in Japanese history, a time when Japan was experiencing upheavals caused by rapid industrialization, modernization, and Westernization. This analysis of the New Woman and her image will shed new light on Japan's modernizing process and demonstrate the importance of gender to the larger historical narrative. I contend that the discourse surrounding the New Woman—and especially the Seitōsha as the representative group—was a means of negotiating the effects of Japan's rapid modernization.[4] Inherent in Japan's push for modernization were two often conflicting desires: the desire to construct the Japanese as a people and as a nation and the desire to be recognized as a civilized and modern state by the West.[5] The anxiety created by these goals is evident in contemporary mainstream definitions of femininity and masculinity. Stated simply, women were supposed to be receptacles of tradition and "good wives and wise mothers" (*ryōsai kenbo*), while men were to adopt Western appearance (hair styles and clothing), thought, and statesmanship. In this way both sexes supported the modern state. But what did it mean when women wanted to be more "modern" than the "good wife, wise mother" role prescribed? Was this desire viewed as progress or as an indication of the evils wrought by modernity?

These questions and the tensions between the "Japanese" and the "modern" were explored in the New Woman debate. Various men and women contributed through actions and words to the construction of this debate. Their often differing goals reveal an assortment of power relations and concerns. Government officials, educators, and intellectuals prioritized the family system, the emperor, and imperialist expansion. These goals required that women know their proper (i.e., subordinate) role in the family and produce and raise sons to serve the nation. Other intellectuals and artists contributed to the debate as a result of their experimentation with Western concepts of the self and individualism. Some men encouraged the activities of New Women as a way of legitimating new space and freedoms for themselves. Others truly believed in equality of the sexes as a fundamental modern quality. Even the New Women varied in their actions and goals. The range of participants in the debate, the differing images of the New Woman, and the divergent visions of what would benefit the Japanese state and individual reveal much about how a nation contends with the modernizing process.

Historical Overview

The New Woman debate did not emerge spontaneously in early-twentieth-century Japan. Rather, it was the culmination of decades of contestation over appropriate gender roles in a modernizing nation.[6] The Meiji period (1868–1912), a time of great upheaval and change, began with the destruction of the centuries-old semifeudal Tokugawa military government and the reopening of trade with the West. Traditional class distinctions (samurai, farmer, artisan, merchant) were abolished, and the government advocated elementary education for all children. The road to success seemed open to anyone. In the 1870s and 1880s, two movements emerged that promoted liberal ideas: the Enlightenment movement, which attempted to "civilize" Japan through the introduction of Western scientific, technological, and social concepts, and the Freedom and People's Rights movement, which sought broad political participation for men and women, a representative government, and a constitution. Both movements helped generate a serious discussion of the position of women and a reevaluation of gender roles.[7] Meiji Japan initially seemed to offer new opportunities for everyone, but it soon proved to be a restrictive society, particularly for women.

The Meiji government also devoted itself to achieving two main objectives: national strength and security, and international recognition as a modern nation. Policies designed to meet these aims included the development of strategic industries, the formation of a conscript army, the creation of a constitutional monarchy based on a uniform code of civil law, and foreign expansion. In the late 1880s, a backlash against indiscriminate borrowing from the West resulted in a renewed emphasis on Shinto ideology—now recast as an "invented tradition"—and on Confucian ideology, which stressed hierarchical structures and social order.[8]

Concomitant with these conservative moves came profound changes in government policies toward women. In 1890, the year of the first Diet session, women were excluded from politics by the Law on Associations and Meetings (Shūkai Oyobi Kessha Hō), which made women subject to fines or imprisonment for organizing a political association, joining a political group, or attending a political meeting. These restrictions were reasserted in 1900 as Article 5 of the Public Peace Police Law (Chian Keisatsu Hō).[9] In addition, the Civil Code of 1898 established the family, or *ie,* system, which emphasized the authority of the household over the individual and firmly entrenched women in a subordinate position within the family. The historian Sharon Sievers summarized some of the code's restrictions on women: "Only men could claim posterity; only men were legally recognized persons. Married women were not able to bring legal action independently; they were classified in the same category as the 'deformed and the mentally incompetent' in the code. Husbands were totally free to dispose of their wives' property as they liked. . . . Adultery, as before, was a punishable offense only in the case of wives."[10] With the establishment of a constitutional monarchy and the enactment of the Civil Code in 1898, Meiji leaders created a family-state ideology in order to provide stability and mobilize the Japanese people in support of modernization. Women were supposed to accept this system for the sake of the nation.[11]

The family system was accompanied by the emerging Meiji feminine ideal of "good wife, wise mother." Starting in the late 1890s, training the "good wife, wise mother" became the main thrust of women's education. The government and some educators advocated domestic science and Japanese ethics as the standard curriculum for girls' higher schools in order to train women for service to the state as mothers and cultivators of future citizens. Much like the Republican Mother in the early United States, the Japanese "good wife, wise mother" publicly served her nation through her private—and now respected—roles within the family.[12]

Like most ideologies, "good wife, wise mother" was not monolithic but multifaceted. The idea incorporated the image of the Confucian-inspired, submissive, self-sacrificing mother and wife, the woman who contributes to the nation through her efforts in the home, and the rational homemaker.[13] Historians Sharon Nolte and Sally Ann Hastings draw a distinction between the Western "cult of domesticity" and the Japanese "cult of productivity." They argue that the Japanese government promoted a feminine ideal that would contribute to economic growth by emphasizing frugality, hard work, and productivity along with modesty and submissiveness.[14] Historian Kathleen Uno suggests that the "good wife, wise mother" was a mixture of old and new. On one hand, the "good wife" was a throwback to the samurai Confucian ideal of the obedient wife and daughter-in-law responsible for the smooth running of the household but morally and mentally unfit to exercise responsibility for child-rearing. On the other hand, the concept of the "wise mother" derived from Western ideas influencing Japanese Enlightenment thought and stipulated that a woman should receive a well-rounded education so that she could raise children properly and interact comfortably with her educated male counterparts.[15]

Some women viewed "good wife, wise mother" as a sign of modern progress. Women were being assigned a public—albeit domestic—role that required a commitment to women's education, however narrowly defined. Conservative female educators like Hatoyama Haruko and Shimoda Utako embraced these advances in women's status. "Good wife, wise mother" gave women respected roles within the family and the nation. More radical women saw "good wife, wise mother" as yet another way government was limiting women's activities in the name of national well-being. Women were to be the site of stability amidst much change. Japanese women would continue to struggle for improved status both within and against the "good wife, wise mother" ideology throughout the twentieth century.[16] The New Woman and her representatives in the Seitōsha presented a major challenge to the state-sponsored position on women.

By 1905 Japan had achieved the external trappings of a modern state. Industrialization was well underway and the unequal treaties with Western nations were repealed. Japan gained recognition and territory in the international arena through two successful military campaigns: the Sino-Japanese War of 1894–1895 and the Russo-Japanese War of 1904–1905. Outwardly Meiji Japan had national sovereignty and international recognition, but uncertainty about national identity and the meaning of modernity still remained. From 1905 to 1932 Japan embarked on a period historians have labeled "Taishō Democracy."[17] Expanded (male) political participation, social reform, increased educational opportunities for both sexes, and the growth of the media and an urban middle class characterized the period. Meiji's legacy of censorship, the barring of women from politics, and the confining marriage and family systems survived as well. Nonetheless, certain male writers, beginning with Kitamura Tōkoku and Takayama Chogyū, gradually transformed the intellectual discourse from an emphasis on self-sacrifice for the sake of the nation to the recognition of self and concern with private interest. H. D. Harootunian sees this not only as a shift toward individualism but also as a search for a "new model of social order." In particular, he refers to the women's movement, free love, naturalism, and socialism in the context of "a new political consciousness" and "new conceptions of community."[18]

This shift from self-sacrifice to self-awareness helped create an atmosphere in which the New Woman debate could surface. The concept of individualism originated in the self-help ideologies of the early Meiji school system and gained further momentum with the Japanese Romantic movement in the late 1880s and 1890s. It emerged as a central concern of social critics in the aftermath of the Russo-Japanese War. The Japanese naturalist movement lasted roughly from 1900 to 1910 and embodied the quest for truth and the search for the individual. Its object was self-discovery. Toward this end, naturalist writers employed the technique of detailed description of the world around them and of themselves. Indicating some of the unrest underlying Meiji society, themes in this writing ranged from life among the lower classes and struggles with family and society to disillusionment and sexual desire. A yearning for reform led to criticism of the existing marriage and family system, with its patriarchal domination and its subordination of women.[19] In an ironic twist, Western concepts of individualism, naturalism, and liberalism were being used to "modernize" Japanese literature and at the same time to critique Japan's early efforts at modernization.

Naturalist men and Seitō women had much in common: the search for inner awakening and personal freedom, and a desire for social change. Nonetheless, the literary historian Janice Bardsley contends that their motivations for writing differed. The men were trying to remove themselves from society, and the women were trying to enter it.[20] Naturalist men were searching for meaning and fulfillment outside the public paths—economic, bureaucratic, or militaristic—deemed masculine. At the same time, many women turned to writing and other artistic pursuits as a means of personal expression and also as one of the few avenues to public recognition and contact and, in many cases, to economic support and freedom. Literary and artistic expression provided a space that was both public and private, a space where men and women could negotiate and experiment with their relationships to modernity, each other, and society.

Japan's New Women

Japanese women's activism in the modern period did not begin with the Seitōsha. The Meiji period witnessed Japan's emergence as a modern nation, and it also provided a legacy of feminist activity. An emphasis on equality, rights, and political participation drew women to the Freedom and People's Rights movement in the 1880s. Kusunose Kita, a widowed household head, argued for political rights to match her status. Kishida Toshiko gave public lectures throughout the country that criticized the family system and argued for women's education and rights. Her words and actions inspired many other women, including the young feminist Fukuda Hideko, to organize, discuss women's issues, and speak out.[21]

Denied any form of political activity in the 1890s, some of the activist women who were forced to give up the public-speaking platform began expressing their opinions in newly emerging newspapers and magazines, especially women's magazines. *Jogaku Zasshi* (Women's Education Magazine), the first major women's journal, published from 1885 to 1904, was in many ways the precursor to *Seitō*. Rebecca Copeland sums up its mission as follows: "The [male] editors were interested in producing, through their dissemination of '*jogaku*,' or studies for and about women, educated and responsible female leaders who would dedicate themselves to improving the social, political, and cultural status of women in Japan—thus contributing to the modernization of the nation overall."[22] Women were encouraged to educate themselves and to be socially active as an extension of their domestic roles. They were also encouraged to read and write. Several female literary talents emerged from the pages of *Jogaku Zasshi* and other Meiji-era periodicals giving voice to women's social, political, and economic concerns.[23] Seitō women also promoted self-awareness and literary expression and envisioned New Women as leaders contributing to a modern Japan, but they demanded options for women beyond their domestic roles and edited their magazine themselves.

Other Meiji women activists, working within the parameters of the "good wife, wise mother" ideology, turned their energies to social and moral reform and to women's education. Yajima Kajiko and a handful of like-minded women had formed the Tokyo Women's Reform Society in 1886; in the 1890s it became affiliated with the international Women's Christian Temperance Union. The Reform Society women campaigned for better education for women, for the abolition of licensed prostitution, and for improved conditions and the end of sexual abuse in factories. They also asserted that the moral character of men needed to be improved. Many women not only attended newly created Meiji girls' schools but pursued careers as educators as well. They considered education the surest path to improving the status of women and believed teaching was an acceptable profession for women. Conservative educators like Hatoyama Haruko, Shimoda

Utako, and Tsuda Umeko supported state-sponsored roles for women, but the schools they established also provided opportunities for girls' higher education. Other educated women like Hani Motoko, Japan's first female newspaper reporter, Yoshioka Yayoi, one of Japan's first female medical doctors, and Yosano Akiko, who wrote passionate poems that celebrated women's sexuality, opened up new options for women and then opened up new schools as well.[24]

In the first decade of the twentieth century, women like Fukuda Hideko, Nishikawa Fumiko, and Kanno Suga experimented with socialist thought and activities as a means of bettering their position in society. Fukuda Hideko published a biweekly newspaper for socialist women, *Sekai Fujin,* from 1907 to 1909. National and international news appeared alongside women's issues and household advice. Nishikawa Fumiko helped lead the first (unsuccessful) campaign for the revision of Article 5 of the Public Peace Police Law, the regulation that excluded women from participating in political activities. Kanno Suga took radical action against the patriarchal structure of Japanese society. In early 1911, she was one of twelve socialists and anarchists executed for plotting to kill the emperor.[25]

Throughout the Meiji period—whether as public speakers, writers, teachers, reformers, or socialists—progressive Japanese women contested their limited role in society and endeavored to improve their status and their opportunities. These women shared many traits that defined New Women in Japan and other parts of the world. For the most part, they were well educated, young, and middle class. They pursued activities and careers that took them out of the home and into public spaces. They challenged the patriarchal foundations of the modern state and called for women's inclusion and even for rights.[26] They sought self-awareness and control over their own lives. However, at least in the early stages of their activism, they did not refer to themselves as New Women, nor were they called New Women by their contemporaries. Most of them were also willing to work within the confines of "good wife, wise mother." For these reasons I categorize them as foremothers of Japan's New Women.

The term *New Woman* was first used and became widespread in the West in the 1890s. It began to have currency in Japan a decade later. Because of variations in Japanese characters and pronunciation several expressions that translate as New Woman emerged; *shin fujin* (the more formal sounding Chinese-style compound) and *atarashiki/atarashii onna* (the less formal sounding Japanese compound) became most popular. Such expressions began to appear in Japanese newspapers and magazines in the early 1900s in connection with reports on women's movements in the West. New Women began to appear in novels as well, both as a term used in conversation and as independent, often sexual, characters. Waseda University Professor Tsubouchi Shōyō is usually credited with being the first to use New Woman as a set phrase in his 1910 lecture series on the plays of Henrik Ibsen and other Western writers. In all these cases, New Women were strongly connected with things Western and modern.[27]

Although some members of Japan's intelligentsia celebrated the New Woman, others disparaged her as an active, vocal, degenerate woman who was out to destroy traditional society and who fortunately existed only in the West. However, the 1911 formation of the Seitōsha heralded the arrival of the New Woman (*atarashii onna*) in Japan. Here was a group of elite women who had received the benefits of modernization and a new educational system but were refusing to quietly become "good wives, wise mothers." Many in the government, the press, and academic circles viewed the topics the Seitōsha women chose to explore as threatening to existing social norms and therefore harmful to society. At the dawn of the Taishō era, Seitōsha women were entering the debate over gender roles, which until then had been dominated by men. Thus, the New Woman had many forms. She was a contested image in the broader discourse on women's role in society. However, she was not simply an object of discussion. She was also an active contributor to the debate and a living example of a new model for women's lives.

The women of Seitō became the figures most identified with the New Woman in the media. Hiratsuka Raichō—founder and spiritual leader of the Seitōsha and first editor of *Seitō*—was the most prominent.[28] Raichō was born in Tokyo in 1886, almost midway through the turbulent Meiji period. She was raised in a wealthy, intellectual household and graduated from Naruse Jinzō's Nihon Joshi Daigaku (Japan Women's College). Finding her course in domestic science to be unfulfilling, she began to study privately both Western philosophy (particularly Nietzscheism) and Zen Buddhism. She also studied English and began to make her way into literary circles. From her youth, Raichō was always searching for ways to expand her knowledge and to understand herself and the world around her.

Raichō's personal life became the object of public scorn in 1908, when newspapers reported that she and male writer Morita Sōhei had attempted double suicide.[29] The incident was scandalous enough to warrant having her name removed from the roster of Nihon Joshi Daigaku graduates. It also led to the dissolution of the literary group led by the writer and social critic Ikuta Chōkō, in which Raichō had actively participated. Raichō removed herself from the public eye by retiring to Kamakura to practice Zen for a few months. This episode had a great impact on Raichō's search for self and identity. Returning to her parents' home in Tokyo, she continued her studies and her practice of Zen. Encouraged by Ikuta, she soon turned her energies to the founding of *Seitō* and the Seitōsha.[30]

Ikuta suggested not only the idea for such a magazine but also the name for it. Seitō is a literal translation of the English term *bluestocking,* which referred to English literary salons hosted by women in the latter part of the eighteenth century. The Bluestocking clubs offered an opportunity for upper-class English women to engage men on an intellectual level.[31] Ikuta was attracted by both the literary and the international connotations of the name, as well as the air of refinement provided by the image of European salons.[32] However, the term *bluestocking* not only referred to the English salons but also came to be used in a derogatory way to imply an eccentric, bookish, pretentious woman. It seems that Raichō reveled in the fact that she and her colleagues were unconventional, and she proudly (if not ironically) chose to use the bluestocking/Seitō name with all its connotations.

With money Raichō's mother had been saving in a wedding fund for her daughter, Raichō and four other women began to put a magazine together. Dividing the work among themselves, they set about gathering colleagues and manuscripts, negotiating with print shops, and arranging publicity. They also produced a prospectus and bylaws for the organization.[33] *Seitō* was first published in September 1911 and continued on a monthly basis until February 1916, when it folded because of financial difficulties and governmental pressure.[34]

Raichō thus initiated the Seitōsha, supplied financial backing, and served as first editor of *Seitō*. She also provided the spiritual backbone for the group. She was a charismatic leader whose early life and writings became emblematic of Japan's New Woman. Raichō's aspiration, never solely literary, was to establish a venue through which women could discover and exhibit their natural talent. The opening lines of Raichō's rousing manifesto in the first issue of *Seitō* remain an important foundation for Japanese feminism. She began, "In the beginning, Woman was truly the sun. She was a genuine person. Now, Woman is the moon. She is a sickly, pale moon, living through others, shining by the light of others."[35] This essay conjured up images of the Sun Goddess, head of the Shinto pantheon and legendary progenitor of the Japanese imperial line. It also recalled the brilliance of women's significant contributions to Japanese classical literature in the ninth to twelfth centuries. At the same time, it revealed Raichō's dissatisfaction with the subordinate status of contemporary women and her desire for spiritual, physical, and economic independence.

Raichō went on to state that it was now time for women to reclaim their position as the sun. She placed the key to women's liberation in *tensai,* a term that translates as "genius" or "natural talent." Women had to strive to discover the hidden *tensai* within themselves. According to Raichō, women had to achieve inner freedom before they could attack the problems of society. This freedom could be gained only through spiritual concentration.[36] In this first declaration Raichō clearly demonstrated that she felt spiritual liberation should be the goal of women.[37] This goal would remain her focus through her Seitō years and beyond, even as she turned to concrete social action.

When news of Raichō and other Seitō members began to appear regularly in the press, many articles included a detailed description of Raichō's office at her Akebono-chō home. There seems to have been a fascination with this woman's "room of her own." And, indeed, it did provide an intriguing combination of elements. The room was divided in two: a Western-style main portion, which was in line with the rest of the house, and a smaller Japanese-style area. The Western space allowed for a paper-cluttered desk, bookshelves overflowing with books and print materials, and art on the walls. The Japanese space was a haven where Raichō could retire to practice Zen meditation surrounded by simplicity and incense.[38] Most reports stopped short of any analysis, but it is important to note that although Raichō was often accused of being out to destroy Japanese society, here she was achieving a sense of balance between East and West in her personal workspace. She should be credited with attempting to do so in her professional life as well.

Seitō included various types of poetry, short stories, plays, translations of Western works, essays, personal reflections, and a monthly piece from the editor's desk. Circulation for the first issue was about one thousand and rapidly rose to about three thousand copies. However, through references and criticism in other publications and because printed materials often were passed from one household to the next, news of *Seitō* reached a far wider audience than the circulation figures suggest. For the first time a magazine in Japan was produced entirely by women for women.

A little more than a year after it was founded as a literary magazine, *Seitō* evolved into a forum for the discussion and debate of women's issues. The issues handled included the marriage and family system, chastity, abortion, prostitution, and socialism. All these topics involved a clash between the rights of the individual and of the state and therefore were central to the project of building a strong nation-state. Debates frequently extended over several issues, giving Seitō members the opportunity to respond to the various arguments presented. In addition to these written "conversations," the Seitōsha also sponsored a lecture meeting and study groups enabling some of these women to articulate their ideas publicly. In these ways, Seitōsha women actively engaged and negotiated the various ideals, images, and realities produced in Japan's struggle to enter its modern era. By discussing a wide range of issues and stressing the importance of self-awareness, they played a significant role in advancing feminist consciousness among middle-class women and the general reading public. With the legacy of naturalism and Western thought to aid them—and with Japanese political, legal, and moral restrictions to hinder them—Seitō women added new dimensions to the New Woman debate.

Historiographical and Theoretical Perspectives

The Seitōsha has a secure place in Japanese women's history and the history of feminism in Japan, as the scholarship by both Japanese and non-Japanese scholars attests. Coverage in both Japanese and English falls into three main categories. The first focuses on the journal *Seitō*'s six-year history, including details about membership, activities, major themes, and points of contention. These works place *Seitō* within the context of a burgeoning mass media and establish the Seitōsha as an essential part of modern Japanese feminism.[39] The second category deals with the lives and contributions of specific individuals within the Seitō organization.[40] The final group examines Seitō's New Women as an alternative to the "good wife, wise mother" or as a precursor of the *modan gāru* (modern girl) of the 1920s.[41] However, for the most part these works do not specifically address the Seitōsha's connection to and significance in Japan's modernizing process.

Works that look at the effects of modernization on the individual or trace the development of an identity crisis in late Meiji and Taishō Japan focus almost exclusively on male intellectuals and writers. Historians Victor Koschmann and Andrew Barshay, for example, examine the male individual and his relationship to an increasingly authoritarian state. Kenneth Pyle explores the sense among youth in the late Meiji period of generational confusion, which was precipitated by rapid cultural change in this period. Carol Gluck reveals a general concern with social upheaval in late Meiji but does not specifically discuss gender roles, sexuality, or women. Donald Roden's early work deals explicitly with the construction of masculinity at this time—at least on an elite level. He offers a detailed look into the character-building mission of the prestigious, all-male First Higher School of Tokyo. He also explores how the boys on the First Higher School baseball team viewed the game as a means of displaying their manliness and thus of bolstering the nation's image.[42]

More recent cultural histories of this period focus on the constructed nature of the modern nation-state but pay little attention to the constructed nature of gender roles and their relation to nation-state formation. Stefan Tanaka discusses the deliberate creation of a historical paradigm that placed Japan on an equal footing with Western nations and in a position of leadership for the rest of Asia. Gender is treated peripherally in the context of a realignment of the Orientalist equation from West = Man, East = Woman to Japan = Man, Asia = Woman.[43] T. Fujitani focuses on the invention, beginning in the Meiji period, of rituals, traditions, and ceremonies that bind the emperor and the Japanese people together as a nation. Here again, the newly emphasized masculine attributes of the emperor (and therefore of the nation) are an indication of the degree of "modernness."[44] Stephen Vlastos's edited volume continues this exploration of "invented traditions." Two essays in this work focus on gender constructs: one examines the invention of domesticity in the late Meiji period; the other jumps to an exploration of cafe waitresses in the 1920s and 1930s. However, neither work refers to the Seitō writers, even though they had much to say about changing family roles and new female occupations.[45]

This book explores the emergence of the New Woman—both creator and subject of discourse—as an event that conceals and also reveals the impact of the modernizing process on Japanese society. This is a study of the construction of a gender role—the New Woman—and its importance to the larger historical narrative. My aim is to integrate Seitō and the New Woman into the growing field of gender history by shifting the focus from Seitō itself to Seitō's controversial and changing role in the broader discourse about gender and modernity.[46]

I use the words *modern* and *modernity* throughout this work. These terms encompass a multitude of meanings, images, ideas, and processes. Part of my project is to examine how the women and men involved in Japan's New Woman/Woman Problem debate used these expressions. For them, modern meant a break with the previous ways of thinking, acting, and being. In other words, it implied a series of social, cultural, political, economic, and psychological changes, as well as a temporal recognition that such changes were occurring. Modernity is used to designate the general time period in which these various changes take place. Historian Miriam Silverberg sheds further light on this issue by offering this definition of modern: "What should be highlighted in a cultural history of the period is the fact that the construction of culture and the consciousness of this construction . . . are what render the era modern."[47] Although she focuses on the 1920s and 1930s, I would argue that her definition also applies to the 1910s. The participants in the New Woman debate—Seitōsha women, government officials, educators, writers, and social critics—had a keen awareness of their historical moment and their ability to contribute to its shape. Individualism and a sense of self were key attributes of the modern subject.

Modernity in Japan in the 1910s was in many ways a work in progress, a goal yet to be attained. Many of the external changes that signified such a break with the past were evident, but the Japanese nation and people were still struggling to define a modern identity. Several groups within Japan continued to seek approval and respect from the West, even as they argued for Japanese distinctiveness. Modernity was often associated with uncontested national independence and a strong sense of nationalism. Drawing on ideas both traditional and modern, Japanese and Western, Japan created its own modern structures. The family system made use of Confucian ideals of hierarchy, order, and control, even as it served as the foundation of the modern state. The system of licensed prostitution combined an unquestioned belief in male privilege with a modern concern for hygiene and containment. "Good wife, wise mother" ideology brought together premodern ideas of wifely duties and the modern concept of educated motherhood. What becomes clear is that modernization in Japan cannot be equated simply with Westernization.[48]

Literary historian Rita Felski defines the controversial term *modernization* as follows: "Modernization is usually taken to denote the complex constellation of socioeconomic phenomena which originated in the context of Western development but which have since manifested themselves around the globe in various forms: scientific and technological innovation, the industrialization of production, rapid urbanization, an ever expanding capitalist market, the development of the nation-state, and so on."[49] Although Felski's definition is useful, I fully recognize that modernization theory has a long and contentious history in Japanese Studies. Initially popularized in the 1950s and 1960s, modernization theory provided "value-free" criteria through which to judge a society's "modernness." Scholars from a variety of disciplines considered modernization a progressive process. Urbanization, literacy, industrialization, political participation, secularism, and the development of the nation-state were all used as markers of such progress. During the early Cold War period, Japan needed to be rehabilitated, and distinguished scholars including Marius Jansen, John Hall, and Edwin Reischauer used modernization theory to remodel Japan's pre–World War II image. They downplayed Japanese militarism and instead focused on the modern, democratic aspects of Tokugawa, Meiji, and Taishō societies. Because the 1930s did not fit into the progressive model, they were written off as an aberration.

Under attack in the 1970s, modernization theory reemerged a decade later looking rather different. In the 1970s historian John Dower, among others, critiqued the prevalence of modernization theory in Japanese Studies.[50] He claimed it foreclosed discussions of conflict, the pros and cons of capitalism, and the fact that modernization did not necessarily lead to democracy. In the 1980s Andrew Gordon, Sheldon Garon, and others incorporated these concerns into a reevaluation of modernization theory. Their Japan did not show Euro-American democratic tendencies, nor did they see fascism and authoritarianism as aberrations. Instead, they viewed these developments as rational, scientific, modern responses. Their works addressed conflict, collaboration, and contending views of what it meant to be modern.[51]

Garon's article "Rethinking Modernization and Modernity in Japanese History" provides a background to modernization theory and indicates ways in which the term *modernization* can still be used as an analytical tool.[52] I agree with Garon that modernity meant different things to different people and that various groups and individuals in Meiji-Taishō Japan were striving to make Japan modern. One of my goals is to uncover how constructions of gender roles and understandings of modernity overlapped and influenced each other. This project includes revealing how a select group of women and men defined modern differently and how the goal of making Japan modern was used to shape appropriate gender roles. While Garon's work focuses on collaboration between various social groups—including women's groups—and the state, I am interested in conflict and resistance.[53] Although many individuals and groups did support state-sponsored views on modernity and gender, I want to examine those who opposed these views—like the women of Seitō—and the definitions of modernity and gender they used to reinforce their own visions.

These images, ideas, and opinions circulated in society in the form of discourse. Discourse includes the various channels through which information is created, exchanged, and reformulated. Michel Foucault explores how discourse is simultaneously restrained by numerous control mechanisms and capable of moving beyond these imposed confines. He argues the need "to restore to discourse its character as an event."[54] It is Foucault's definition of an event that I find most relevant to my own research. "An event," he explains, "is not a decision, a treaty, a reign, or a battle, but the reversal of a relationship of forces, the usurpation of power, the appropriation of a vocabulary turned against those who had once used it."[55] Through their participation in the New Woman debate, Seitōsha women turned the discourse on appropriate gender roles into an event.

For a definition of gender I turn to Joan Scott's groundbreaking article "Gender: A Useful Category of Historical Analysis." According to Scott, "Gender is a constitutive element of social relationships based on perceived differences between the sexes, and gender is a primary way of signifying relationships of power."[56] She emphasizes the need to historicize the construction of gender roles, to analyze connections between gender and power, and to examine the "reciprocal nature of gender and society." This analysis of the New Woman debate in early twentieth-century Japan attempts to answer this call.

Japan's New Women shared many of the traits linked with the modernizing process in Japan. They, too, can be seen as a work in progress as they struggled to define their place(s) in society. They sought approval and respect. They asserted their independence and their desire to contribute to society. They drew on a variety of sources in creating their visions of a new modern woman, including Zen training, Western writings and ideas, and Japanese morals and arts. They also tried to open up new spaces for female activity beyond the confines of "good wife, wise mother." We can follow their efforts through the numerous writings they left behind. Their story brings together issues of modernization and gender construction under a common discourse at a specific moment in time. New Women were an inevitable product of Meiji period changes in education and the status of women, and they played an important part in Japan's struggles to define what it meant to be modern.

Using the New Woman of Seitō as the focal point, I assess the trajectory of the New Woman in Japan from her start as a Western phenomenon through her varied Japanese incarnations in the 1910s, all the while analyzing her impact on the wider debates over appropriate modern gender roles. During the 1910s, socialist and other leftist activities were suppressed in the wake of an assassination attempt on the emperor; the Japanese empire expanded as Korea was officially annexed; the Meiji emperor passed away; the New Woman emerged; Japan benefited economically, territorially, and diplomatically from its limited participation in World War I; and democracy seemed to be taking root as political parties exercised increased power. All these events, as well as many others not mentioned, were a part of Japan's modernizing process and therefore were in many ways interconnected. However, the New Woman debate sheds little light on the role of women and gender in Japan's colonizing efforts, economic activities, or political developments. Seitō women made it clear that, for the most part, they had little interest in class issues and national or international events. They felt it necessary to concentrate on their own internal development first. Their critics helped to broaden the debate a little, but the focus remained on opportunities for women and appropriate gender behavior, models, and morality for a modernizing nation.

Throughout the book we will hear a variety of voices that represent Japan's New Women, their supporters, and their critics. Hiratsuka Raichō's words and actions will be discussed regularly. Because she was the guiding force behind *Seitō,* the quintessential representative of the Japanese New Woman, and a prolific writer, this focus is only fitting. We will hear from and about several other women involved with the Seitōsha as well. To get a glimpse of the diversity, these include (but are not limited to) Yasumochi Yoshi and Kiuchi Tei, two of the original founders of the organization and the magazine; Katō Midori, working mother and future newspaper reporter; Otake Kōkichi, young artist and central figure in Seitō scandals; Itō Noe, radical-feminist-turned-anarchist and second editor of *Seitō;* and Araki Ikuko, independent owner of a boardinghouse for university students. Women who earned their New Woman status from activities distinct from the Seitōsha also add their voices. They include Yosano Akiko and Tamura Toshiko, established literary figures; Iwano Kiyo; participant in the 1905 campaign to revise Article 5 of the Public Peace Police Law and to increase women's political rights; Fukuda Hideko, feminist activist with ties to the Freedom and People's Rights movement in the 1880s and the socialist movement in the 1900s; and Matsui Sumako, considered by many to be Japan's first modern female actor. Many supporters of the New Woman came from the literary world. Critics included educators, scholars, government officials, and other New Women. The range of voices involved is a tribute to the richness of Japan's New Woman debate.

I begin with the emergence of the New Woman debate. Chapter 2 examines the introduction of New Women to Japan in the form of European dramatic heroines. In late Meiji Japan, Western plays by Henrik Ibsen, George Bernard Shaw, Hermann Sudermann, and the like were discussed

Figure 1. Early Seitōsha members. Back row from the left: founding members Kiuchi Tei, Hiratsuka Raichō, Nakano Hatsuko. From reprint of *Seitō 2*, no. 1 (January 1912). *Courtesy of Fuji Shuppan.*

and performed as part of a campaign to modernize Japanese theater. The female protagonists of these plays—characters who rejected the conventional roles of wife and mother in favor of self-discovery and egalitarian relationships—prompted the discussion of New Women as a by-product of modernity. This chapter focuses on the initial responses to this new phenomenon by analyzing the reactions of the media in general, and Seitō members specifically, to Ibsen's heroine Nora from *A Doll House*.

The interconnections between New Theater, New Women, and modernity continue to be explored in Chapter 3. This chapter examines the performance of Sudermann's play *Magda* and its subsequent censorship. The heroine, Magda, rejects male authority by defying her father and refusing to marry. These actions added to the perception of New Women as destructive and dangerous beings—dangerous, that is, to the patriarchal foundation of Japan's modern state. The government's reaction raised questions about acceptable modern behavior and freedoms. Although censorship can be a powerful silencer, the reactions of Seitō women and others to the ban on performance reveal different visions of modernity.

In Chapter 4 the New Woman shifts from a Western phenomenon to a Japanese reality. Seitōsha women were targeted as representatives of the Japanese New Women when a series of scandalous activities made headlines in the summer and fall of 1912. Word that Seitō women were interested in alcohol, pleasure quarters, men, and other women marked them as immoral and, once again, dangerous. This chapter explores how the women of Seitō pushed the boundaries of acceptable feminine behavior; in doing so they added to the negative public perception of New Women and transformed them from dramatic characters to genuine individuals.

Seitō women actively engage in some gender construction of their own in Chapter 5. Tired of being defined and misunderstood by others, they used the pages of *Seitō* to redefine and re-create the New Woman in their own terms. Based on their writings, I analyze how these women envisioned their place in society. Although the Seitō women presented a variety of approaches, concerns, and definitions, they all argued for a broad, diverse image for themselves. They also felt that New Women could contribute positively to Japan's modernizing process. Articles continued to appear in virtually every issue of *Seitō* that refined, defended, or promoted a particular vision of the New Woman. Their efforts also brought about in the general press a discussion of the New Woman that was more serious than previous commentary had been.

Chapter 6 investigates the formation of a second New Woman's group, the Shinshinfujinkai, or True New Woman's Association, as another example of how the image of the New Woman became varied. The members of this group offered an alternative vision of New Women as wives and mothers. They argued for a modern vision of women that did not completely reject Japanese traditions and morality. The rivalry between the two groups, in part fabricated by the press, helped to enrich the New Woman debate and provide additional options for women.

In Chapter 7, the book concludes with a brief comparative look at the New Woman as she emerged in several other countries around the world. After examining the general characteristics associated with the Euro-American New Woman, I turn to case studies of Egyptian, Chinese, and Korean New Women. This exploration of variations in the definition of New Woman offers insights into the effects of and reactions to modernity in different nations. Finally, the chapter returns to the Japanese New Woman. It ends with her legacy and the activities of the women who succeeded her in the 1920s and 1930s.

For her critics the New Woman embodied the destruction of home and nation that excessive imitation of the West would bring to Japan. For her supporters she represented progress and personal freedom. For both she represented a rejection of "good wife, wise mother." Seitōsha women—as representatives of the New Woman—triggered a public reaction disproportionate to their numbers and influence by providing a site where the need to modernize and the need to remain Japanese were contested. The New Woman may have originated in the West, but Raichō and the women of Seitō helped to make her a notable figure in Japan's modernizing process.

CHAPTER 2

Ibsen's Nora

THE NEW WOMAN DEBATE BEGINS

During the summer of 1910 Tsubou-chi Shōyō—a well-known writer, translator, critic, and educator—gave a series of lectures in several major cities entitled "The New Woman in Modern Plays." As part of his continual efforts to introduce Western literature and to promote a new, modern theater in Japan, he described for his audience some of the works of Henrik Ibsen, Hermann Sudermann, and George Bernard Shaw. The New Women of these works were female characters who in various ways rejected the conventional roles of wife and mother in favor of self-discovery and egalitarian relationships. In a scholarly setting, Tsubouchi presented the New Woman in a positive light and concluded that women should be given the same opportunities as men in order to reach their full potential.[1]

In September 1911, Tsubouchi Shōyō's Literary Society staged the first Japanese production of Ibsen's *A Doll House* in its own small theater.[2] It was such a success that it moved to the Imperial Theater for a week-long run that November. Although Tsubouchi had translated and lectured on *A Doll House* the preceding year, it was the performance that prompted active media attention. Literary critics, scholars, journalists, and feminists began to write articles in newspapers and journals to explain, analyze, admire, and critique the play.

At the center of the discussion were the women of Seitōsha, the feminist literary organization founded the same month *A Doll House* premiered. Journalists were quick to label these independent, creative women "Japanese Noras" and "New Women" (*atarashii onna*).[3] These terms were used both to dismiss these women as frivolous and immature and to warn of their dangerous and destructive nature. However, several Seitōsha women decided to engage in the discussion and to provide their own serious examination of the play, its female protagonist, and Japan's existing gender roles. In the January 1912 issue of their magazine *Seitō,* they included a 110-page supplement devoted to *A Doll House*'s Nora.[4] I will situate these writings within the critical context of the day and explore how they enriched the exchange of ideas. *A Doll House,* New Women, and the Woman Problem would continue to be topics of debate in the press in subsequent years, but this chapter focuses on the immediate reactions to the play in late 1911 and early 1912.

I examine the discourse that surrounded the performance of Ibsen's *A Doll House* for ways it marked the emergence of the New Woman debate in Japan. Here I specifically address the beginnings of a conscious and self-conscious use of the term *New Woman.* A product of increased access to education and careers, the New Woman was economically independent; socially, politically, and sexually active; and a decidedly Western phenomenon. She also represented a rejection of the dominant ideology of "good wife, wise mother."[5] Although women who in many ways fit the description lived, worked, and made an impact throughout the Meiji period, the expression itself had not been coined yet. The contributions of these Meiji women to Japanese society are significant but usually are viewed as individual achievements and not part of a larger feminist project. Debates over gender roles and their relationship to modernization and national identity had started in early Meiji as well.[6] Therefore, the reactions generated by *A Doll House* examined here can be seen as part of an on-going Meiji interest in the role gender had to play in the modernizing process, and we can also view the women who involved themselves in the discussions as following in the footsteps of a variety of pioneering women. However, in this particular gender debate both men and women actively engaged with and responded to each other.

This chapter addresses four elements that overlapped in the discourse surrounding the emergence of the New Woman in Japan. Initially, she was inextricably linked with Japan's New Theater movement. This connection in turn helped to forge a link between the New Woman and Japan's efforts to establish itself as a modern nation. In addition, there was tension between treating the New Woman as an object of discourse and recognizing her as an embodied social reality. Finally, the New Woman presented a challenge to established gender roles.

Who was the New Woman? Did she exist in Japan? Was she useful or detrimental to Japan's modern image? Seitōsha women added their voices to the abstract discussion of New Women and their impact on society. At the same time, their unconventional life-styles marked them as concrete examples of both modernity and potential danger and made it hard to ignore the presence of New Women in Japan.[7] By analyzing Seitō women's responses to Nora and *A Doll House* alongside those of male scholars, critics, and reporters, I explore how women's voices contributed to and altered the beginning of Japan's New Woman debate by offering different perspectives on, concerns for, and visions of Japan's future.

The Play

The performance of *A Doll House* in Japan set the stage–both literally and figuratively–for the emergence of the New Woman debate. Although Norwegian playwright Henrik Ibsen contended that he was more interested in human rights than in specifically female ones, the majority of people who have viewed *A Doll House* since its inception in 1879 have considered it a feminist statement. Nora, the heroine of *A Doll House,* took on a life of her own as a model of the self-awakened New Woman. She inspired heated debates throughout Europe and the United States about the role of women in the home and in marriage, the restrictions that society places on women's mental and spiritual growth, and the duties of women to family, to society, and to themselves. These debates, first in the abstract, then concretely, were waged in Japan as well.[8]

The play tells the story of a young woman's path to self-awareness. In Act I we find Nora, wife of the strait-laced lawyer and banker Torvald Helmer and mother of three, flitting about the house preparing for Christmas, secretly munching on macaroons. Doted on by Helmer, who calls her his squirrel and his lark, she is young, attractive, and unschooled in the ways of the world. We soon discover Nora's great secret. Early in their marriage her husband had fallen gravely ill, and she had borrowed a large sum of money so they could spend a year in southern climes, thereby saving his life. Over the years, by taking in piecework secretly and wheedling extra money out of Helmer, she had almost succeeded in paying off the loan. Now Krogstad, the moneylender and a clerk in Helmer's bank who is about to be fired for his crooked past, appears and asks Nora to intercede on his behalf. If she does not, he will reveal not only that she borrowed money but also that she committed the crime of forging her father's signature in order to do so.

In Act II Nora pleads with Helmer to keep Krogstad on at the bank, but to no avail. Nora begins to realize the seriousness of her situation. She considers requesting the remaining money she owes from Dr. Rank, a close family friend, but when he declares his love for her she feels she cannot take advantage of him and refrains from asking. Krogstad, having received his notice, arrives with a letter revealing all to Helmer. This he leaves in the locked mailbox. In an effort to prevent Helmer from retrieving the letter, Nora begs him to help her rehearse a dance she will perform at a costume party the next night. She proceeds to dance a wild Tarantella, knowing that her secret soon will be revealed.

With Act III we see the happy Helmer home unravel. Nora's Tarantella at the party is a huge success, and Helmer whisks her back home soon after. He heads to the mailbox to make room for the next day's papers and discovers the letter. Nora meanwhile is preparing to leave so that her husband and children will not have to bear her shame. Helmer's reaction to the letter is extreme. Instead of offering to shoulder her burden, as Nora expected, he rails against her, calling her a criminal and an unfit mother. Another letter from Krogstad arrives containing her forged note and a promise that her secret will never be revealed. (Krogstad has reconciled with a former lover and has new hope for the future.) Helmer's reaction is "Nora, I'm saved!" and he then completely forgives her. Nora awakens to the realities of her marriage and home life and realizes she can no longer live as a doll trapped in a dollhouse. She must educate herself, learn about the world, and discover who she is. She must be herself before she can be a wife and mother. The play ends with the door slamming behind her as she steps into the world.[9]

Initially, the media concentrated not on the New Woman in the West or Japan but on the actual performance of *A Doll House,* from preproduction through opening night.[10] It was an event, a spectacle, a cornerstone in the creation of a modern, Japanese theater. The articles focused on the construction of the theater itself, the rehearsals, and the actors—especially the lead. Women had been banned from the Japanese stage as commercial theater was developing in the seventeenth century because the sexual content of their performances and their links with prostitution often led to public disturbances.[11] Now, in the early twentieth century, New Women were being portrayed in the New Theater by new actors.

The Literary Society's production of *A Doll House* received favorable reviews largely because of Matsui Sumako, the woman who played Nora and who is considered by many to be Japan's first modern female actor. Tsubouchi, whose lectures began the New Woman debate, founded the Literary Society as both a study group and a training ground for modern

FIGURE 2. Matsui Sumako as Nora. From reprint of *Seitō* 2, no. 1 (January 1912). *Courtesy of Fuji Shuppan.*

actors. It was also coeducational. The New Theater movement that emerged in the 1900s provided, or rather required, a space for women on the stage. Women's presence on stage would prove that Japan was as modern as the West because it too could produce talented *female* actors.[12]

According to the reviews Japan had indeed succeeded in generating modern theater. One enthusiastic reviewer asserted, "It is no exaggeration to say that the Nora of this actress will long be remembered as having solved for the first time Japan's actress problem and as having liberated women on the stage."[13] Another gushed, "I was deeply moved and delighted to hear, for the first time, natural lines spoken by an actress born in Japan." And again, "I have never been more astounded than by the Nora in *A Doll House* performed by the Literary Society. How enormous the power of an actress that we now see on the Japanese stage, how great the presence of an actress!"[14] Matsui Sumako was a triumph as a Japanese actor.

Even before the play opened, it drew some attention in the press as a theatrical event. It was to be the first production staged at the new, private theater of the Literary Society. The *Yomiuri* newspaper ran an article in late August providing details of the newly constructed, five-hundred-seat theater and of the preparations for the opening. It also revealed how Tsubouchi sold off a third of his private residence in order to finance the construction of the theater (and a smaller residence) on the remaining grounds.[15] The journalist commended Tsubouchi for his willingness to sacrifice for the sake of a new, modern theater. Considering the connections being made between the development of a modern theater and that of a modern nation, it is possible Tsubouchi viewed his gesture as a contribution to the advancement of the nation as a whole.

An article in the September issue of *Waseda Bungaku,* a literary journal published by a leading private university, also discussed in detail the layout of the theater and the stage. In addition, it disclosed specifics about rehearsals. The group carefully studied the script before beginning to rehearse on stage three times a week for several hours. Sometimes sections were repeated numerous times in order to achieve the proper effect. There were constant adjustments and modifications to the actors' delivery. And they had to work with construction noise in the background, on an unfinished stage, with incomplete props and scenery. Even under these poor conditions, rehearsals seemed to be going well.[16]

In early September, Shimamura Hōgetsu—a critic, leader in the New Theater movement, and director of *A Doll House*—provided some background for the play to the press. Like Tsubouchi, Shimamura discussed it as a modern European work that addressed a modern European problem, namely the Woman Problem. On the one hand, he seemed to assure the Japanese public that this was not a serious issue in Japan, but, on the other hand, he warned that Japan would soon have to contend with it. He indicated that *A Doll House* and the Woman Problem it depicted caused a "great commotion" in Europe and was the "sole topic of conversation in social circles," a conversation that was "especially heated among women"; but in Japan "such a reaction is not expected."[17] He called the Woman Problem in Japan a "frivolous thing" and declared, "There is still no Woman Problem in Japan." Yet, he cautioned, "if Ibsen's proposal to try and emancipate women's individuality is a reality in Europe now, it will be our country's next problem."[18] In any case, it seems the Literary Society chose *A Doll House* for its status as a modern play, not because of its central theme.

Shimamura promoted awareness of the play, its complexities, and its importance as part of modern theater. Through his writing and directing he also urged the Japanese public to become aware of women as an important part of modern society. Additionally, he supported women in their efforts to become self-aware. He even offered praise for *Seitō:* "There is now a literary magazine formed only by women. It would not be significant if they were simply doing what men do with a female hand. But the literature is of the poignancy of their lives, of their awakening. Here is a women's magazine that lifts a truly female voice. And it deserves attention."[19]

The actors who appeared in *A Doll House* also had a few remarks about the play. Unlike the critics, they concentrated on the challenges the play presented. As an amateur group attempting to establish a precedent for realistic, modern productions in Japan, they were concerned about the quality of their performances and conscious of the difficulties of successfully bridging East and West. Doi Shunsho, the actor who played Helmer, wrote: "When rehearsing, one of the joys is that this is a famous script. When you imagine staging such a script, the feeling while rehearsing is as if there are the two extremes of West and East, and the two cannot meet, and your heart is close to despair. But gradually as the rehearsals pile up, the two extremes come closer and you feel as if there is not such a great distance."[20] Matsui Sumako (Nora) worried about her inexperience and the difficulty of finding the right emotion for her lines. She and Tōgi Tetsuteki (Krogstad) both declared that modern plays were far more complex than plays set in the past. They all struggled with making New Theater viable in Japan.[21]

In late September the *Yomiuri* carried the news of the opening performance. The final dress rehearsal also served as a preview, to which reporters were invited. "A tent surrounded with a red and white striped curtain was set up on the open grounds. White, cloth-covered tables held baskets heaped with pears and apples, floral wreaths and cut flowers. Beyond that you could see the construction of Professor Tsubouchi's new home." The reporter went on to describe the purple satin stage curtain embroidered with gold thread, the photos taken of cast members prior to the performance, the stage set for Act I, difficulties with the lighting, and the director's summary of Act II, which led to the performance of Act III. The opening itself was the event. Little mention was made of the play's plot.[22]

Critical Discussion in the Popular Press

Critical discussion of the plot and its implications began in newspapers and journals after the initial performance was declared a success and as the date of the performance at the Imperial Theater approached. The emphasis shifted from form to content, with much discussion of Nora, her awakening, and her decision to leave home. Some critics discussed below stressed that the play should be "properly" understood and provided alternative ways of reading Nora's actions. They hoped to introduce theatergoers and the general public to modern thinking, while explaining away the disruptive elements of the story.

An article by Sawada Bushō in *Fujin Kurabu* (Women's Club), a popular women's magazine, attempted to alleviate anxieties about the New Woman by presenting Nora not as a role model but as a warning. Sawada questioned the value of women's awakening.

> Women's awakening [*kakusei*] seems to be actively advanced of late. According to this view women are also human beings. As human beings they should be able to do all things. They should not be resigned to being slaves to men all their lives, as they have been until now. It goes without saying that this is an imported, Western thing. These Western, imported things seem to be in considerable demand. . . . However, are such awakened women really happy as individuals? Does women's awakening really benefit the nation? For our country, there is certainly doubt.[23]

In short, did Japan have to follow the path of Western nations or could it offer its own version of modernity? After establishing Nora as the Euro-American model of an awakened woman, Sawada proceeded to devote the majority of the article to a detailed synopsis of the plot. He credited Ibsen with creating a captivating and sympathetic character in Nora, but one that should not be emulated. "Nora cried out that she was a human being, but it was not clear what this meant. There is no reason that you cannot become human without trampling the relationship between husband and wife, parent and child. Rather, it is through these relationships that one is able to be human. . . . Today's so-called awakened women are women who . . . should be pitied as they have no one to rely on."[24]

Sawada concluded by blaming education and its emphasis on individualism for creating so many pitiful awakened women. "In order to rescue women from such a dangerous state, we should cultivate a sacrificing spirit.

All told we must educate them as human beings, while at the same time not letting them forget that they are women."[25] This opinion complied with the government-supported educational policy of "good wife, wise mother." In other words, Japan had the right idea: women could be modern but within limits. The smooth functioning of state and family—not self-awareness—was the surest path to personal happiness and fulfillment.

Another article the following month continued in a similar conservative vein. Asai Shōzō, a dean at Japan Women's College, expressed his belief that "modern, young women lead a meaningless life, a thoughtless, shallow, frivolous life." If only these women considered themselves "members of society" and "elements that constitute the nation" their lives would be so much richer.[26] Again, women's lives would be enhanced by focusing on their place within the Japanese community, not by trying to discover their individuality. Asai then related a conversation he had overheard between two theatergoers heading home after the play. Unable to understand Nora's decision to leave home, they concluded she must have been someone else's mistress. This little aside lends support to the idea that women could not—or should not—make their way in the world without a man. Asai himself dismissed the play's "dangerous" ending as nothing more than a theatrical stunt. Imagining himself as Nora he writes: "I will always be here. I will always work for the sake of you and the children. This is what I wanted to say, but it doesn't make for a play, it's not interesting. But the real world is not a play, and in a real situation I would remain at home. It's only natural to endeavor to do the things a woman should."[27] Thus, women were to realize their full potential within society-sanctioned roles; otherwise their lives would be meaningless.

A major Tokyo newspaper serialized a lecture given by Professor Ukita Kazutami entitled "Nora and the Woman Problem."[28] He reiterated the theme that Japan was progressing apace with other modern nations. "Today people have advanced to the point where they can no longer bear external dominance. Politically speaking, it is an age that has shifted from autocracy to constitutional monarchy or republicanism."[29] Japan too had made that shift. Yet, Ukita asserted, each country must handle its problems, including grappling with the Woman Problem, according to its own laws and customs. Ukita placed the Woman Problem with the labor and peace problems as the major worldwide social movements. Understanding the Woman Problem was part of being globally aware. However, nations approached these issues differently. "Nora's beginning a new life, discarding three kids, discarding her husband, is truly radical and European-style—in other words, it is not at

all Japanese-style."[30] Japan needed to establish an alternate method of dealing with the Woman Problem that would accommodate its laws and customs
and would contribute to the nation's progress. Ukita suggested a "modern"
view of the relationship between the sexes. Instead of the theory that makes
men superior and women inferior, he argued for a complementary, separate-
but-equal approach. Men had muscular strength and courage. Women had
patience and endurance. Both were needed to make society work. Both were
important. Nora missed the whole point by thinking she could make it on
her own.[31]

Professor Ukita developed these ideas in detail in another article for a
women's magazine. He argued that the definition of appropriate gender roles
and behavior affected men as well as women. "Women are not the only ones
who are trapped by custom, men are too," he wrote. "Women's awakening
is necessary, but men must awaken too."[32] In other words, this was a gender
problem, not just a Woman Problem. He also offered an alternative reading
of the play's ending, similar to Sawada's.

> The ideal of the play positions a wife before a mother, a woman be-
> fore a wife, a person before a woman, but the play in fact argues the
> opposite. . . . In other words, the Nora play does nothing more than
> strongly indicate the order of woman's awakening. . . . In exerting
> oneself in the duties of daughter, wife and mother, one becomes a
> person, one causes one's character to advance. It is not that one must
> discard husband and children in order to enter a new life. To awaken
> or not to awaken is in one's heart. If you awaken yourself, that is the
> new life.[33]

He thus emphasized the need to awaken, not the need to leave home. The
process leading Nora to self-awareness, not her final action, was important. These arguments supported his contention that men and women need
each other and must work together in order to improve society. Although
he still stressed the community over the individual, he advocated an egalitarian approach to male-female relations and accepted women's need for
personal growth.

Three of the aforementioned articles appeared in women's magazines,
namely *Fujin Kurabu* (Women's Club) and *Fujin no Tomo* (Woman's Companion). Since the 1890s women's magazines had flourished in Japan. Run
largely by men, although with some female contributors, many of these magazines aimed at instructing women how to be "good wives" and "wise mothers." *Fujin Kurabu* and *Fujin no Tomo* were serious, high-quality, progressive

magazines that fit this category. Contributors to *Fujin Kurabu* constituted a long list of noted educators, both male and female. Contents covered female education, moral training, child-rearing, cooking, and hygiene, as well as fiction, poetry, and biographies of famous women. *Fujin no Tomo* emphasized rational, efficient household management in both theory and practice. Both magazines promoted women as valued members of society through their efforts as homemakers.[34]

Not surprisingly these articles on *A Doll House* reinforced the concept of female domesticity as a linchpin in Japanese modernity. Japanese women would reap more benefits from contributing to their nation, community, and families than from focusing on their individuality. True happiness came from relationships, not from being all alone. Women deserved respect and status as competent wives, mothers, and household managers. Keeping informed about trends in other nations did not necessarily mean having to follow them. The alternative approaches to Nora's dilemma offered in these articles by scholars and critics provided a way to engage in the modern discourse on female gender roles within a Japanese context.

Critical Discussion in *Seitō*

The next circle of critics to join the discussion of *A Doll House* contributed to a different type of women's magazine, one that emphasized women's inner awareness and strength and that rebelled against the "good wife, wise mother" standard enforced through laws and education. *Seitō* and *A Doll House* both debuted in Japan the same month, September 1911. *Seitō*'s January 1912 issue included a supplement with reactions to Nora.[35] The contributors delved deeply into the plot and personalities of the play's main characters in an effort to reveal their own thoughts on women's duty to themselves and society. What were the Seitō women's initial perceptions? Although one expressed a highly critical reaction to Nora, the others responded more enthusiastically. Some had reservations, most had worries, but they generally approved of Nora's awakening.

Hiratsuka Raichō, the founding editor and spiritual backbone of *Seitō*, reacted most critically to Nora's actions. Although the others used *A Doll House* somewhere in their titles, Raichō addressed Nora directly in her title, and at the beginning of each paragraph, with a "Dear Nora." In this letter format, Raichō expounded on each one of Nora's faults as she saw them. Her chief concern was that, in the end, Nora had not awakened to her true self.[36] Taking Nora's doll-like, naive behavior at face value, Raichō wrote, "Dear

Nora, as a Japanese woman it is hard to believe that a woman as impulsive and blind as you is a mother of three children and not a girl of fourteen or fifteen years."[37] She focused on Nora's innocent, unaware nature by implying that Nora's awakening was only half-baked. "Dear Nora, you left home blindly," she continued. "Your thoughts differed from those of your husband. When you suddenly felt as if he were a stranger, you left half-impulsively in what seemed to me like an act of self-defense. However, it was not your true intention."[38] Nora, Raichō argued, reacted instinctively, not rationally. And again she noted, "Dear Nora, the sound of the door you slammed echoed with authority. But one step outside and you were in total darkness. You didn't know east from west. Your footsteps were so uncertain."[39] Raichō felt this was immature behavior—no plan, no foresight.

Even though Raichō offered a spiritual solution, she demanded that Nora follow a well-defined path paved with hard work and dedication. Raichō believed that awareness could not be attained instantly but required knowledge and discipline. Raichō continued, "Dear Nora, saying that you were first of all a human being, you threw away the Doll House. However, you had not yet become human. You had only finally become aware that you must become a human being. What kind of being that was you still didn't know."[40] She bemoaned not only Nora's childlike innocence but the fact that Nora had not struggled on her way to self-awareness as well. Nora was mistaken if she believed she could "awaken" (*jikaku suru*) so easily.

Raichō believed Nora was also mistaken in her understanding of love. "Dear Nora, you said that 'for eight years I've been living here with a stranger, and that I'd even conceived three children—oh, I can't stand the thought of it! I could tear myself to bits,' as if you truly couldn't bear the mortification. I'm sure it was regrettable. On hearing these words many women cried. However, this is something that any woman who has fallen in love has experienced at one time. Your awakening [*anata no sameru no wa*] is rather late."[41] It appears Raichō felt there was a "right time" for awakening and that it was a woman's duty to herself before getting married and having children if possible. She went on to lecture Nora about the meaning of love. Nora committed forgery and then kept it secret out of love for her husband. However, she expected his love, her dreamed-of "miracle," in return. Raichō believed that true love was given freely, happily, with no strings attached. One should not love in order to be loved. She berated Nora for her "beggar-like" disposition.

Raichō devoted the rest of her "letter" to Nora's need to struggle in order to find true awareness. Predicting that a spiritual encounter with her inner self awaited Nora, Raichō wrote, "Dear Nora, your true awakening will be from now on. Along your way the second tragedy awaits. It's the tragedy of throwing away this false inner self. It's the spiritual problem that boils up from the depths of your heart as a more miserable, serious, sad individual, not as the gay person you were when you threw away your husband and children."[42] Again, she was only just beginning to know herself. She had to dig deeper. Raichō continued, "Dear Nora, this second tragedy that I spoke of is to curse this false, illusory self. It is denial. It is the struggle for the eradication of self."[43] Raichō had for years studied and practiced Zen Buddhism, which greatly influenced her ideas about spiritual awakening. She presented Nora with a mystery to unravel. "Dear Nora, when you experience this second tragedy, when you have killed, exhausted all traces of that being called Nora, won't that be when you have truly gained self-awareness? Won't that be when you become from the depths of your soul what is truly meant by a New Woman?"[44] If the goal was to extinguish the self then one's gender becomes insignificant. It could no longer be an obstacle. Yet Raichō did not explain how a woman could be genderless and a gender-conscious New Woman at the same time.

Raichō demanded so much more from the character Nora than was revealed in *A Doll House*. Although some might feel she intended self-awareness to be the privilege of an elite few, I would argue she wanted all women to delve deeper than they thought possible. She was urging women to gain inner fortitude before slamming the door and facing the hardships of the outside world, a world that discriminated against them because they were women. Then again, if women worked on self-awareness first, maybe they would not need to slam doors.

As a counterpoint to Raichō's rather negative appraisal, Katō Midori's "*A Doll House*" advanced a more positive view of Nora. Katō contended that Nora was self-aware from the beginning but camouflaged it. She acted like Helmer's little lark, singing and dancing around the house, secretly nibbling sweets, Katō wrote. "But that is nothing more than the shadow of Nora that is revealed externally, it's not the true Nora. What Nora herself said is true, she's not as stupid as others think." And Katō added, "This is not something limited only to Nora. . . . There are any number of women like this in the world."[45] So, unlike Raichō, Katō chose to imagine that Nora's childish behavior was all literally an act, a mask she wore out of love for her husband. This interpretation definitely helps to make Nora's awakening in the last scene more believable than in Raichō's interpretation. It also gave Nora more agency. She was not simply a doll who moved when Helmer pulled her strings. However, Katō did not question the societal norms that made this behavior necessary. She did not try to explain why it made a man happy to have his wife act childishly and helplessly or what the woman gained by this behavior.

Katō read the play as a gradual unfolding of Nora's inner personality, not a sudden awakening at the end. "Nora's self-deceiving outer personality and her hidden inner personality run parallel in Act I, but gradually her inner self starts crying out and her inner personality begins to appear. . . . At the beginning of Act II, even though to this point Nora believed that what she did was right, she comes to realize that it was against the law, and at the same time she feels uneasy as if the peace and affection of the home she has had will instantly vanish."[46] By mentioning some of Act II, Katō brought attention to the fact that Nora was indeed beginning to experience pain and suffering.[47] She did not remain throughout the innocent girl Raichō bemoaned. Katō recounted Nora's conversation with the children's nurse regarding the effect her absence would have on the children. She was thinking ahead and beginning to realize what might happen.

By the end of Act III the meaning of Nora's life became clear. Katō saw that "Nora's eight years—eight years of hardships for her husband, of laughing and crying for her husband, of bearing three children—for Nora this was merely the difficult path for reaching self-awareness," all part of a process.[48] Contrary to Raichō, Katō felt Nora did suffer and learn and grow in order to gain self-awareness by the end of the play. In the end Katō exclaimed, "Isn't the act of throwing away the 'Doll House' in fact a splendid one?"[49]

In her article "Reading *A Doll House*," Ueda Kimi positioned herself somewhere between Raichō and Katō. Like Raichō she took the initial doll-like Nora at face value. But whereas Raichō upbraided Nora for her lack of agency, Ueda used this missing element to excuse Nora. Going from her father's home to her husband's and then having three children, "the beautiful Nora who was loved like a doll *never had a chance to see her own self.*" Again Ueda noted that "Nora is a person who *can not escape from* her innocent pride, her lack of common sense, and her fanciful emotions."[50] All agency was removed, and Nora became an even more pitiful character than she was in Raichō's reading." However, like Katō, Ueda felt that in the end Nora discovered her true self. Her earlier lack of agency did not prevent her from ultimately becoming self-aware. In response to Helmer's abusive reaction Ueda wrote, "How unexpected from the husband she felt would give his life for her sake. This caused the heart of poor Nora who had decided to go to her death instantly to rebel; . . . in that heart her true self suddenly flashes, and the shock of awakening from years of sleep leaves her blood cold."[51] Unlike Raichō, who saw Nora's childlike disposition as an obstacle to true self-awareness, Ueda believed that such a transformation could indeed occur.

Yasumochi Yoshi's response in "Concerning *A Doll House*" was more complex than Ueda's. Yasumochi started by discussing how unnatural Nora's awakening seemed and gradually worked her way to an appreciation of it and a projected happy ending. She argued, "Can't we think that Ibsen, in order to cause Nora—especially at the end—to be more active and in order to keep the audience from getting bored, portrayed the change in personality to an extreme?" Yasumochi felt the change was too sudden, "a mere three days."[52] Like the male critic Asai, Yasumochi reminded her readers that she was discussing a character in a play, not an actual person, and that certain techniques were used to keep an audience's interest. But while Asai used this approach to dismiss Nora's final action, Yasumochi employed it to justify Nora's abrupt transformation.

Yasumochi characterized Nora's awakening as a progression from feminine qualities to masculine ones. In discussing Nora's doll-like treatment, Yasumochi wrote, "But Nora did not have the self-awareness to complain about such treatment. She thought it natural and the finest of womanly virtues to do things like a slave. . . . She was thus simply . . . like a little girl, an innocent woman."[53] On Nora's final decision to leave her home and family she remarked, "There is no other way to educate the self than to leave this home. . . . Thus, in the end, with *firm, manly free will* [*ketsuzen ōshikumo jiyū ishi*] and guided by reason, she acts *manly* [*isagiyoku*] for the sake of *truth*."[54] It is unclear whether Yasumochi consciously shifted her language from womanly to manly virtues or if she was simply using the conventions of the day to highlight Nora's change in behavior. Although she began by calling Nora unnatural, near the end she wrote, "I admire Nora's courage and determination."[55]

Yasumochi also speculated about what would happen next. Maybe Nora would join a group of entertainers, earn a living, learn about the world.

Gradually she will think of her children and her husband. She will have a second spiritual awakening and return home. No, as an awakened woman she *must* return home. And she finally will have the miracle marriage she hoped for. She will obediently serve her husband with body and soul. He, with the same heart, will love her.

Together they will educate the children. Moreover, they will respect each other's individual free will and help each other work toward the perfection of their character.[56]

In Yasumochi's interpretation, the story would end on a happy note. While Raichō turned to a Buddhist spiritual solution, Yasumochi seemed to espouse a more Christian one.[57] In her vision, a woman's place was in the home with a family, but men and women were equal before God. "In the God-created being there was originally no distinction between man and woman, they had the same value. If you are a person devoted to the perfection of character, there is no difference between male and female, high and low."[58] Raichō envisioned a genderless state of being, Yasumochi one of gender equality.

Ueno Yō in "From *A Doll House* to the Woman Problem" combined Yasumochi's Christian-sounding ideal of marriage with a dash of "good wife, wise mother" ideology.

Women must gain their own perspectives and nurture their abilities, so that they can become good conversation partners to men, good consulting partners to them, and even their right hand in managing their lives. When this happens, man would treat woman with proper respect; woman on the other hand would encourage, console, and respect man, without resentment but with her characteristic submissiveness, standing with the self-awareness and pride of being his high-minded helper and partner in life.[59]

Ueno approved of Nora's struggle for self-awareness but disapproved of her decision to leave home. The real challenge was to work this conflict out within the family.

Ayako Kano speaks of the "re-wifeing" of Nora—the need to reharness her energies to the image of "good wife, wise mother"—as a frequent response to *A Doll House* in Japan.[60] I contend that while some of these women's arguments resembled a reworking of "good wife, wise mother" rhetoric, they were in fact rebelling against this constraining image. Many Seitō women opposed marriage as it was defined under the existing Civil Code.[61] Some experimented with free love, others entered a series of monogamous relationships, others made lifelong commitments to a single partner. The marriages they envisioned included equality, respect, character building. They were not against all marriages, just those that relegated women to subordinate status. Like Nora, they realized they had to walk away from the social conventions that stifled them.

Most of the public criticism and commentary was directed at Nora and her awakening. Little attention was given to Helmer and his behavior. Raichō only briefly noted that Helmer too was an unawakened soul; then she returned to chiding Nora. Ueda mentioned Helmer's tirade against Nora only to analyze the effect it had on Nora's awakening. Ueno accused Nora of being stubborn when she rejected Helmer's attempts to make amends in the end. Katō and Yasumochi, however, had a few harsh words to say about Helmer. And Matsui Sumako, the actress who played Nora, raised the issue of audience reactions to Helmer.

A two-page interview with Matsui appeared in the 1912 *Seitō* Nora supplement; it was titled "What Gave Me the Most Trouble on Stage." Half of the interview concerned mechanical difficulties. For instance, in Act II her hair did not come down during her frantic dancing, or it came down too quickly. In Act III she had difficulty with Helmer's cloak, worrying whether she was pulling it on inside-out or upside-down, and whether it was tied tightly enough to stay on, but loosely enough for Helmer to pull off. The remainder addressed a more troubling difficulty: the different reactions to the confrontation between Helmer and Nora. In the play's final scene two dramatic shifts in Helmer's attitude helped Nora realize she needed to leave home for her own sake. Before reading Krogstad's letter, Helmer claims, "You know what Nora—time and again I've wished you were in some terrible danger, just so I could stake my life and soul and everything, for your sake."[62] After reading the letter he rants, "Oh, what an awful *awakening!* In all these eight years—she who was my pride and joy—a hypocrite, a liar—worse, worse—a criminal! How infinitely disgusting it all is! The shame! . . . Now you've wrecked all my happiness—ruined my whole future."[63] Later, after learning his reputation is saved, he reverts to "But you think I love you any the less for not knowing how to handle your affairs? No, no—just lean on me; I'll guide and teach you. I wouldn't be a man if this feminine helplessness didn't make you twice as attractive to me. You mustn't mind those sharp words I said—that was all in the first confusion of thinking my world had collapsed."[64] Matsui commented, "It seems many people were surprised when Nora became a self-aware, strong, cool woman."[65] Yet she wondered why people were not surprised by the sudden shifts in Helmer's personality as well, and she bemoaned the unquestioned attitudes that kept Helmer beyond reproach.

Katō pointed out, "In the end, Helmer showed his true self. He showed the true character of a human being—no, of an egoistical, individualistic male. Helmer's male personality, which to this point was above

Nora's female one, fell to the ground. At the same time, Nora's moved several steps up."[66] Katō obviously was pleased with Nora's awakening and disappointed in Helmer's lack of growth. But one could argue that Nora's decision to leave home was as egoistic and individualistic as Helmer's behavior or that by putting her own needs first she was moving "several steps up" because she was behaving more "male" than he. I feel Katō believed Nora was pursuing a more noble cause than simply honor or reputation. Ueno found Nora's decision to leave home both childish and self-centered, an interesting combination of "female" and "male" traits. Katō did not delve into these questions but remained focused on Nora's awakening and the situation of women.

For Yasumochi, the problem of self-awareness applied to both women and men, as it had for Ukita earlier. She wrote, "*A Doll House* sketches the process of a woman going from an unaware state to one of awareness. At the same time it explains to men the pressing need for awareness and urges this on them."[67] Men too had to awaken from their dreams. After discussing Nora's shortcomings, she turned to Helmer's faults. "I don't feel Helmer is a person of depth and refinement who endeavors to cultivate himself and who attaches importance to character. He is, all things considered, a man of superficial morals. That is to say, rather than using his cultivation to become a source of societal morals, he is instead governed by existing customs, morals, and laws."[68] He did not have the strength of character to see beyond his own reputation. He did not have the self-awareness that would allow him to try to better society. He lacked humanity. It was Nora who returns him to the fold. "Through the Krogstad incident, Nora rather than her husband gains awareness. It is Nora's leaving that causes Helmer to return to being human."[69] In this way Nora was saving not only herself but potentially Helmer too.

These five *Seitō* women and the actor Matsui Sumako did not present a united front. Yet they all expressed a desire for women to advance internally and externally. For them, the New Woman was clearly someone who demanded respect as a woman and equal treatment with men. They focused largely on inner spiritual awakening, yet they also realized that external customs, laws, and attitudes were obstacles to women's development. They did not clearly denounce these obstacles in these writings, as some of them would later on.[70] Although they railed against the conventions that keep Nora doll-like, ignorant, and essentially unaware within her marriage, not a single one questioned the law that prevented Nora from signing her own name to a loan. This was the early stage of their own self-awakening. They had only just begun to define the New Woman and her place in a modernizing Japan.

At this early stage in the New Woman debate Seitō women and the male scholars and journalists did not differ greatly. They all shared an interest in the development of modern theater in Japan, and they all engaged in the discussion of the New Woman. These two elements were part of a quest to be "modern." For the Seitō women being modern meant creating for women (and men) a new image that they felt was necessary for a new, strong Japan. For the other critics it meant appearing modern to the outside world without dismantling Japan's own customs and laws. In analyzing *A Doll House,* many of them disagreed with Nora's decision to walk out on her husband and children. Some also acknowledged that both women and men needed to discover their true selves.

Yet, differences emerged. The male critics emphasized the community over the individual and upheld the government line that women served the nation by serving their families. They tried to reinterpret Nora's behavior in order to bring her back into the "good wife, wise mother" mold.[71] The Seitō women opened up new directions. They moved beyond "good wife, wise mother" to talk about strength, independence, and self-awareness for women. They wanted to create an individual who functioned within a community, not one who was subordinate to it. They did not just mention the existence of a Man Problem too but examined Helmer's character alongside Nora's. They spoke of men and women in relation to each other and of the need for respect, equality, and true partnership. They did not want women to be subservient to men. As the women of Seitō continued to push in these new directions, the gap between them and the conservative critics widened, as did the variety of options concerning gender construction.

CHAPTER 3

Sudermann's Magda

NEW WOMAN CENSORED

*I*n May 1912, the Literary Society followed up on the success, themes, and sensation of *A Doll House* by staging a public performance of German playwright Hermann Sudermann's *Magda,* a story of a defiant daughter turned successful career woman.[1] Once again a New Woman strutted across the stage. Once again critics talked about the play, the lead actor, the New Woman's unconventional behavior, and how modern (or not) Japan was becoming. But this time the government intervened and prohibited any future performances unless the ending was altered to be in line with accepted morals. Revisions were made, many critics objected, and Seitō women once again added their thoughts.

Magda proved to be the sequel to *A Doll House* in many ways. *A Doll House* left most viewers wondering what would become of the New Woman once she left home. *Magda* focuses on what happens when the New Woman returns home. Nora was sheltered and naive, with little experience outside the home. Magda suffered hardships, learned how to survive on her own, and became a successful, independent woman. Nora walked out on her husband and children; Magda defied her father and supported her child alone. Nora's conduct prompted animated discussion of the New Woman; Magda's behavior drew the ire of the government censors. Nora challenged established gender roles embodied in the "good wife, wise mother" image; Magda defied patriarchal authority in general. If *A Doll House* helped launch the New Woman debate in Japan, *Magda* helped clarify what made the New Woman distinct, modern, and potentially dangerous.

The four intersecting elements discussed in relation to *A Doll House* are evident in relation to *Magda* as well. The production of *Magda* was another step in the development of Japan's New Theater, with Matsui Sumako advancing her reputation as a fine actor.[2] New Theater and New Women continued to be integrally linked to discussions of what it meant to be modern and how Japan was faring on this front. Whether the New Woman (and the Woman Problem) was a reality in Japan continued to be pondered and debated. The New Woman's opposition to the patriarchal order on which Japan's modern state was based elicited both enthusiasm and alarm.

The Home Ministry decided Magda's defiance of her father and subsequent actions were dangerous to public morals and, after the initial ten-day run of the play in Tokyo, banned any future performances. The banning of *Magda* helped solidify the connection between New Women and unacceptable behavior, which the activities of Seitō women would soon reinforce. This chapter explores how *Magda* came to be performed, censored, revised, and restaged; it focuses on the critical reactions to the both the play and its censorship. This examination enables us to see how governmental concerns, women's liberation, artistic license, and notions of modernity conflicted and overlapped. In so doing, it also contributes to our understanding of the development and definition of the New Woman in Japan.[3]

The Play

Magda represents the clash between the modern spirit of freedom and individualism and old-fashioned repression. The entire action of the play takes place in the home of a retired lieutenant-colonel named Schwartze. Twelve years earlier his eldest daughter, Magda, had rejected a match with the pastor Heffterdingt and was cast away from home. When she sent a letter the following year saying she was making her way in the world as an actor, the break was complete. Schwartze, as patriarch of a strict, old-fashioned household, was deeply concerned with preserving family honor. There was no room in his world-view for "modern ideas." Meanwhile, most people in this provincial German city are caught up in preparations for a music festival. Magda's aunt and the pastor discover that the famous opera singer everyone is fussing over is none other than the prodigal daughter Magda. With the pastor paving the way, the stage is set for a father-daughter reunion and a renewed clash between old and new thought.

In Act II, Magda returns home after her long absence. She seems to desire acceptance as she is, rather than forgiveness for past deeds. Once again the pastor serves as mediator convincing Magda to remain at home for a few days rather than return to her hotel. In her world—the outside world, the modern world, the theater world—she acts by her own will. At home she immediately feels the weight of her father's will. Magda is saddened to learn from the pastor that her decision to become an actor many years earlier caused her father to suffer a stroke and consequently to be discharged from the army. Her independent choices had repercussions, and Magda feels the weight of these consequences. She agrees to stay at home for a few days on one condition: she must not be questioned about her life away from home.

Act III reveals even more the gap between Magda's world and her father's. She is financially independent enough to provide the funds necessary for her younger sister, Marie, to marry her suitor, Max. With the pastor she talks about being different, about not being submissive but instead using her voice to bend men's wills to her. She appalls the society ladies who visit her father's residence by emphasizing the need for a vocation over a home. And when City Councilor Von Keller, who had walked away from a youthful romantic liaison with Magda in Berlin years earlier, attempts to reestablish ties with the now-famous actor, he learns that their union produced a child. Magda's father, who has been obsessed with confirming that she remained chaste in her years of wandering, questions Von Keller to no avail and finally orders Magda into his room.

Magda apparently reveals all behind closed doors, and Act IV begins with her begging to leave in order to make the house "pure again." Schwartze refuses and then storms out of the house saying he will restore her honor. While he seeks out Von Keller in order to exact a marriage proposal, the pastor once again smoothes the way by convincing Magda to accept the proposal for the sake of her father, her family name, and her child. She initially accepts, but on learning that Von Keller expects her to give up the stage to become a "proper" wife and to send their child away to spare his reputation, she refuses. Schwartze, unable to bear his daughter's dishonor and disobedience yet again, threatens to take Magda's life and his own, suffers a second stroke, and dies.[4]

As with *A Doll House,* the media initially focused on the theatrical aspects of *Magda,* not on Magda's status as a New Woman. The New Theater movement was still in its early stages and was being discussed as part of the many debates linked to Japan's development as a modern nation. Shimamura Hōgetsu, translator and director of the Literary Society's *Magda,* was at the center of efforts to create a legitimate modern theater in Japan. As with *A Doll House,* which he also had directed, he seemed more interested in *Magda*'s status as a modern (Western) masterpiece than in its controversial content. He trumpeted the importance and popularity of *Magda* in Europe, asserting that Magda was "the most analyzed heroine in modern European theater."[5] Other critics focused on the quality of the play itself, critiquing both Sudermann's writing and Shimamura's translation. The general consensus seems to have been that *A Doll House* was the superior piece of writing, but the acting was better in *Magda*.[6]

The quality of the acting in *Magda* was proof that the Literary Society was succeeding in creating a modern theater with modern (female) actors. *Magda* was the Literary Society's third production, and it is natural to expect that the actors' abilities would be improving. But the reviews were almost unanimous in their praise, especially when it came to Matsui Sumako, who once again played the female lead. Not only was she the star of the play, but she also had become the star of the Literary Society. One critic noted, "There is a remarkable difference in Sumako's artistic development

FIGURE 3. Matsui Sumako as Magda. From reprint of *Seitō* 2, no. 6 (June 1912). *Courtesy of Fuji Shuppan.*

between Nora and Magda."[7] She had developed into a "first-rate, modern, talented actress" who "single-handedly carries the Literary Society on her back."[8] There were a few complaints about her high-pitched voice, but even the critic who called her performance "unimaginative" still noted she had a "promising future."[9] In general, the actors were praised for their progress, seriousness, and enthusiasm, even when their performances were not quite up to par.

Even the *Magda* supplement *Seitō* appended to its June 1912 issue concentrated more on the theatrical than the critical. Playwright and novelist Hasegawa Shigure applied her expertise and contributed a basic review of the play. She devoted the majority of her essay to an evaluation of the various actors' performances, particularly praising Matsui Sumako and the actor who played the pastor.[10] Otake Kōkichi provided commentary on the acting and other technical aspects of the play. She admired the performances of Doi Shunsho (Schwartze) and Tōgi Tetsuteki (Von Keller), praised Matsui's skill and earnestness, and accused Hayashi Nagami (Marie) of making "the biggest mess of things." She complimented the lighting, noted that the backdrop needed to be upgraded, and worried that the rattling set would cause a prop to fall from its high perch. She did not discuss the contents of the play.[11] Again, as with *A Doll House,* a serious, critical analysis of the plot and its ramifications would soon follow. Journal articles comparing and contrasting the characters of Nora and Magda and the central themes of the two plays and discussing also the connections to the Woman Problem began to appear that same month.

The Ban and the Revision

Although these general comments on the play were in response to the Literary Society's performances in early May 1912, the subsequent ban on performance triggered a heated discussion of censorship-related issues. Why was the play initially approved but then banned? Why ban *Magda* and not *A Doll House?* What were the reactions to the ban? Should the Literary Society have revised the script? An examination of reactions in the media will begin to answer these questions, illuminate some of the major concerns of the day, and reveal how the government used censorship to help enforce "appropriate" moral and gender behavior.

Initially the authorities had viewed the play as a harmless contribution to modern Japanese theater, as well as a sign of Japanese modernity in general. Prior to the opening of the play at the Yuraku Theater, the script had been submitted to the government censors and approved. Police Chief Naruzawa Sadayuki gave three reasons for its approval. First, it was a foreign play written by a non-Japanese. The implications here are twofold: the staging of foreign (i.e., Western) plays made Japan seem modern, and its foreign origin and mind-set meant it would not (or could not) be readily absorbed into the Japanese consciousness. As with *A Doll House,* the emphasis was on form over content, on the appearance of modernity over its permeation into society. Second, *Magda* was a Literary Society production. The Literary Society was respected for its efforts to reform and develop Japanese theater, endeavors that contributed to Japan's attempts to appear modern. Third, the society also was credited with cultivating modern artistic knowledge and tastes among the viewing (and reading) public. The authorities were confident that the spectators *Magda* would attract would have the proper critical abilities to handle the play.[12] It thus appears that government officials approved of *Magda* because it seemed to fit with Japan's modernizing project. One wonders whether the script was even read.

Once *Magda*'s contents were made public on the stage, a negative evaluation quickly swept away the positive reasons for initially approving the script. Five days after *Magda* closed its initial ten-day run, the Tokyo Metropolitan Police Department officially prohibited any future performances. Home Ministry Security Head Ishihara Raishi indicated that although the script itself had raised no objections, the performance of it revealed its dangerous elements.[13] An Osaka newspaper pinpointed the moral problem. The 1890 Imperial Rescript on Education, issued shortly after the Meiji constitution, provided a moral foundation for the new nation-state by emphasizing loyalty and filial piety. The authorities felt that Magda's unfilial behavior went unpunished in the play and thus the play contradicted Japanese mores.[14] In supporting the ban, Police Chief Naruzawa noted this "discrepancy in moral standards" between Japan and the West and questioned the acumen of the Japanese audience. "Even if this script has not been banned to date in Europe and America, it was inevitable in Japan where sympathies are different. I feel the ban on performance is a little late as the play has already closed. In other words, at some point it must have been performed in front of people lacking in critical ability and I fear in what direction this may lead."[15] Being a modern, foreign masterpiece was thus not enough to keep a play from being censored if its message ran counter to "national morals." And although the Literary Society was to be commended for its contributions to modern Japanese theater, government officials decided its choice of plays was flawed and its education of the public incomplete.

It seems the authorities were relying on a modern "critical ability" to help the Japanese distinguish between their own sense of morality and the errant ways of the West. Without this ability the Japanese would remain backward and easily swayed by new thought, regardless of the dangers it might present. The Japanese needed to acquire a modern sensibility in order to be able to distinguish the useful from the threatening and to create a distinctively Japanese modern nation. The drive to be modern involved borrowing extensively from the West but not slavishly imitating it and thereby experiencing the same social and moral upheavals.

All these justifications beg the question: Why ban *Magda* and not *A Doll House?* Was allowing *A Doll House* to be performed merely an oversight on the part of the censors, or was Magda's behavior deemed more disturbing than Nora's? Nora walked away from husband and children, effectively discarding the state-supported role of "good wife, wise mother." Magda broke away from her father and family, showing a disregard for filial piety at a time when Japan was defining itself as a "family-state" with the emperor as a "father figure."[16] Both women transgressed fundamental ideologies of a modernizing Japanese state. By banning *Magda,* was the government indicating that defying the family-state—an image/entity gendered male—was potentially more damaging than defying the image of "good wife, wise mother"? Seitō member Kiuchi Tei's reaction suggested the real issue. She writes, "In Nora, the play ended with [Nora] leaving home. However, Magda, dismissed as a daughter, returned to her father's home as a great success, as a winner. Don't you think Magda is truly a New Woman?"[17] Nora's future was uncertain. Could she survive on her own in the world? Would she return home and beg forgiveness? Would she end up relying on another man? Magda proved that she could make it on her own, without a man to support her, and that she could return home on her own terms. Magda's success made her the more alarming example of female independence.

Interestingly and sadly, these issues were not deeply discussed in the critical response to *Magda.* The government, concerned about morality and control, would not tolerate opposition to the patriarchal social foundation of the modern state. Press regulations that dated back to the early Meiji period and would remain basically intact until 1945 reinforced an earlier pattern of self-censorship. Because written materials were reviewed only after the costs of printing already had been incurred, publishers and writers were well aware that censorship would be financially damaging.[18] Possibly, fear of censorship helped to stifle open debate of gendered issues like "good wife, wise mother," patriarchal authority, and female independence. The fact that *Seitō*   ·

had been issued its first ban on publication the previous month could help to explain the general reticence of Seitō women.[19]

Rather than touch on these deep issues, many connected with the literary world came to the play's defense and opposed the ban on other, often contradictory, grounds. Some argued the plays weaknesses, others its merits. Many spoke generally of a conflict between old thought and new thought and identified the new as modern and progressive. Others argued that the play was outdated, offered nothing new, and therefore was not dangerous. Some even mentioned that censoring *Magda* was ineffective because it drew more attention to the work than was warranted. So many voices speaking out against the ban on performance is not surprising. Writers had a vested interest in protesting any infringement on artistic expression. Even though they did not necessarily support or defend the New Woman and her actions, they used the commotion she generated as a springboard for expressing their own concerns.

Critic, writer, and translator Uchida Roan, who had seen his own work censored, argued against the censorship of *Magda* by claiming the play was outdated and by disparaging Sudermann's talents. He was quick to note that the play was twenty years old. "And it is not the clash of old and new thought we have today. . . . Today's is becoming sharper, not that sentimental stuff of the past."[20] Uchida accused Sudermann of being more interested in theatricality than in good writing, of pandering to the masses instead of trying to elevate them. In a dismissive way he commented, "So even though he [Sudermann] occasionally includes new trends, he doesn't show them keenly. So he doesn't have the power to be a strong stimulus to people." For Japanese authorities who banned the work of this mediocre playwright Uchida used the word "spineless" (*ikujinashi*).[21]

Magda's translator and director, Shimamura Hōgetsu, added his voice in an article for the Yomiuri newspaper, making light of the whole issue of censorship. This article calmly explained his reasons for choosing *Magda*. He claimed that he was innocent of espousing any particular ideology and that he was promoting art for art's sake. He asserted that he chose the play as a good showcase for Matsui Sumako and because it was a modern play that would promote modern thought, not because of its feminist or ideological issues. In fact, he claimed, Sudermann did not care about ideological issues. Shimamura agreed with Uchida and others that Sudermann was famous for his stage technique and not for the depth of writing.[22]

Mrs. Penlington, a foreign critic writing in the Yomiuri paper, used the issue of censorship to question Japan's modernity. She was "shocked" when *Magda* was banned, noting that it had been performed in the West for many years without any ill effect. She hinted at the lingering backwardness of the Japanese people. "Weak people may follow in Magda's footsteps. Strong people would take her life as a warning." Penlington indicated her own views on morality and Japanese theater by mentioning that many foreigners viewed Kabuki plays—the majority of which are set in the pleasure quarters—as "the height of vulgarity." Her final judgment of the censors was that "they are clearly ignorant of the true spirit of good theater."[23]

Even Professor Ukita Kazutami, who in his essays on *A Doll House* maintained that Nora should not have left home because men and women need to work together to better society, did not find censorship of *Magda* warranted. "I can't say that it doesn't include some dangerous elements, but in the end it takes the position of social improvement. . . . I don't feel it is something that will damage public morals or ideology."[24] Ukita worried about the Japanese being too narrow-minded and welcomed the Literary Society's efforts to expand their horizons.

Some critics opposed the ban and argued for a more practical approach that involved understanding and addressing the issues raised by the play. One reporter wrote of being between two worlds, between old and new. Because "no country in the world can escape the clash of old and new thought," it is necessary to "strive to cultivate our power of understanding."[25] Religion scholar and Tokyo University professor Anesaki Masaharu believed that "parental thought and youthful thought are completely and mutually contradicting" and that the clash portrayed in *Magda* "is a reflection of actual society."[26] He argued that the ban on *Magda* drew attention to the play and created its own problem. Anesaki felt censorship was an ineffective means of preserving national morality. Instead he argued that seeing the clash performed as art enabled the spectator to objectively evaluate both sides. Change is inevitable, but all that is old need not be discarded and all that is new should not be accepted. Anesaki questioned, "How can we improve dangerous, modern thought? How can we guide the future?"[27] Another reporter agreed that although the authorities were justified in their concerns about the play's contents, the solution involved coming to terms with new ideas, not suppressing them. He stated, "In the eyes of an old thinker, a new thinker appears rash and unreasonable. To the ears of a new thinker, the words of an old thinker sound like the ramblings of a fool. How should old and new advance together to harmonize this gap? This is today's problem."[28]

Although the ban on the performance of *Magda* drew considerable media attention, the Literary Society's decision to revise the ending of the play also proved newsworthy. Headlines proclaimed "*Magda*'s Comeback" and even "Watered-Down *Magda* Dissolves the Ban."[29] These articles reported that changes had been made to the final scene, the ban on performance had been lifted, and preparations were under way for a Kansai-area tour. The revisions involved Magda's talking more gently with her father, admitting that her selfish, new ways had caused the downfall of the household, and accepting all the blame.

Director Shimamura clarified his reasons for modifying *Magda* and for wanting the play to appear even in altered form. "In short, because the art of these actors and the theatrical skill of the playwright are rare things in modern Japan's art world, it is for these reasons that I don't want to bury it, that I want to bring it to Osaka. In other words, the Society has a responsibility and the work should be modified."[30] Because he was more interested in promoting modern theater than in engaging in gender or moral debates, he was thus willing to alter *Magda* to appease the authorities. Clearly he had an economic stake in staging future performances of *Magda* as well.

Shimamura justified the revision for art's sake, but not everyone in the literary world agreed with this assessment. A number of academic men expressed their dissatisfaction with the Literary Society's willingness to modify *Magda*, wondering why the group had not replaced it with another play or simply retained their artistic integrity by observing the ban. "They are losing the central meaning of the work. What is this thing called *Magda* they will present to the public?"[31] Unlike Shimamura, these disgruntled men of letters felt a revised *Magda* was a disservice to the public, the play, and the prestige of the Literary Society. Another critic, unimpressed with *Magda*'s artistic quality, feared the Literary Society would "turn toward profit making and make popular appeal its main point" and requested that the society engage in more "serious projects."[32]

Defining the New Woman

By early June newspaper coverage of *Magda* had largely diminished, and lengthier journal articles began to appear. Many of the same issues continued to be discussed, including the quality of the acting, the merits of the play, and the pros and cons of censorship. The clash of old and new and the need for some middle ground were explored in more detail than in the newspaper articles, and connections with Japan's efforts to become modern became more explicit. In addition, new issues emerged concerning motherhood and the definition of the New Woman.

In the six months between the performances of *A Doll House* and *Magda* the existence of the New Woman and the Woman Problem in Japan became less questioned and more acknowledged. Some still denied the problem, claiming that "there is as yet in our country little women's awakening. The Woman Problem as yet does not seem to be occurring."[33] Others began to accept it. "In Japan today, Magda is rare and Schwartze is everywhere. Magda is the faint light of dawn, Schwartze is a hot day. . . . Although Magdas are few, their light faintly is rising above the horizon."[34] Many openly admitted that Japan had a Woman Problem too. One writer claimed, "Like many of Japan's daughters recently, Magda wants to escape from a cold, oppressive household and live a free and independent life."[35] Another declared, "To cover up offensive things and pretend not to see them . . . is cowardice."[36] These writers shared a growing realization that the Woman Problem needed to be studied, discussed, and understood. Only then did Japan have a chance of minimizing its ill effects. Japan must not make the same mistakes as the West and allow the Woman Problem, and its companion the New Woman, to run rampant.

Part of the reason the Woman Problem came to be accepted in Japan was because of its connection with modernity. Progress meant changes not only in science, technology, industry, and government but in social relationships as well. The conflicts between household and individual, between old and new morals that these two plays portrayed so clearly were inevitable signs of the times. One commentator noted that "as society advances and becomes more complicated, these conflicts cannot be avoided."[37] Another linked the scientific and the social by referring to women's (and men's) awakening as part of "the evolution of all things."[38] Yet another wrote of a worldwide progressive spirit that pushed all else aside. "There is nothing to do but strive to make the advantages [of this spirit] many, and the evils few."[39] Coping with the Woman Problem and the New Woman was part of "being modern," but Japan needed to create a Japanese-style modernity.

Higuchi Hideo sought to connect Japan with general trends, but not with Euro-American outcomes. He mustered an extensive knowledge of Japanese and Western history in order to prove that the Woman Problem was an inevitable consequence of modernity and that Japan needed to comprehend it prior to its reaching the country's shores. "The direct origin [of the Woman Problem] is in the revolutionary spirit of the modern world of thought and the great changes in the industrial world that accompanied it."[40] This "modern world of thought" encompassed the French Revolution, Jean Jacques Rousseau and the theory of the social contract, and Japan's own

Freedom and People's Rights movement in the 1870s and 1880s. He traced the women's movement from Olympe de Gouges and Mary Wollstonecraft to the Women's Rights Convention in Seneca Falls, New York, and similar developments elsewhere in the West. He crisscrossed continents and time periods, presenting the historical background to Japan's impending situation. He viewed the Woman Problem as a serious threat to social morals and organization and urged that it be seriously studied.

Tsutsumi Kito, a female contributor to *Fujo Shinbun* (Women's Newspaper), argued for a different view of awakening than the one provided by Nora and Magda. "I can assert one thing—throughout our country's history women have always been awakened. They have always had an important relationship to the ups and downs of the nation."[41] Japanese women did not need suddenly to come to their senses. For her, awakening was not about selfishly pursuing one's own independent life-style but about striving alongside men to improve the family and the nation. "When the male-female relationship is morally bound together you can compensate for the strong and weak points on both sides. You can navigate a happy life . . . and expand the welfare of the human race."[42] Both Higuchi and Tsutsumi presented an enlightened, yet conservative perspective on the Woman Problem. They showed an awareness of the historical origins—both Japanese and Western—of modern trends but argued for a Japanese approach to modernity that emphasized the family and the nation, not the individual.

The serious social threat posed by *Magda* had resulted in harsh criticism and censorship. It also produced a call for a middle ground, for some kind of compromise between individual and community. Several critics expressed the need to temper the lack of discretion in modern thought. Although they sought balance and moderation, they focused almost exclusively on Magda and her disturbing behavior, with little mention of modifying Schwartze's oppressive behavior. Two male critics writing in women's magazines, T. Shirai and Miyake Yujirō, questioned whether the quest for self-discovery replaced completely one's obligation to others. Shirai applauded Nora's and Magda's assertions that they had a "duty to themselves" and believed that all people needed such an awareness. However, he cautioned, "the advance of individualism and egoism this far is destruction. If all women awakened and took up this attitude, what would happen to society?"[43] Miyake Yujirō also expressed concern that "[Nora and Magda] knew freedom well, but they did not seem to know the reasons to control it. Even though it is good to do the things you want to do, you are not alone in this world. You should not be a self-centered person."[44] Miyake emphasized the need for compassion in dealing with others. Shirai added, "When you think about Magda's psychology, no matter how much she tried to persevere at individualism, she could not cut the string of love for her father and sister. This suggests that you cannot be free from responsibility."[45]

Critics questioned the benefits of behavior such as Nora's and Magda's not only for society but for the women themselves. The general consensus was that such behavior did not lead to happiness. Shirai asked, "Is such a life-style truly enjoyable?"[46] Another critic, even while arguing that modern young women were misunderstood and oppressed, asserted that Magda herself "could not find peace of mind in such depraved surroundings."[47] Others wrote of the loneliness of an empty room at the end of the day or suggested that "behind that cheerful talk and laughter is the echo of a deep sadness."[48] Hasegawa Shigure, who contributed to *Seitō,* admired Magda's strength of character but pitied her lonely life.[49] For these critics true happiness was to be found in the resolution of the clash between family and individual, not in pursuing one or the other to an extreme.

Even Seitō leader Hiratsuka Raichō added her voice to the call for a balanced resolution. She did not feel Magda had emerged victorious in the end. Raichō asked, "What will become of Magda after her father's death? . . . Can she be free again? Does this show that old and new thought can never completely be harmonized, that with the defeat of old thought, new thought finally wins out? No, I do not think so."[50] She recognized that Magda was still in search of a place to call home. Magda's new life-style had not provided a new home and her old one was no longer sufficient. She needed to discover a "true home," one that allowed her to be herself and to enjoy the warmth and security of family. Even though Raichō was opposed to the restrictive government-sponsored family system, her aim was not to destroy the family but to create a model that allowed for individuality and variety.[51]

The reactions of other Seitōsha women ranged from the theater reviews already mentioned to critical analysis. As with *A Doll House, Seitō* devoted a supplement to *Magda* in June 1912. The *Magda* supplement was far less substantial than the Nora supplement in both length and content. One might have expected a critical evaluation of Magda and a Nora-Magda comparison, but instead most of the articles were about the mechanics of the play, and few were about the New Woman debate. At a mere twenty-one pages, why bother publishing a supplement at all? Perhaps the Seitōsha was simply staying abreast of the general trends of the day. The members kept current with the theater world and regularly discussed it in the pages of their magazine. The early media attention to *Magda* had focused on the performance itself and then on the issue of censorship, while barely mentioning the New Woman or the Woman Problem. *Seitō* followed suit.[52]

Even so, a few Seitō members did draw some comparisons between Nora and Magda and found Magda the more powerful image. Hasegawa felt more of a bond with Magda and her battle between old and new than with Nora and her experiences. "More than the highly acclaimed Nora, Magda had a far stronger effect on me."[53] Magda's struggles and successes in the face of confining familial and social conventions resonated deeply with Kiuchi Tei as well. As already noted, she too felt Magda was the better role model than Nora because Magda succeeded in living an independent, self-supporting life. Magda provided an example of a woman who had challenged societal norms and won.

Only Hiratsuka Raichō offered a detailed critical evaluation of *Magda* and its lead character. Like many other critics, she found the quality of the writing and its power to persuade inferior to that of *A Doll House*. She believed that most people were familiar with the clash between old and new thought and that this play toyed with the emotions not the intellect. Raichō declared, "Rather than seeing *Magda* as a problem play or an assertion of new thought . . . I see it as the complicated, rich emotions of a female protagonist, as the pure thoroughly irremovable feelings between parent and child, between sisters. . . . Rather than appealing to the head, *Magda* is a play that echoes in the heart."[54] Raichō also asserted that Magda was not truly a New Woman. Five months earlier she had questioned whether Nora was truly awakened. Now she had her doubts about Magda as well. While Nora's awakening "did not seem to stem from her internal self but from external oppression," Magda's was driven by her personality, not by a conscious awareness of self. Raichō contended that this "hasty, strong-minded, theatrical daughter did not fit in the home of her strict, unsympathetic, unnecessarily severe father" and that Magda saw in her rejection of the arranged marriage a "good opportunity" to escape.[55]

Although Magda is not credited with being a New Woman when she set off to make her way in the world, Raichō did concede that "if Magda awakened it was after her carnal sacrifice to the frivolous Von Keller resulted in an illegitimate child."[56] Only then does Magda suffer the hardships of life—the scorn of others, the struggle to support herself and her child, the difficulties of building a successful career. Raichō believed hardship and struggle were vital elements in creating a greater sense of self, as well as an independent life. Earlier she had bemoaned the fact that Nora had not suffered enough to become a truly awakened individual. This was clearly not the case with

Magda. Raichō, like Magda herself, noted that Von Keller deserved a bit of credit for enabling the creation of a New Woman. She reasoned that by fathering a child and then abandoning Magda, Von Keller provided the stimulus for Magda's awakening.[57] This interesting role reversal reduces a man's usefulness to his contribution to the reproduction process.

Not just her suffering but her devotion to her child made Magda a New Woman in Raichō's eyes. Raichō chose to focus on Magda the loving mother rather than on Magda the independent, career woman. "For Magda, the one sacred thing, the one true life, is not art but to love as a mother. She had to pursue the life of a performer in truth because of her fatherless child. Her art which receives respect from all, for her is nothing more than what gives bread to her child."[58] Here too, Magda differed greatly from Nora, who walked out not only on her husband but on her children as well. Raichō opposed the government-dictated role of "good wife, wise mother" but defended motherhood as a source of women's strength.[59] For Raichō, New Women rejected patriarchal oppression, not their own maternal instinct. For other critics less concerned with defining the New Woman, Magda's maternal instinct was her one saving grace and helped to make her character a sympathetic one.[60]

For all the uproar over Magda's lack of morality, the focus was on her unfilial behavior toward her father, not on her having a child out of wedlock. Both actions threatened the government-prescribed family system. Why focus on the clash of old and new thought without getting specific about the chastity issue?[61] One explanation is that the authorities felt a breach of familial and gender hierarchy was more damaging to the patriarchal order than a breach of morals. Nora had challenged established gender roles, Magda brought into question the very structure on which the modern state was built. Nora's behavior was lively debated; discussion of Magda's behavior was stifled. One wonders, if Magda were a son walking away from family obligations and asserting his independence, would his behavior have been cause for censorship?

Magda continued to facilitate the discussion of New Theater, New Women, and the connections between gender and modernity that *A Doll House* had initiated. Many of the issues were similar, and, in some cases, answers to questions were becoming clearer. *Magda* proved that modern theater in Japan was improving in quality and gaining in recognition. Japan was indeed becoming modern, and, for better or worse, New Women were becoming a reality. A number of critics, scholars, and writers now accepted the

New Woman and the Woman Problem as signs of modernity and explored ways to incorporate gender-related issues into existing Japanese society.

With *Magda* the government intervened and used censorship to control and suppress unacceptable (female) behavior. The government labeled the play "injurious to public morals."[62] The general consensus was that Magda's defiance of her father was the cause. Changing the play's ending to depict a repentant and once-again filial daughter allowed it to be restaged. But *Magda* challenged the patriarchal order in other ways as well. Magda lived, worked, and raised a child without relying on a man. None of these issues were addressed in any great detail, nor were any of the male characters taken to task for behaving badly. It seems that both actual censorship and the threat of censorship were instrumental in limiting critical responses. Seitō women participated in the discussion of this New Woman as well but did not make any particularly bold statements. Their voices would become increasingly radical once they were personally under attack.

Male and female critics found common ground in opposing the ban on the play and praising Magda's devotion to her child, even though their motivations often differed. Much of the critique of censorship was made in the name of artistic freedom and couched in terms of Japan's modernity. Female independence, a central theme of the play that resonated deeply with many of the Seitō women who were pursuing self-sufficient lives, was not particularly explored or advocated in the analysis of *Magda.* Instead, first the censors and then many critics wanted to see Magda securely entrenched back in the hierarchy of the family system. Although Magda was decidedly a New Woman, both detractors and supporters noted her dedication to motherhood. For detractors, it was a redeeming feature that would help reincorporate the New Woman into acceptable society. After all, one of women's chief "modern" duties was to bear and then successfully raise the next generation. Supporters, notably Seitō leader Hiratsuka Raichō, viewed motherhood not as an obligation but as a source of women's strength and uniqueness. New Women could oppose the patriarchal order and still make a vital contribution to a modern nation through their role as mothers.

The performance, censorship, revision, restaging, and analysis of *Magda* reveal important aspects of the emergence of New Women in Japan and their connections to visions of modernity. New Theater and New Women were becoming accepted as signs of a modern society. Even so, censorship was an important tool in monitoring the thoughts and behavior of people in Meiji-Taishō Japan, and we saw it at work in controlling the breadth and depth of discussion. Although interested in keeping up with Western trends and gaining Western approval, many in the Japanese government and intelligentsia were also concerned with creating a modern state that was still Japanese in character. *Magda* was widely viewed and discussed in the West, but not censored or revised. The play ends with no clear resolution or judgment. Will Magda repent and mend her ways or leave and continue her independent existence? The Japanese censors passed judgment and required that Magda be repentant. The Meiji constitution, the Imperial Rescript on Education, the Civil Code of 1898, and other laws and edicts defined the modern Japanese state as one based on hierarchy, loyalty, and obedience. Male authority was central to this vision, with the emperor as head of state and the father as head of the household.[63] There was little tolerance for female individuality and independence.

The New Woman, represented by Nora and especially by Magda, was increasingly perceived as a negative product of modernity, as a figure intent on destroying the very basis of modern Japanese society—its patriarchal order. Seitō women and their supporters tried instead to promote a positive vision of New Women as those who through self-awareness, independence, and even motherhood would strengthen the modern state. The activities and self-exploration of Seitō members soon made them the focus of the debate and reinforced the negative view of New Women.

CHAPTER 4

Sexuality

NEW WOMEN BEHAVING BADLY

*T*he controversy over *Magda* had barely died down when two scandalous incidents took the New Woman debate in a new direction during the summer of 1912. News of New Women drinking "five-colored liquor" (*goshiki no sake*) and visiting the Yoshiwara was splashed across the pages of several Tokyo newspapers.[1] Both of these unladylike activities involved Seitō women, and both were instrumental in the transformation of New Women from fictional heroines of European dramas into living, breathing, Japanese individuals. The press reports inconsistently accused New Women of being man haters, of being on the prowl for husbands, of having an unnatural proclivity for alcoholic beverages and younger men, of associating with prostitutes, and of having an affinity for same-sex love. The public was both tantalized and horrified by these accounts, and active female sexuality quickly became a defining characteristic of the Japanese New Woman.

Nora and Magda had challenged the established gender roles of subservient wife, mother, and daughter and thereby questioned the patriarchal foundation of the modern nation-state. The actions of a handful of Seitō women in the summer of 1912 further transgressed the boundaries of acceptable female behavior. These New Woman not only defied gender norms but flaunted their sexual nature as well. They went out in public unescorted and visited places—like drinking establishments and pleasure quarters—that were typically considered male territory. They interacted socially with both men and women and wrote about their emotional and sexual experiences. In their quest for personal awareness and fulfillment, they defied male authority and privilege in both the private and the public spheres. Stories about their unconventional life-styles increasingly filled the pages of newspapers and magazines and heralded the emergence of Japan's own New Women.

The "good wife, wise mother" ideology was the standard against which the New Women were measured. Actively promoted by government officials and educators since the late 1890s, the "good wife, wise mother" image defined appropriate conduct for women: women served the nation through their roles within the family.[2] Some women did gain limited access to society at large. Under certain circumstances women's work outside the home was seen as a necessary contribution to the household. For example, the young girls who filled the textile factories were credited with being filial daughters for their contributions to the family's well-being. They also helped fuel Japan's economy.[3] In other cases women exercised the roles of wife and mother publicly in their efforts at social reform, playing an active role in temperance and antiprostitution movements.[4] Gender norms had some elasticity. The Japanese woman could broaden the roles of "good wife, wise mother" and filial daughter as long as she still put society's needs ahead of her own. She was not tagged as a New Woman and a danger to society unless she displayed both open sexuality and selfishness.

The general public did not view prostitutes as New Women, nor were they considered a threat to society. In fact, some of the arguments in favor of continuing the system of licensed prostitution contended just the opposite: legal prostitution helped make the streets safe for good wives and daughters by giving men an outlet for their natural sexual urges. Moreover, because many of the girls came from poor, rural families and by being sold into prostitution helped feed their families, they too could be praised as filial daughters.[5]

New Women distinguished themselves from other women by resisting the "good wife, wise mother" standard and the concept of separate spheres it supported and by pursuing their own self-interest. Part of the media attack on New Women can be viewed as an attempt to protect male privilege. These New Women were infringing on a masculine world that included literature, drinking establishments, and access to pleasure quarters. Meiji-Taishō society, through custom and law, condoned male heterosexual activities. Adultery was not a crime for men according to the Meiji Civil Code, and prostitution was kept legal and well-regulated to satisfy men's needs.[6] These examples of male sexuality were not perceived as a threat to Japanese society, but female sexual intercourse outside of marriage threatened not only the family structure and lineage but the coherence of the entire family-state. Japanese women were to enrich society (and themselves) through their roles as women. The New Woman's self-centered, unconventional behavior was cause for alarm.

Japan pursued modernization in order to strengthen the nation, not the individual. Women were to benefit from and contribute to Japanese modernization in specific ways. They benefited from increased access to education, and they were expected to use this education to contribute to society as efficient household managers and as wise mothers.[7] Even men, although they enjoyed greater freedoms than women did, were supposed to be modernizing for the sake of the nation and not for themselves. Men and women were expected to contribute to the nation in different ways. Male emulation of Western technology, diplomacy, and statesmanship helped strengthen Japan. Female emulation of the New Woman threatened the foundations of Japanese male privilege as well as national strength and stability. At least this was the image created in the press.

The paths these New Women pursued and the reactions they provoked reveal much about attitudes toward change as Japan's first modern era—the Meiji period—came to an end and the Taishō period began.[8] A sense of ambivalence is evident throughout the media attention to the New Woman. Both men and women were grappling with what this image meant on a national and an individual level. Was the New Woman a harbinger of Japan's decline or of its success as a modern nation? Should she be embraced or discarded? The political, economic, social, and cultural changes of the Meiji period had conditioned the Japanese people to view change as inevitable, but they also learned to be wary of excessive borrowing. The multiple reactions to the emergence of a Japanese New Woman indicate a continued negotiation with modernity: How much change was necessary, at what rate, for whom, to what end? The media discussion concerning the New Woman provides a variety of responses to these questions. Some writers championed the New Woman, others dismissed her as frivolous, but many took an equivocal stance.

The scandalous stories that began appearing in the summer of 1912 and that linked Seitō women with alcohol, prostitutes, and deviant love affairs precipitated increased scrutiny of the lives of these Japanese New Women. Their various relationships and life-styles were recounted as examples of female sexuality gone astray. The press had discovered Japanese New Women and was heaping abuse on them. Raichō bemoaned, "Even the denunciation as imitators of Nora and Magda inflicted on us previously was insignificant when compared with the intensity of this personal attack."[9] This chapter examines the events and relationships that fueled the negative media onslaught, analyzes the various reactions, and reveals how closely entwined attitudes about Japan's emerging New Woman and modernity were.

Five-Colored Liquor, the Yoshiwara, and Unrestrained Sexuality

The "five-colored-liquor incident" helped establish a negative view of New Women. (Five-colored liquor was a French drink that was all the rage in Japan.) According to a variety of articles, Seitō members could be found consuming alcohol on a regular basis. They imbibed alcoholic beverages at their organizational meetings and New Year's gatherings, and they frequented bars where exotic beverages were served. They even wrote about alcohol and sexual encounters in their magazine. One reporter opined, "These people have a lover-like fondness for strong Western liquor."[10] He also quoted a Seitō member as saying, "I find the shape of a whiskey bottle unbearably cute."[11] Several reporters used the actions, words, and writings of Seitō members to draw a picture of women who had a fascination bordering on obsession with the look, smell, and taste of alcohol. By the summer of 1912 New Women and drinking were inextricably linked.

A young woman by the name of Otake Kōkichi played a central role in the five-colored-liquor incident and in the ensuing controversy surrounding Japan's New Woman.[12] Kōkichi was born into an artistic family—both her father, Etsudo, and her uncle Chikuha were noted painters—and was raised in the Osaka area. After graduating from a girls' higher school, she was sent to live with her uncle in Tokyo for a short time. During that stay she first heard of the newly formed Seitōsha and its magazine. She was immediately intrigued, and although she soon returned to her family in Osaka, she began writing letters to the Seitōsha office in general and to Hiratsuka Raichō in particular. Her letters were filled with a childlike enthusiasm, passion, and rambling that earned her the reputation within the Seitōsha as "the strange person from Osaka." Raichō finally sent a reply agreeing to accept Kōkichi as a new member and inviting her to draw up a new cover for *Seitō*. Kōkichi's design debuted in March 1912.

Kōkichi and Raichō met for the first time that April. Kōkichi was nineteen years old, and Raichō was twenty-five. Their initial reactions to each other set the tone for what would become a lifelong friendship. Raichō was struck by the younger woman's appearance, noting that "Kōkichi was a lovely, boy-like person who wore a delicate, splash-patterned men's kimono and haori with serge hakama and had a big, tall, roundish body and a full, round face."[13] Her eccentric demeanor was coupled with a youthful exuberance that made her well-liked within the Seitōsha and the subject of gossip without. Raichō found her delightful and treated her with much affection.

Kōkichi's reaction to Raichō was more awe-filled. She raved, "The word sublime doesn't suffice to express the overflowing beauty coming from inside her. Perhaps it's the brilliance of wisdom."[14] Kōkichi immediately felt a "fated connection" with Raichō. Individually and together, these two New Women drew considerable media attention.

In an effort to solicit an advertisement for *Seitō,* Kōkichi visited the Swan's Nest Cafe, a famous gathering place for young artists and writers. The proprietor placed a glass of five-colored liquor in front of her.[15] Whether she drank it is open to debate. However, the artistic Kōkichi was clearly captivated by the colorful beauty of the exotic, Western beverage and incorporated the image into several of her writings.[16] Her repeated fictional invocations of five-colored liquor helped forge the link between New Women and alcohol in the public's eye.

However, the evolving image of the New Woman in the media was not merely about intoxication but about sexual predation as well. These women used alcohol to help them seduce members of the opposite sex. They visited cafes and bars, like the Swan's Nest Cafe, where five-colored liquor first appeared, in order to mingle with writers, artists, and actors and to flirt with students. Some were in search of a husband; others were out simply to have a good time. In either case, many writers, intellectuals, and officials viewed the bold behavior and brazen sexuality of these New Women as an infringement on male territory and a violation of feminine norms.[17]

Almost immediately another incident solidified the connection between New Women and atypical sexual activity: three Seitōsha women spent a night in the Yoshiwara. Kōkichi's uncle Chikuha suggested the trip and made all the arrangements. Because he was well-connected and well-acquainted with the pleasure quarter, he presented the women with a rare opportunity to enter a world usually closed to them and to experience the conditions firsthand. Kōkichi, Raichō, and another Seitōsha member, Nakano Hatsuko, agreed to go. According to Raichō, first they were taken to a teahouse and then on to the highest-ranked brothel in the quarter. They spent the evening speaking with the highly ranked courtesan Eizan, and the three women stayed the night with her while the uncle slept separately. They left the Yoshiwara the following morning.[18]

An early newspaper account of the "Yoshiwara incident" paralleled Raichō's account but condemned the visit as an inappropriate activity for women. A later report added to the perception that Raichō and company were merely "amusing themselves" by extending the visit to three days and mentioning intoxication. The three women were depicted as frivolous, morally bankrupt, and out of line for crossing sexual, gender, and class boundaries.[19] Not only did they enter a world to which only men had free access, but they did so out of curiosity and not with the intent of social reform.[20] They were not conforming to the behavior dictated by their privileged middle-class backgrounds. For these Seitōsha women, the Yoshiwara visit was a new experience, but it did not inspire them to take up the cause of their less fortunate sisters. Their blithe association with loose sexuality and lower-class society allowed their demands for women's awakening and rights to be easily dismissed.

The Yoshiwara incident also provided the media with the chance to highlight the "unfeminine qualities" of one New Woman in particular, Otake Kōkichi. Few reporters could resist commenting on her unusual height, overall size, and style of dress. One declared, "I'm sorry to say but she did not look like a woman."[21] Another listed her height as 5'6" and her weight as 144 pounds, both above average for Japanese women even today.[22] Her habit of wearing somber men's clothing also drew comment. Now, in addition to her striking physical presence, reporters fixated on her fondness for the company of prostitutes.

After the Yoshiwara incident, Kōkichi maintained a correspondence with Eizan, the courtesan who had entertained the Seitōsha women. This relationship, which bridged occupational, social, and class differences, intrigued the press. Kōkichi was quick to remark that Eizan had received some formal education and to compliment her excellent handwriting, a sign of intelligence and refinement. Rather than focus on this novel female friendship, reporters used it to assert Kōkichi's irregular sexual proclivities. One newspaper account suggested that Kōkichi had developed her affinity for the Yoshiwara as a child by accompanying her uncle on his visits. Another rumored that she sought out female companionship and conversation among the prostitutes of unlicensed brothels as well.[23] It was well understood that men consorted with prostitutes, women did not. As we will see below, a series of articles soon focused on Kōkichi's lesbian leanings. The fact that Kōkichi pursued inappropriate relationships set her apart from the female norm, and such tendencies became a distinguishing feature of New Women in general.

Araki Ikuko, another Seitōsha member, represented a different aspect of the New Woman both within the Seitōsha and without. She did not share the privileged upbringing that most of the Seitōsha members had enjoyed. Araki's father died when she was young, and she took on the responsibility of supporting her mother and siblings. She ran a boardinghouse for Waseda

University students and then an inn that served as a meeting place for a varied clientele including literary types, socialists, and refugees from the Chinese revolution. Through her customers she was exposed to and became grounded in literature. When Seitō cofounder Yasumochi Yoshiko's mother arrived from Shikoku to attend her daughter's college graduation, the two of them stayed at Araki's inn. This chance meeting resulted in an invitation to join the Seitōsha. Araki with her unique background added a little color to the list of Seitō's founding members, which consisted largely of Japan Women's College graduates.[24]

Like Kōkichi, Araki contributed to the negative media image of the New Woman by writing about and pursuing inappropriate relationships, this time of a different sort. Her short story "The Letter" caused *Seitō*'s April 1912 issue to be banned. It raised the censors' ire because it told of an adulterous affair in glowing terms.[25] This was the first—but not the last—time *Seitō* would be censored. The story is in the form of a letter that a married woman writes to her male lover telling of her delight in their past secret meetings and hoping for more. The woman rails against the confines of marriage and celebrates the joy of free love. She explains, "In this world where so many things are but superficial formalities, none is so bizarre as the relationship between husband and wife. . . . Because you haven't yet lived in this suffocating realm of 'husband and wife' or 'marriage,' you wouldn't know this. . . . I write this so that you will understand the happiness of lovers."[26] Although she mentions a mutual show of affection between husband and wife, she also claims, "I have never once won his heart, and he has never tried to touch mine."[27] She rejects the limitations of such a marriage in favor of a true connection.

By championing an adulterous affair over a loveless marriage "The Letter" clearly ran counter to "good wife" ideology. The woman boldly asserts, "Although I, too, can be a chaste lady, I have no desire for such an empty honor. Rather than that, if indeed I am a human being, then I wish to be engaged by a deep and human love. Even if such an act were condemned as a terrible sin, I want a life that allows your heart and mine to touch."[28] Although she never explicitly talks about ending her marriage, she does envision her lover making a secret nocturnal visit while the rest of the household is asleep. She ends the letter by mentioning that, "at the beginning of next month, my husband will be away" and imploring her lover to meet her once again at the place they used to frequent.[29]

Araki's illicit and sensual subject matter offended the moral sensibilities of the government censors, but because the prohibition of sale was not issued until April 18, little real damage was done to *Seitō*. As the April issue of the magazine was already sold out, when the police came to the *Seitō* offices to seize the run, they walked out with only one copy. However, the incident did result in the *Seitō* offices being evicted. The following month *Seitō* moved to rooms rented from a Zen Buddhist temple.[30]

Araki's personal life was cause for gossip as well. In its four-part series "The So-Called New Woman," *Kokumin Shinbun* (Citizen Newspaper) devoted an entire article to Araki's uninhibited love life and flaunting of convention. At age twenty-six Araki was still single, running a boardinghouse, and in love with a twenty-two-year-old university student, Masuda Atsuo. The older woman–younger man paradigm was yet another deviant pattern that helped distinguish New Women.[31] The boardinghouse was in financial trouble, and a wealthy Mr. Komatsu—who happened to be the more appropriate age of thirty—agreed to take over and expected Araki's hand in marriage as part of the bargain. Araki, who had been living with Masuda at another boardinghouse, gathered her belongings and ran away. Masuda found her several days later in a disheveled state back at her own boardinghouse, seemingly having chosen the option of financial and marital security. But when she once again saw the face of her lover, she decided to flee from the city with him, disregarding personal and professional commitments in order to satisfy her own selfish passion.[32]

Ambivalent Reactions to the New Woman

The *Kokumin Shinbun* was among the first newspapers to publicize the scandalous activities of these brazen New Women, creating an on going association of Seitōsha women with five-colored liquor, the Yoshiwara, and unrestrained sexuality. The tone of its "So-Called New Woman" series was sensational and trivializing. These were "absurd" women who obviously could not be taken seriously. Their "frivolous behavior" had caused internal dissension and would inevitably lead to the dissolution of the Seitōsha. Nowhere in the articles was there discussion of the writings or ideas of the women mentioned, unless they revealed elements of past or present love affairs. The emphasis was on loose women and liquor.[33]

However, these articles also indicated an increase in the number of women who needed or desired to make it on their own and provided examples of women trying to free themselves from dependence on men. Araki Ikuko's struggles to keep her boardinghouse running, her need to turn to a rich patron, and her decision to choose love over money already have been mentioned. A brief sketch of Kitahara Sueko, a new Seitōsha member and daughter of a respectable provincial family, appeared in another one of the articles. She and her sister came to Tokyo after her parents' death and eked out a living giving lessons on the koto, a traditional Japanese instrument. The reporter indicated that the two sisters allowed themselves to become the "playthings" (*omocha*) of two university students in order to protect their female household from burglars and other hazards. They soon found themselves discarded and turned to various women's magazines to express their anger through writing.[34]

In both dismissing the New Woman as a corrupting influence and recognizing the necessity for some women to be self-sufficient, the "So-Called New Woman" series demonstrated Japanese society's sense of ambivalence toward the New Woman and the modernizing process in general. The articles explored the extremes some of these New Women went to in their search for freedom. In addition to merely making for good gossip, these accounts also helped the general public identify (and steer clear of) these women and served as a warning to other women about the dangers of rejecting appropriate feminine roles. Yet the articles also publicized the need for feminist activity by acknowledging an increase in the number of women fending for themselves. These women expressed frustration at the obstacles standing in their way and sought out like-minded individuals and organizations. Seitōsha membership grew, as did the number of real New Women.

The press continued to focus on the unconventional behavior and love lives of these New Women, and Raichō and Kōkichi continued to serve as prime examples of female sexuality gone astray. In late November 1912, a reporter for the *Tokyo Nichi Nichi Shinbun* (Tokyo Daily Newspaper) began a ten-article series entitled "Strange Love" that shifted the discussion of New Women from *Seitō*'s summertime scandals to "a Love Problem that should be studied." He dismissed the visit to the Yoshiwara and the drinking of five-colored liquor as "novel amusements" that were "colorfully exaggerated." Instead, the reporter claimed he would examine the more insidious behavior identified as "same-sex love."[35] In actuality his scope was broader than that as he focused on three main characters and how they each inverted sexual norms to produce a variety of "strange loves."

The first of his main characters was Seitōsha leader Hiratsuka Raichō. Following the now-established pattern of portraying New Women as transgressors of accepted boundaries, the reporter depicted Raichō as an atypical female. In addition to having received a higher education, Raichō was loath to show weakness, liked to be unconventional, and was full of ambition. The

FIGURE 4. Hiratsuka Raichō around the time of *Seitō*'s first issue. *Courtesy of Otsuki Shoten.*

implication was that these were masculine traits.[36] While at Japan Women's College Raichō had studied philosophy, developed an interest in hypnotism, and independently sought out instruction in Zen meditation—all further evidence of her unconventional nature.[37] Even as he established Raichō as a manly woman, the reporter reasserted a male-female distinction by stating, "[Raichō] is very bright for a woman. Some people say she is even brighter than Shimoda Utako. But when compared with men, she is still a woman."[38]

The general public was familiar with Raichō's aberrant and sensational behavior well before the first issue of *Seitō* was published. In the spring of 1908 newspapers had noised about her alleged double-suicide attempt with young married writer Morita Sōhei. Morita was a teacher at the English school where Raichō was studying and a protégé of the famous author Natsume Soseki. This promising young man and the well-educated, upper-middle-class Raichō journeyed into the snowy Shiobara mountains in March 1908 carrying a pistol and a knife. Raichō left behind two cryptic notes that hinted she was going to her death. After a long, cold night, the two of them were found uninjured.

Raichō recounted what became known as the Shiobara incident in her autobiography. According to her, Morita envisioned the experience of killing her as a means of enhancing his literary talents. Her reasons for going along with the scheme are less clear. This incident occurred shortly after she had achieved a stage of Zen enlightenment, and perhaps she was even more open to experimentation than usual. Raichō explained it as part of her effort to act on her own will, create her own identity, and tap into her internal strength. She maintained that she was not in love with Morita but followed his plan out of curiosity. It was Morita who did not have the fortitude to see it through and spent the evening getting drunk instead. Raichō absorbed herself in the meditative aspects of her surroundings.[39]

The press treatment of the Shiobara incident created a far different impression. The public perceived Raichō as Morita's lover, which meant not only that she was sexually active but that she was having intimate relations with a married man! Calling the incident an attempted double suicide supported the notion that they were hopelessly in love and saw no other way out of their dilemma.[40] Although some considered this attempt a romantic gesture, in general the public viewed Morita and Raichō as foolish, spoiled youngsters corrupted by Western ideas of love and individualism. Morita's identification as a naturalist writer strengthened this view.[41] Morita would provide the most lasting public impression by publishing *Baien*, a fictional account of the incident, the following year. His portrayal of the female protagonist as a headstrong woman who led a bewitched male writer toward destruction reinforced the public's image of Raichō as a brazen and dangerous woman.[42] For years to come Raichō was often identified as the "Baien woman."

The "Strange Love" series revived the Shiobara incident as another example of the inversion of sexual norms through its depiction of Morita Sōhei, the second main character in the series. The reporter portrayed Morita as an innocent rustic from Gifu Prefecture who fell victim to the urbane Raichō. Roles were reversed as the teacher fell for the student, the man was smitten with the woman. The reporter described Morita as effeminate and stated, "As is usual with men of such disposition, they choose strong-minded women. They like women with many male elements. For [Morita] this was [Raichō]."[43] Yet, Raichō continued to blur the male-female distinction. On the one hand she attracted Morita with her intelligence and manly qualities. On the other hand she ensnared him with her feminine looks and wiles. To top it off, she allegedly declared to Morita, "I am asexual." This statement, inspired by the Zen concept of a genderless being, seemed to draw Morita to Raichō even more.

Installments three and four of the "Strange Love" series offered a synopsis of the Shiobara incident. The reporter continued to emphasize the contrast between a weak, bumbling Morita and a strong, calculating Raichō. Raichō, fond of experimenting and pushing boundaries, toyed with Morita while remaining aloof. He would do anything to win her love, and she knew it. Finally, the reporter revealed, she decided that for the two of them to draw close required the most dramatic of changes: they must die together.[44] In the early spring of 1908 they would walk deep into the snow-covered Shiobara mountains, Raichō carrying a short sword, a family heirloom, Morita carrying a newly purchased pistol. Raichō was accustomed to taking unconventional, eccentric actions and like a sweet puppy dog Morita followed her.

Yet, as the reporter noted, the great drama to be enacted on the snowy mountain turned into a great farce. Once they entered the mountains and stopped to rest at an inn, Raichō began to come to her senses. However, not wanting to appear fickle, she continued as planned, relying on Morita to be incapable of going through with the suicide. Indeed, Morita came across in the article as an incompetent coward. Although he was willing enough to follow Raichō into the mountains, the pistol he carried had no bullets, and in his backpack he had stashed a styptic pencil and some bandages. They both found a way out when they were discovered the next morning. Raichō wanted to distance herself from the whole situation, but Morita persisted in pursuing her.[45] He never won Raichō's heart, but his subsequent novel, *Baien,* helped launch his literary career.

According to Raichō, she initiated her first sexual encounter soon after the Shiobara incident. The *Tokyo Nichi Nichi* reporter used this encounter as yet another instance of "strange love" from Raichō's past. He recounted the story of Raichō's affair with a Zen Buddhist monk named Nakahara and portrayed her as a self-centered snob who used people like Morita and Nakahara for her personal ends without any regard for their feelings. Indeed, he claimed, she preferred men who were in some way inferior to her for this very reason. Her aim was not romantic love but to expand herself through a variety of experiences. The reporter remarked, "For [Raichō] it was not first love or anything. Nakahara sometimes said Zen-like things. This is what made her happy, what she loved." It was Nakahara who learned that "loving [Raichō] was a disaster."[46] Another man fell victim to the aloof Raichō.

But men were not the only ones captivated by Raichō. With the introduction of Otake Kōkichi as the third main character in the *Tokyo Nichi Nichi* series, a whole new tale of "strange love" unfolded. The reporter delved into Kōkichi's past in order to establish a pattern of powerful female-female bonding that had its roots in her childhood. He related two stories that he clearly felt had a formative influence on Kōkichi's adult sexual orientation. Although he never explicitly labeled the emotions or actions of the women involved as lesbian, he implicitly suggested as much. Kōkichi had only vague memories of these events but recalled since childhood having a "mysterious [*fushigi na*], different feeling" and a sense of being "caught in a mysterious fate."[47] She previously had expressed a similar sentiment to another reporter: "Since I was a child I've had a curious feeling. It is a feeling I alone enjoy, and one I've never put into words."[48]

Both stories focused on the strong attachment of a beautiful young woman around twenty years old to a seven- or eight-year-old Kōkichi. In the first case, the young woman's affection—which is likened to that of a big sister—turned to obsession. She could not stand to be separated from Kōkichi and ultimately went mad.[49] The second case involved another young beauty who carried the child Kōkichi out of town one night. She took Kōkichi into the mountains to a small shrine above a waterfall and made her drink the holy water as she repeatedly intoned that they would never be parted.[50] As Kōkichi grew up she was repeatedly approached and befriended by other young women. With her family connections to the art world she came to know many women involved in the arts and entertaining. This reporter also joined in the rumors that Kōkichi had enjoyed the company of courtesans from an early age.

With these numerous female "friendships" as a background, the reporter turned his attention to the relationship that developed between Kōkichi and Raichō. According to him, Kōkichi returned to Tokyo in April 1912 not simply to actively join the Seitōsha but because she was drawn to Raichō. He claimed Kōkichi was unaware of the Shiobara incident until she read Morita's autobiography that January. She felt a strong affinity for the Raichō she found in those pages and immediately arranged to go back to Tokyo. The two women met and immediately "formed an affectionate friendship in which [Raichō] acted like a big sister and Kōkichi like a little sister."[51] Over the next several months they became inseparable. The article mentioned the closeness of the relationship without overtly labeling it as unnatural.

In their own writings it is apparent that Kōkichi and Raichō viewed their strong bond of friendship differently. Kōkichi acknowledged the intense emotions being near Raichō generated in her, and she chose to interpret Raichō's affections romantically. In the June issue of *Seitō*, Kōkichi wrote about the previous month's organizational meeting and how she and Raichō had pledged their love to each other. She was ecstatic over Raichō's attentions and likened herself to an infatuated boy.[52] In *Seitō*'s July issue she penned a fictional account of a romantic liaison between Raichō and a handsome youth. It was common knowledge within the Seitōsha that Kōkichi envisioned herself as the handsome youth, who, after drinking a glass of five-colored liquor, pays a nocturnal visit to Raichō.[53]

Raichō was certainly fond of Kōkichi and treated her like a younger sister who needed to be nurtured, encouraged, and protected. She was drawn to Kōkichi's unconventional appearance and lively, childlike enthusiasm. They spent an increasing amount of time together, both working on *Seitō* and by choice. Raichō knew of Kōkichi's romantic feelings toward her but did not share them, or at least never admitted as much.[54] She noted, "[Kōkichi] had lots of male friends, but she seemed to be not at all attracted to the opposite sex. She was intent on becoming closer to me."[55] Although they saw each other almost daily, Kōkichi initiated a rather one-sided letter exchange, sending about ten letters for every one she received in return. Raichō felt a bit overwhelmed and claimed, "All along I tried to regulate [our relationship] and not get too close to Kōkichi."[56]

However, Raichō rushed to Kōkichi's defense when the press and even some Seitōsha members harshly attacked her involvement in the five-colored-liquor and Yoshiwara incidents. Kōkichi felt she should leave the Seitōsha to help make amends, but Raichō urged her to bear the criticism and to continue to grow within the organization. In the midst of this turbulent period, Kōkichi's health began to noticeably decline. At Raichō's behest she saw a doctor. In mid-July 1912 Kōkichi was diagnosed with a mild case of tuberculosis and was sent to a hospital in Chigasaki to convalesce. Raichō went along both to keep Kōkichi company and to escape the gossip in the city.[57]

Other Seitōsha members and friends soon joined Kōkichi and Raichō and passed the summer in Chigasaki as well. It was a happy time of walks along the beach, boating excursions, and relaxation, and Kōkichi thrived surrounded by friends. But there was also work to be done, and Raichō's lodgings became the provisional editing room for the one-year anniversary issue of *Seitō*. Kōkichi even arranged for a publisher to come to the hospital to discuss taking over *Seitō*'s business affairs.[58]

The publisher happened to bring a young artist, Okumura Hiroshi, with him. This chance occurrence would permanently alter the relationship between Kōkichi and Raichō. Okumura left early that day but said he would come again with his painting equipment. Kōkichi had sensed a connection between Raichō and Okumura and secretly sent a note to Okumura indicating that Raichō wanted to see him again. Okumura returned and joined in their summer amusements. Kōkichi's generosity quickly turned to jealousy as Okumura and Raichō began to fall in love. She even wrote a threatening letter to Okumura in which she declared her love for Raichō.

For her part, Raichō maintained that she felt a strong connection to Kōkichi but that it was not of a carnal nature. In her autobiography she recorded, "For me, even though it is true I was captivated by Kōkichi's innate, unique, personal charm, I did not receive Kōkichi with so-called lesbian (*doseiaiteki*) feelings."[59] Raichō continued to protest: "The place Kōkichi occupied in my heart was no small thing, but this was not same-sex love (*doseiai*)."[60] She contrasted her affectionate feelings toward Kōkichi with her strong physical attraction to Okumura.

Events in the summer of 1912 only reinforced the *Tokyo Nichi Nichi* reporter's negative view of Raichō. He used her relationship with the "Young Swallow," her pet name for the fledgling artist Okumura, as another example of Raichō's domination over men. The reporter described Okumura as "an easy mark and suitable to become [Raichō]'s toy."[61] At first he appeared uninterested, but Raichō persisted and won him over.

Raichō's pursuit of Okumura broke Kōkichi's heart. The continuing saga of "Strange Love" reported: "Kōkichi could not watch this situation. In twenty years she had never been abandoned by a person who loved her as a little sister. The women who had taken hold of her hand had not been able to let go and she believed she had some mysterious, magical power."[62] But Raichō shattered this belief and left Kōkichi feeling betrayed and bewildered.

Raichō tried to maintain her friendship with Kōkichi while developing her relationship with Okumura; however the situation was apparently untenable. Even though the reporter detailed a female-female relationship, he relied on a male-female dynamic to explain it. Raichō used reason and logic in her arguments; she "shined with worldly wisdom" and the "pretense of philosophy and foreign things." Kōkichi was not argumentative but "rich in poetic disposition" and "always moved by emotion."[63] The more manly Raichō triumphed over the more womanly Kōkichi. Raichō drew Kōkichi to her and then treated her coldly. Perhaps this abandonment explained Kōkichi's comment: "I feel like I resemble [Morita] in certain ways."[64] Although Kōkichi's masculine appearance was often noted and her interest in same-sex love raised eyebrows, her emotional nature and deferential position in her relationship with Raichō were clearly feminine traits. The reporter tantalized the readers with hints of retaliation. Would Kōkichi seek revenge for her broken heart? Yet the series closed quietly with Raichō and Kōkichi appearing to part ways.

The romantic encounter between Raichō and Okumura during the summer at Chigasaki compounded the sense of alienation from the Seitōsha that Kōkichi had begun to feel after the five-colored-liquor and Yoshiwara incidents. Kōkichi resigned from the organization later that autumn, but she and Raichō remained close friends for life. In 1914 Kōkichi submitted to convention and married the artist Tomimoto Kenkichi. Their turbulent marriage produced three children and ended in separation in 1946.

As opposed to the examination of same-sex love promised in the first installment, the "Strange Love" series discussed a variety of relationships that contradicted the dominant male–subservient female relationship accepted as the norm. Morita, Nakahara, Okumura, and even Kōkichi were depicted as innocent victims ensnared by Raichō's charms. Their only weakness was having succumbed to romantic emotions. Raichō was portrayed in the most unfavorable, unnatural light. She used her feminine looks and wiles to attract people, her masculine traits to dominate relationships, and an asexual stance to remain aloof from amorous entanglements. The selfish, manipulative, and unsentimental behavior of a woman like Raichō was depicted as far more alarming than feminine men and same-sex attraction. All the stories of "Strange Love" made for good gossip, but the woman who toyed with conventional gender and sexual attitudes was most maligned.

In addition to the writers and readers of these titillating articles, many members of the intellectual elite also perceived Raichō's aberrant behavior as symptomatic of New Women in general. Such behavior was considered both distasteful and a danger to society. The emergence of New Women in Japan caused a great deal of consternation among, for example, the members of the Social Policy Association (Shakai Seisaku Gakkai), which convened in Tokyo in late October 1912; the New Woman was frequently addressed in the lectures and discussions of this group of economists, social scientists, bureaucrats, and businessmen.[65] Members of this association considered the New Woman movement an "undesirable phenomenon" and used some examples from England to prove their point. A newspaper account cited their main arguments. They regarded the English New Women as antagonistic man haters. Even though the Church of England had modified the wedding vows that required a woman to "honor and obey her husband," New Women still refused to take these vows. Also, "when the *Titanic* sank, it was praised as male chivalry that women and children were placed on boats first and escaped danger." However, New Women viewed these actions as symptomatic of the self-serving condescension that kept women weak and dependent on men. Many members of Social Policy Association lamented that not only in thought but in appearance too New Women wanted to be like men, and some went so far as to grow facial hair! They argued that New Women were not just a problem in England but in Japan as well, where their numbers were increasing. This growing horde of New Women was becoming a threat to the smooth functioning of Japanese society.[66]

Professor Tsumura of Kobe Business School participated in the Social Policy Association meeting and linked the New Woman to a potential population problem: "They don't want to be someone's wife. With Magda and Nora as ideals, they do not care to be household dolls. Rather than being pressured by the old beliefs and customs of married life, they desire the ease of single life."[67] Tsumura predicted that the number of marriages would decrease, and even if New Women married they would not want children, so the birthrate would decrease as well. At the same time, he was concerned about an increase in illegitimate children. He urged people to take heed of the New Woman not simply as a threat to male privilege but as a population threat that could affect the well-being of the nation as a whole.

As alarming as Tsumura's dire predictions were, they had little basis in fact. The ideal woman in Japan was not a "household doll" but a productive, responsible, and educated wife and mother. The number of New Women was increasing, but societal constraints limited it to a small, albeit vocal, group. Tsumura failed to take into account the hardships a woman in Taishō Japan would face trying to pursue a single, self-sufficient life—with or without children—and the reasons she would choose such a life over a conventional marriage. Also, although a declining birthrate was a concern in some European countries, Japan's population was growing at this time.[68] Nonetheless, the idea that New Women posed a threat to national well-being became hard to dislodge.

New Women not merely were being discussed by policymakers and gossip columnists but were drawing the attention of literary men as well. Writer Satō Kōroku complained about the eccentric behavior of New Women in a dismissive way. He felt that the women who either claimed the title New Woman or were given it were superficial and were acting in unconventional, outrageous ways with no particular purpose or design. They were undeserving of the designation "new." Satō joined those who trivialized the actions of New Women and ridiculed them as absurd. "Becoming a New Woman demands a new effort," he wrote. "It demands a new principle. I don't know what the so-called New Woman of today demands."[69] They were not the first to speak of the expansion of women's rights, he argued, nor were they the first to break with accepted conventions, but they did so without any valid political intent.

Satō complained that by drinking alcohol and visiting brothels they "wanted nothing more than to imitate men and be eccentric."[70]

Another writer, Mizuno Yōshū, shared Satō's skepticism about the import and novelty of the New Woman. Mizuno viewed New Women as "vulgar" beings with "superficial polish." To him, their posturing was more about external appearances than about internal awareness. He questioned, "How fine are these people's tastes? And are they able to understand them? To appreciate them? To pursue them?"[71] Just because they looked and behaved differently on the outside, he did not feel they had changed on the inside. For Mizuno, the behavior of New Women raised issues of class and classiness.

Both Mizuno and Satō trivialized the New Woman, but Satō was unable to completely dismiss her impact on society. He clearly was concerned with keeping distinct the worlds in which men and women functioned. Satō wanted women to enrich their (and others') lives while still staying within certain boundaries. "The New Women must work to cultivate new space *as women,*" he asserted.[72] He took an essentialist position that emphasized women's ability to give birth to and nurse infants, as well as their "natural gifts" of "long hair, soft bodies, and smooth skin." He continued, "This argument of mine is a very . . . common argument; however I feel that there is new ground to be cultivated hidden within it."[73] He supported the "good wife, wise mother" ideology as a means for women to advance within proper feminine bounds. Women should take pride in the womanly virtues that enabled them to contribute to family and society, he believed.

As part of continuing debates about Nora and Magda, Satō invoked Nora as the perfect example of a selfish, willful woman who wreaked havoc on her family by refusing to accept responsibility for her role within it. Her husband left the home each day in order to provide for his family, while it was her duty to attend to her husband's and children's happiness within the home. Satō lamented, "It is regrettable that she did not awaken and say, 'It was bad of me to be dependent on my husband 'til now. Just as my husband goes out to work, I too with feminine ways must make my husband happy. That I made a mistake on this path has brought us to this.'"[74] To Satō she represented a reckless person, not a New Woman. In his view, a New Woman would not walk away from her duties but would create new solutions as a woman—that is, as a wife and mother.[75]

Satō tenaciously advocated an untainted masculine sphere of activity. Throughout his essay he argued, "It's not good that women forget about living in a feminine world and recklessly oppose men, much less that in a woman's way they imitate men." Satō exposed his true personal concern

etry, who attended scholarly lectures, who were former (an
aper reporters. But they also drank liquor, visited brothels, an
urtesans and female actors. Seitōsha women maintained tha
sparaged and misunderstood. Yet they held onto the hope that
r true selves will be understood," as they continued to put out
ne.⁹² It is unclear whether the reporter also looked forward to
he seemed to admire their dedication. His vacillating attitude
e of the ambivalence many involved in the New Woman debate
apan's modernizing process in general. As the Seitōsha women
find their own identities, they too vacillated.
andals arising from the initial attempts of several Seitōsha wom-
er their "true selves" created quite a commotion. The largely
ntion to the New Woman in the press caused problems inter-
e Seitōsha. Many members left because of family pressure or
rsonal convictions. Several schoolteachers cancelled subscrip-
fear of being fired. Of those who remained, some asked to have
withheld from the pages of *Seitō* altogether; a few assumed pen
general trend was to dissociate themselves from the uproar and
om the term *New Woman*.⁹³ Nonetheless, under Raichō's charis-
rship, a streamlined Seitōsha would turn its efforts toward mak-
ge of the New Woman broad and positive as 1912—the last year
d the first year of Taishō—drew to a close.

when he declared, "Even in literature they imitate men. They must think about whether or not as women they can become first-rate literary people."[76] He obviously felt threatened by the competition from women writers. He supported the emergence of New Women who would stay within a feminine world that did not infringe on the masculine one. Satō's New Women had to awaken within the subordinate roles that many found so restricting. He fretted, "Under the notion of being 'new,' to what extent will many young women damage their feminine virtue? Become vulgar in actions? Indecent in speech? I hear 'New Woman' and get a loathsome feeling."[77]

Some men of letters offered a more positive vision than Satō's of the New Woman's contributions to society. Instead of viewing her as a threat, they welcomed her as a means of promoting alternative behavior in general. By advocating intellectual awakening, social change, and equality, they legitimated their own life-styles as well as those of the New Women. They bolstered their position by arguing that progress in these directions was a sure sign of Japan's modernity and would improve society.

Influential literary critic and novelist Uchida Roan presented his own interpretation of what constituted a New Woman. She was a woman who was not bound by existing morals and customs, who behaved "freely and boldly" according to her own will. To prevent the New Woman from being labeled as frivolous or superficial and to distinguish her from the mentally impaired and the insane, Uchida added that her behavior "must be accompanied by intellectual awakening."[78] He viewed Japan's so-called New Women as a work in progress. They were breaking with tradition and behaving daringly. To Uchida, variety improved society: "Just one color, one path is very dull, monotonous. Having various kinds of people enriches our social colors. Even just livening up our surroundings is a good thing."[79] Japan's so-called New Women were both following and creating a general trend, and Uchida contended that general trends lead to social change. On the one hand he made light of their behavior by accusing them of merely being fashionable and experimenting with unusual behavior as they would with a Western hairdo. On the other hand he asserted that they were contributing a new energy that would help to transform women. Uchida believed that when this energy combined with intellectual self-awareness, Japan would have its own true New Women.

Another writer-critic, Baba Kōchō, shared in the feeling that the New Women of his day were not a finished product. Baba admitted that those labeled as New Women had not yet progressed far on their own. He contended, "There are not many examples of women through their own ingenuity developing to the point of no longer being inferior to men."[80] Like Satō, he saw women imitating men, following their lead, and embracing their ideas without any sense of what "new" truly meant. However, rather than dismissing the behavior of these New Women as superficial, Baba asserted that this "parroting" was a step in the right direction: "Even women who are interested simply in mimicking new thought, clearly have moved ahead a level."[81] He argued that male leadership was still a necessary element for women's progress but the number of capable women would increase over time.

Baba declared that to become "new" women needed equality. He insisted, "Women too should be permitted individual independence. Women should claim for themselves the same independence of thought as men."[82] Convention and a firmly entrenched double standard made many men and women fear such an occurrence, but Baba contended that equality would change society for the better, strengthening the husband-wife relationship, not destroying it as many imagined. He drew this analogy from Japan's recent past: "Those who deeply oppose women's emancipation and women's defiance today are the same as those who opposed our ancestors abolishing the wearing of swords and cutting off their topknots. They are shackled by custom and rooted in useless worry."[83]

Critic-at-large Yamaji Aizan also likened women's awakening and equality to the Meiji Restoration, which started as a fantasy, gathered strength, and ultimately became a reality. But just as with the Restoration, women's advancement necessitated major societal changes. Yamaji asserted that women's awakening became meaningful only when backed by access to economic self-sufficiency. "Put plainly, women's awakening is a great misery if it does not come with economic strength."[84] Becoming aware of one's lot in life without the means to improve it was an exercise in futility. Yamaji explained, "This is the situation of a class of women who have education and knowledge. They are mentally awakened, clamoring for women's freedom, advocating women's rights and independence. But since they do not have the real economic power to make this viable, even while they cry out for freedom, rights, and independence, as before they fall into the wretched contradiction of living subordinate to and dependent on men, and they anguish in vain."[85] He stressed that the family and property systems had to change and that this change was just another transformation Japan had to accept in its march to modernity. Yamaji also emphasized that "women's independence . . . would not become an obstacle to the well-being of humanity."[86]

For Baba, the key to equality was education. Women needed to feed their minds just as men did. Baba was dissatisfied with women's education,

which emphasized old-fashioned wives and mothers. Instead he adv training to become a person. It's a have."[87] Through education women new ideas and helping society progre that caused women to be dependent and men. Women could contribute t their minds as individuals, not just a

*W*hether attacking the New the abstract, reporters, scholars, wri discussed this new Japanese phenom acteristics were clearly delineated: t from others of her sex by her unconv ality, and her repudiation of "good wi New Woman was bad or good, disrup for celebration would continue to be

In October 1912 the *Tokyo Ni* ry entitled "Women Who Want to added some gossipy items, yet also h Seitō women.[88] The reporter began b over the "unladylike behavior" of Ne at Seitō members and their organizati for daily drinking alcohol, loafing arou also acknowledged, "If you read their are very serious."[89]

This *Tokyo Nichi Nichi* reporter Otake Kōkichi and Hiratsuka Raichō, vacillated between mockery and quiet Kōkichi's physical presence and noted moved from topic to topic, he also comm ty and mind." The two engaged in serious ing, and the prizes she had won at exhil seemed intent on uncovering personality Yet, he and Raichō also had intelligent Zen meditation.[91]

Throughout the six articles the repo tween portraying New Women as compete and as frivolous and base on the other. A

who wrote p future) news befriended c they were d "someday o their magaz that day, bu was indicati felt toward attempted t

The s en to disco negative att nally for th wavering p tions out of their names names. The therefore f matic lead ing the ima of Meiji an

CHAPTER 5

Discourse

"I AM A NEW WOMAN"

As a result of the 1912 summer activities of a handful of Seitōsha women, the media depicted Seitō members (and by extension the New Woman in general) in a distorted, derogatory, and monolithic fashion. Such a portrayal prompted Hiratsuka Raichō to publish the following appeal in the editor's notes at the end of *Seitō*'s December 1912 issue:

> I do not know when or where the term New Woman came to be in vogue, but recently it appears to be revealing its charm in newspapers and magazines. It looks as if journalists have manufactured a kind of toy balloon. And it looks as if the members of Seitō have the good fortune to be seen as that toy balloon and are being held aloft. In our editing room, we are now talking of trying to use our New Year's issue to write openly our thoughts and opinions concerning this infamous creature called the New Woman. . . . We differ completely from the journalists' interpretations; therefore let us try to consider seriously and earnestly the subject of this so-called New Woman, and the real New Woman.[1]

The New Woman, like a balloon, floated in the air for all to see but was empty on the inside. She was showy, but lacked substance. Raichō's sarcasm revealed that she did not believe this to be so. She argued that if others could impose the term *New Women* on the women of Seitō, then these same women could construct and define the term themselves. She called on New Women in and around *Seitō* to offer their own thoughts on what it meant to be a "real New Woman."

Raichō encouraged members of Seitō to confront the New Woman onslaught in the press with a positive alternative in *Seitō* and in other press

79

organs. She wanted them, together, to redefine and re-create the New Woman. She felt that such a step was important for both society at large and Seitō specifically. The generally derisive view of the New Woman current in society was a result largely of the media's accounts of the scandalous personal lives and activities of Seitō women, as opposed to any serious consideration of their ideas and writings. However, Raichō not only was concerned with challenging the bad press but was also worried about the tendency within Seitō for women to avoid or deny the New Woman appellation. She wanted the women of Seitō to create and to own an image in which they could take pride.

Raichō's December 1912 statement urging women to engage the New Woman heralded the opening of what could be called the "Year of the Woman Problem" in Japan. *Seitō* would produce special supplements dealing specifically with Japan's Woman Problem and the New Woman in each of its first three issues of 1913. Other major journals would follow suit with their own special issues on the Woman Problem. This expanded coverage broadened the Woman Problem/New Woman debate by moving beyond scandalous accounts

FIGURE 5. A Seitōsha gathering, 1913. From the right: Hiratsuka Raichō, Yasumochi Yoshiko, Araki Ikuko, Nakano Hatsuko, Iwano Kiyoko, Kobayashi Katsuko. *Courtesy of Otsuki Shoten.*

of the lives of a handful of New Women to a serious discussion of a wide variety of woman-related issues. Also, a second New Woman's group would soon emerge, adding even more depth to the debate.[2] Raichō recalled in her autobiography that the year 1913 was unparalleled in the extent to which the phrase *New Woman* appeared in the media.[3] The trajectory of the New Woman debate continued to reveal the concerns of a modernizing nation in flux.

This chapter examines this expanded discourse surrounding the New Woman. The thoughts and words of Hiratsuka Raichō, Katō Midori, Iwano Kiyo, Hori Yasuko, Itō Noe, and Fukuda Hideko are explored here. These Seitōsha women presented alternative views of the New Woman and argued for a meaningful, varied, and positive assessment of her. They emphasized the importance of self-awareness and the need to translate this awareness into action. They stimulated a serious evaluation of practices and institutions that restricted women's lives by talking about inequitable family and marriage laws and the need for economic self-sufficiency. *Seitō*'s New Women challenged both the negative press and each other as they reevaluated their position in Japanese society.

Some reporters continued to sensationalize accounts of New Women—especially with the emergence of the "rival" New Woman's group, the Shinshinfujinkai—but their accounts now competed with a wider range of opinions and a more in-depth analysis of the New Woman and the Woman Problem than they had in the past. The Seitōsha women, in their efforts to reclaim their image, not only kept the discussion of the New Woman alive but linked it with the comprehensive discourse on the position of women in Japanese society.

Raichō's Redefinition of the New Woman

In January 1913, Raichō responded to her own appeal and began the serious contemplation of the Woman Problem that would continue throughout that year. The New Year's issue of *Chūō Kōron,* a leading general-interest journal of the time, ran Raichō's essay "New Woman," in which she boldly claimed the controversial label. This piece appeared as part of the special section devoted to the writings of fifteen "accomplished women."[4] With this essay, Raichō began the process of redefining the New Woman, a process that others within Seitō would continue.

The style of "New Woman" was reminiscent of that of Raichō's longer essay "In the Beginning, Woman Was the Sun," written for the premier issue of *Seitō* in 1911. The new essay even employed the same sun imagery used in the original essay.[5] But there were differences. This time, instead of lamenting that women had lost their status as the sun and needed to regain it, Raichō looked ahead to what women could achieve through concerted effort. As in the earlier essay, Raichō's writing is sermonlike, with its repetition of key words and phrases, and it is laden with spiritual undertones. Raichō's Zen training clearly influenced her emphasis on concentration and awakening in this, the early stage of her career.

> I am a New Woman.
> At least, everyday I pray, everyday I strive to be the truly New Woman I want to be.
> In truth, and eternally, the new being is the sun.
> I am the sun.
> At least, everyday I pray, everyday I strive to be the sun I want to be.
>
> . . . The New Woman curses "yesterday."
> The New Woman cannot bear to walk meekly, silently the path the Old Woman walked.
> The New Woman is not satisfied with the life of the Old Woman, who was made ignorant, made a slave, made a piece of flesh by the selfishness of men.
> The New Woman desires to destroy the old morality and laws that were *constructed* [*tsukurareta*] for the convenience of men.
>
> However, the various ghosts that haunt the minds of Old Women persistently pursue New Women.
> When "today" is empty, it is then that "yesterday" invades.
> New Women battle daily all kinds of ghosts.
> A moment of neglect and the New Woman is an Old Woman.
>
> I am a New Woman. I am the sun. I am simply a person. At least, everyday I pray, everyday I strive to be the being I want to be.
>
> The New Woman desires everyday . . . to *create* [*sōsaku suru*] a new realm where new religion, new morality, and new laws will be put into practice.
> In fact, herein lies the mission of the New Woman. So, what is this new realm? This new religion? This new morality? These new laws? The New Woman does not yet know.
> She will study, train her mind, strive and agonize for the sake of that which she cannot yet know, for the sake of her personal mission.

The New Woman at present simply desires strength.

She desires the strength to endure the studying, training, striving, and agonizing she must do for the sake of that which she cannot yet know, for the sake of fulfilling her mission.

The New Woman at present does not desire beauty. She does not desire virtue. She is simply crying out for strength, strength for the sake of *building* [*tsukuran*] the as-yet-unknown realm, for the sake of her noble mission.[6]

In this essay, Raichō acknowledged that men were the main source of women's oppression, but she seemed more concerned with the dichotomy of New Woman/Old Woman than with that of Woman/Man. Raichō was conscious of the difficulties women faced in separating themselves from the past and tried to instill a sense of determination. She wanted women to gain the inner strength necessary to release their true potential without placing boundaries or restrictions on that potential. Raichō stressed the artificiality of the gender roles assigned to both the Old Woman and the New Woman. These roles were social creations, as the highlighted words in her essay reveal. Exposing this artificiality, she was opening the way for Seitō women to create their own gender roles, roles that would liberate women and not suppress them. This essay, published outside of *Seitō,* was a response to the trivializing press coverage that reduced the New Woman to a morally deviant, destructive, and dangerous woman. It was a powerful, positive declaration—by a New Woman herself—of who the New Woman was, what she was trying to change, and what she wanted to accomplish. More important, it was a rallying cry to women within Seitō who were struggling with their public image and evading the term *New Woman.*

Although Raichō spoke broadly about women's oppression, she did not offer concrete causes or examples. She also did not indicate how the New Woman was to go about destroying the "old morality and laws." This lack of specificity was typical of Raichō's style at the time. She offered images, ideas, and spiritual fervor, but solutions remained individual and personal. She was still emphasizing spiritual awakening and inner freedom, not concrete social action. Women needed time and courage to discover themselves first. This prescription may sound like an emphasis on the individual inspired by Western thought, but Raichō was more likely drawing on her Zen background and the Eastern concept that mental focus and concentration lead to inner strength and awareness. Raichō also insisted that the New Woman was not merely a destructive force but a being who envisioned a better world.

The negative media attention to the New Woman forced Raichō to reevaluate her position and consider the broad implications of the Woman Problem. Claiming that her own thoughts were not fully formulated, Raichō decided to introduce the Swedish feminist Ellen Key instead. For *Seitō*'s first New Woman supplement, Raichō prepared a preface to Key's *Love and Marriage* that credited Key with helping to trigger her interest in the Woman Problem.[7] In her preface, Raichō admitted, "I often do not think of myself as a woman. . . . When I am meditating, writing, or even in love . . . I do not have a consciousness of being a woman. It is simply a consciousness of self."[8] In addition to providing a preface to Key, Raichō translated the foreword to Key's work that was written by the English sexologist Havelock Ellis. Later, in *Seitō*'s February supplement she would publish a partial translation of Key's first chapter. These publications marked the beginning of Raichō's long-term engagement with the work of Ellen Key.

In her preface to Key, Raichō again tried to disassociate the Seitōsha from the negative image in the press, while reiterating the need for women to attain inner liberation before they could hope to confront society at large. She wrote, "Right now, we Seitō women must strive, as new beings, as true New Women, to free our souls and become complete individuals. If there are to be social movements they will necessarily come after this."[9] She engaged the women of Seitō as New Women but also as "new beings" and "complete individuals." Again, she left the way open for individual interpretations and personal applications, welcoming a variety of images instead of a single, confining one.

Seitōsha Pleas for a Meaningful Redefinition of Women's Roles

Several Seitō women responded to Raichō's call-to-arms. They offered a variety of images, ideas, and concerns to counter the seemingly monolithic and negative image of the New Women offered by the press. One tactic was to take a "we-are-not-who-you-say-we-are" approach. Raichō used this idea in her "From the Editing Room" appeal quoted above, noting that "we differ completely from the journalists' interpretations." Katō Midori, who developed as a writer under Seitō and would later become a reporter for the *Osaka Mainichi* (Osaka Daily) newspaper, extended this approach and also employed Raichō's image of the New Woman as a toy balloon that people liked to poke and prod. Katō bemoaned the fact that "the New Woman is easily tossed about like a toy balloon."[10] However, she managed to strike a blow at the critics and place New Women in the vanguard of Japanese modernity when she likened the critics to "those in Paris salons who pose in front of a cubist painting and without any true understanding assume a knowing look and offer criticism."[11] Thus, Katō argued that the New Women were the truly modern(ized) individuals of Taishō Japan, and their pretentious and ignorant critics were the ones who exemplified some of the worst traits of modernity. Katō joined Raichō in urging women to attack these uninformed, inaccurate critics. Being modern did not entail superficial knowledge, slavish imitation of trends, or feigned appearances. It required moving beyond conventional practices. Like the cubist painting, New Women were about breaking boundaries and encouraging new thinking.

Iwano Kiyo, a Seitōsha member who had been an activist for more than a decade and was a strong believer in women's equality, also responded to Raichō's appeal. Iwano had a strong, outgoing personality and believed in backing up her words with actions. Around 1905 she joined a small group of feminist activists petitioning the Diet to rescind the restrictions on women's political activity. This group worked (unsuccessfully at that time) for revision of Article 5 of the Public Peace Police Law of 1900. Recalling this campaign, Iwano noted, "I wanted women, as women and as citizens, to have an understanding and knowledge of law and politics. I wanted them to see a life and society outside of the home."[12] In 1909, Iwano married the controversial naturalist writer, critic, and poet Iwano Hōmei. Within the Seitōsha, she was a steady advocate of political and economic rights for women. In her first contribution to *Seitō*'s 1913 New Woman supplements, Iwano presented a variation on the "we-are-not-who-you-say-we-are" approach. Raichō and Katō accused their critics of misconstruing the image of the New Woman, but Iwano argued that it was the image of Woman in general that journalists portrayed inaccurately.

Iwano attacked ideas from both Western Social Darwinism and Eastern Confucian and Buddhist thought that had been used to proclaim women's inferiority. She declared, "I cannot abide the superficial comparative framework of many of the people discussing women today. They do such things as compare the strengths and weaknesses in the physical constitution of men and women, offer up physiological factors, line up the mythical good and evil of men and women, and boast of the development of men's inherent intelligence."[13] Iwano's method was to expose weakness in each of these positions through rational arguments of her own. First, she negated physical strength as a standard for male superiority by arguing that "if we conclude that according to logic those with superior strength are naturally superior beings, then wouldn't sumo wrestlers necessarily be superior to everyone else? What's more, bears, boas, tigers, elephants, crocodiles, and the like would be superior to humans. . . . However, it is said that humans are higher beings than these fierce animals. In other words, the question of brute force has no relation to the theory of the superiority and inferiority of animals. However, men violate this premise by comparing themselves with women and saying they are inherently superior because they are stronger."[14] Dismissing (irrational) claims made about women in general, Iwano implicitly offered the New Woman as the model for a strong, modern, female persona.

With the strength argument reduced to nonsense, Iwano moved on to one of the other physiological factors. Women were told that they were unable to participate in society on a par with men because menstruation and pregnancy hindered their activities. Iwano exposed this as an excuse, not a reality. She explained, "A woman's period is a natural process. It is by no means a sickness. For a healthy woman it is not so painful that it causes her to discontinue her work or duties."[15] As for pregnancy, Iwano defined it as a temporary condition that need not hinder women's social, political, and economic rights.

Iwano also disputed the images of good and evil promoted through myth and religion. Many Buddhist sects maintained that women were evil and defiling. In Judeo-Christian traditions, the story of Adam and Eve associated women with sin. Iwano claimed that men created these images as a means of suppressing women. She did not believe that sin was limited to women and virtue was limited to men. She did believe that society was built through the joint efforts of men and women.

As far as intellectual prowess was concerned, Iwano admitted that at the moment men were generally superior to women but insisted this difference was due to circumstances, not ability. She argued, "It is wrong to conclude that women, who have been forbidden entry to the realm of knowledge, who have long been trapped in the home, when compared with men who freely enter the realm of knowledge, have no intellectual capacity."[16] Iwano drew a comparison between the position of Japanese women vis-à-vis men and the position of the Japanese nation vis-à-vis Western nations at the time of the Meiji Restoration. Just as Japan, over time, was able to gain equal status as a modern nation, so too would women prove themselves to be the equals of men as members of a modern society. The advancement of women should be seen as a natural part of the modernizing process.

Hori Yasuko served as a critical voice from within in her contribution to *Seitō*'s New Woman supplements. In her article "I Am an Old-Fashioned

Woman," Hori admonished Seitōsha members for making limiting assumptions similar to those of their critics. At the time she was writing, Hori was involved in a common-law marriage with Osugi Sakae, a leading socialist/anarchist of the day.[17] Although seeking a socialist point of view was clearly part of the Seitōsha's efforts to present a variety of opinions, Hori took the staff to task for being careless in their assumptions about her personal politics. "I cannot understand you sending a letter to someone like me because you want a socialist woman's view of the Woman Problem," she scolded. "Of course, I am living with a socialist man. However, I do not think of myself as a socialist and I do not recall calling myself one."[18] Hori's article highlighted the fact that Seitō women had to become aware of the conventional ideas and assumptions that still saturated their thinking and use of language; they had assumed a unity between Hori and her partner. As Hori pointed out, the Seitōsha leaders needed to be aware that within any term or definition there was room for much variety. The press was also guilty of making unwarranted assumptions and of collapsing distinctions in thought, she said. But, as New Women, the women of Seitō needed to be both more careful and more open-minded than the press in their thinking. Hori's sharp criticism, sarcasm, and use of the term *old-fashioned woman* (*furui onna*) called attention to the fact that not all New Women held the same views or acted for the same reasons.

Seitōsha Pleas for Self-Awareness and Action

Seitō women used other tactics as well to argue for a serious, diverse view of the New Woman. In her "New Woman" essay, Raichō not only asserted a positive New Woman image but also advocated a focus on self-awareness and inner, spiritual awakening for women. Several other Seitō women also voiced the need to cultivate strength from within. In this approach, too, the women drew on both Eastern and Western concepts in making their cases. They clearly were influenced by Raichō's Zen-inspired enthusiasm.[19] They were also following the lead of Japanese naturalist writers, who turned inward to an exploration of the self and championed the individual. The Seitō women turned to similar Western notions of self and individual as alternatives to the increasingly confining roles for women within contemporary Japanese society.[20] Although the new roles remained unclear, the women focused on a broad range of options and opportunities.

Itō Noe, who took over as editor of *Seitō* when Raichō stepped down in 1915, initially espoused views on self-awareness and individual solutions similar to Raichō's. She would soon, however, concentrate her energies on gaining social and legal rights for women. Itō first appeared at the Seitōsha offices in June 1912, when she was only seventeen. She had just run away from an arranged marriage and was living with her former high school teacher turned lover, Tsuji Jun. Over the next few years she was attracted to anarchism, and her life ended tragically in 1923 when she was murdered in prison along with her common-law husband and fellow anarchist Osugi Sakae (formerly partner to Hori Yasuko).[21] The short essay Itō contributed to *Seitō*'s January 1913 supplement, "The Path of the New Woman," emphasized her desire for each woman to discover her own course and become a leader. Itō poetically depicted the hardships this leader, this New Woman, must inevitably face, while at the same time she glorified such a life. She described the New Woman clearing a path thick with overgrowth, cutting through rock, wandering in mountain recesses, scaling cliffs, and being stung by poisonous insects. With dramatic flourish, Itō offered her own definition of what it meant to be new: "New is a word whose meaning should be used only for the few leaders. It is a word that should be monopolized by those who live and die tragically, those who, knowing themselves and believing in themselves, open up their own path and advance. . . . Leaders are firmly confident. They are strong. They are courageous. They are responsible for their own lives. Leaders do not allow others to interfere with their work under any circumstances."[22]

Itō emphasized that the New Woman, first and foremost, had a responsibility to herself. She too insisted that "leaders above all else require the completeness of their inner being."[23] The New Woman needed to rise above public criticism and discover who she was for herself. She had to be strong, for her path was full of hardships. Through self-awareness, which each woman had to attain independently, women would come to understand and fulfill their needs. Like Raichō, Itō addressed the New Woman but used terms that were gender-neutral. Itō wrote of leaders, of those who blazed trails, of those who stepped forward into the unknown, into the modern. She rejected conventional ideas that viewed leadership as being determined by lineage, wealth, or male privilege. The New Women were new leaders not by virtue of their birth but by virtue of the choices they made and the actions they took. According to Itō, New Women disregarded the limitations placed on them by law and society and instead explored new, modern ways of being. Itō put her words into practice during her all-too-brief lifetime.

Raichō and Itō used a gender-neutral approach to promote equality for women. They wrote about individuals, human beings, and leaders who had inner strength and talents and who were vital to Japanese modernity. Two other Seitōsha members argued for a more woman-centered approach than that of

Raichō and Itō. Katō Midori agreed with Raichō and Itō that self-awareness was the first step toward change for women, but she called on women to take a stance as women. Katō provided a brief historical context for her position by claiming that New Women had existed throughout the ages in various forms. As an example she cited Japanese women like Fukuda Hideko, who in the 1880s participated in the Freedom and People's Rights movement.[24] Katō admired the enthusiasm of these earlier New Women but censured them for merely following in men's movements without asserting a position as women. Katō explained the conditions that led to the birth of the New Woman. She underscored the subordinate position of women within the family. According to the three obediences espoused by Confucianism, a woman spent her life dependent on men: first her father, then her husband, then her son. The New Woman appeared when women rejected such an oppressed life and decided to take action to change it. As another example of women breaking free from their circumstances, Katō referred to some of Ibsen's heroines. Women like Nora had had enough of their monotonous, unfulfilling lives. Events and pressures in the home caused them to become aware of their situation and to desire a more gratifying life than the one they were leading. New Women emerged when self-awareness led them to challenge their conventional (middle-class) role and to explore new possibilities. Katō believed a New Woman was born when a woman used her awareness to take action.[25]

In her "Explanation of the New Woman," another Seitō member also insisted that women needed to become self-aware as women. This was the necessary foundation from which to improve their lives. Nishizaki (Ikuta) Hanayo argued, "To be given this name 'woman' was not a cause for pride or shame, nor for superiority or inferiority. Being born a woman should mean the same amount of freedom and bright future accorded to men."[26] This conviction enabled women to see themselves as human beings. Nishizaki felt that this level of consciousness would allow women to grow. She declared, "Women are people too. This is a simple thing, but when said by a woman it is a great thing. All progress should be pursued from this base."[27] She believed that New Women were those who attained this level of consciousness, while Old Women were those who still followed old customs and ways of thinking.

Seitōsha Pleas for the Resolution of Marriage and Economic Problems

In their attempts to wrestle with the New Woman image, Seitō women not only offered broad new definitions and options but also focused on specific problems and demands. One particular source of concern centered around legal restrictions, especially the family and marriage laws instituted in the Civil Code of 1898. Seitō women also called for women's economic independence. Late Meiji and early Taishō Japan allowed a space for Seitō women to explore their "spiritual" or "literary" sides, but when these same women challenged specific laws or customs, they drew the censors' attention.

When it came to the marriage and family laws, New Women reacted from a variety of vantage points. In April 1913, Raichō wrote an article for *Seitō* in which she condemned the existing marriage system. Her stance caused the magazine to be banned. Her offending essay, "To the Women of the World," combined her Zen-inspired quest for self-awareness with a critique of society's confining attitudes and laws. First, Raichō took women in general to task and questioned why it did not occur to more of them to "fundamentally doubt the conventional ideas that women ought to marry once, that marriage is the only path for women, that every woman should be a good wife and a wise mother, and that this is all there is to a woman's life."[28] Second, she boldly and clearly stated her reasons for rejecting marriage as it was then defined: "Though we do not object to marriage itself, we cannot submit to the concept of marriage today and the existing marriage system. In today's social structure, isn't marriage the relationship of obedience to authority throughout a lifetime? Isn't a wife treated in the same manner as a minor or a cripple? Isn't it true that wives have neither proprietorship over their assets nor legal rights concerning their children? Isn't it true that adultery is not considered a crime when committed by husbands, but it becomes a crime when committed by wives? We will not think of getting married if it means submitting to such an unreasonable and irrational system."[29] Raichō backed her beliefs with action. She lived out her convictions during twenty-seven years of cohabitation with artist Okumura Hiroshi before agreeing to a formal marriage to prevent discrimination against their children. Many critics of the New Woman chose to depict her actions as immoral and destructive, but Raichō clearly demonstrated that it was possible to reject a conventional marriage and still engage in a committed, monogamous relationship.

Raichō used the issue of marriage to reinforce her contention that women needed to forge a new identity. Raichō and many of the women of Seitō chafed at the restrictions of Japan's family system, yet they were uncertain about the kind of life choices that should be available to women. They found that there were no concrete answers. However, one thing was clear: Raichō believed women should have more options, both personally and professionally, than simply those of wife and mother. She announced, "While we continue to have internal anxieties, and while we also struggle against so much unreasonable external persecution, we are fundamentally doubting, inquiring, and investigating just what kind of life a woman's true life should be."[30] New Women were those who took these important first steps of questioning and reevaluation, which would lead to a more fulfilling life than they now had.

Raichō believed in the concept of marriage but not in the legalized inequality it entailed. Katō Midori, who had mocked the uninformed criticism of journalists, followed the conventions of her day but did not believe in the concept of marriage. Katō viewed marriage as a temporary necessity and believed that ideally women should remain single in order to remain true to themselves. She implied that such a condition would be possible when society evolved and women were no longer dependent on men. She argued, "After all, men and women can never possibly understand each other. The worlds of men and women are completely separate. You can think you have drawn near, but it is only the momentary knowledge of external appearances. Men and women live their lives in opposition to each other."[31] However, society had not yet entered a completely modern period, so such a life was still difficult to achieve. Therefore, while society was still struggling with old and new, women had to seek some kind of union with men for support and stability. Katō herself was married to a reporter.

Hori Yasuko's views on marriage combined Raichō's sense of commitment with some of Katō's practical concerns. Hori continued to press Seitō members to free themselves from the conventional assumptions they found objectionable. She criticized the Seitōsha for addressing her as "Osugi's Wife" in the letter requesting her contribution to the special supplements. This appeal would have been acceptable from an old-fashioned woman but not from a New Woman, she stated. Furthermore, it was incorrect: "When a woman becomes one with a man, the woman must give completely both her thoughts and her feelings, and also her name to the man. These are the regulations of us old-fashioned women. In truth, I want to do the same, however my man will not comply with this. And, according to my man's wishes, I remain Hori Yasuko."[32]

In her essay, Hori ironically positioned herself as an old-fashioned woman and demonstrated just how complex the issue of marriage was for women. She wanted to enter a union with her man in which they became one spiritually and emotionally. This relationship differed from a legal marriage, in which she would have to sacrifice her individual rights. It also differed from her man's views. He advocated open relationships, in which both parties lived separate, independent lives and were free to associate with whomever they pleased; either party could break off the relationship if he or she fell in love with another.[33] Even though Hori was still at the mercy of her man's wishes, in her desire to be with the man she loved and her willingness to forego conventional marriage, she confirmed that she was indeed a New Woman. However, she was aware that this was a precarious situation. Women could experiment with free-love relationships but had to deal with the personal and public costs of their actions in a society that expected female fidelity but not male. Women could create freer, more equal unions than they had, but without the sanction of marriage they were stigmatized by society, as were any children from the union. In addition, the economic situation for women was often tenuous at best. New Women needed other aspects of society to change as well if they were to realize their full potential and develop practical alternatives to marriage.

Although several Seitō women looked to self-awareness and inner freedom as preconditions for concrete change, others focused on economic change as the key to liberation. Katō Midori argued that women would be more capable of avoiding (and ultimately changing) the inequalities of the family and marriage laws once they had more economic power of their own. First and foremost, she emphasized, women needed to become self-sufficient—emotionally and financially. Katō noted that New Women often had artistic careers, supporting themselves as artists, writers, or actors, because "there are many instances of the arts . . . waking up the naturally sleeping self."[34] She not only offered the arts as a possible path for women to pursue but encouraged those women already following it by professing that the self-awareness and inner strength they gained from being economically independent would help them face the public scrutiny such careers entailed.

In addition to refuting general assumptions of women as inferior beings, Iwano Kiyo, like Katō, believed women needed to prepare themselves for economic self-sufficiency. In her second contribution to *Seitō*'s New Woman supplements, "Ideological and Economic Independence," Iwano expounded on the two factors—awakening and practice—she felt were most important to the women of her day. She contended that a woman could not truly have one unless she also had the other. "If by chance a situation arises where independence of thought is hindered, a woman who has no preparation to live life alone as an individual has no other choice than to depend on men or parents. If this happens, she must reluctantly make concessions to these people. In so doing a part of her thought is destroyed. Life and thought become completely separate things."[35] For Iwano, spiritual awakening and concrete practice had to go hand in hand.

Fukuda Hideko, Katō's model for the activist woman, took the call for economic change a step further and pressed for the realization of a communist society (*kyōsan shakai*) as a solution for women. Fukuda, like Katō, felt that capitalist economics both necessitated and marred the institution of marriage. "Indeed," she claimed, "the family that will exist once the system of private property has been destroyed, . . . once economical and profitable marriages die out, will be based on true love."[36] Like Iwano, Fukuda came to the Seitōsha with a history of prior activism as an advocate of women's rights. In the 1880s she had participated in the Freedom and People's Rights movement and also had been imprisoned for radical activity. The Seitōsha sought her contribution as a well-recognized feminist from an older generation and as a socialist. But her background and reputation probably influenced the government's decision to ban the February 1913 issue of *Seitō,* which carried Fukuda's article "The Solution to the Woman Problem."[37]

Fukuda's controversial voice was one of the few within the pages of *Seitō* that raised the issue of class and addressed the needs of a broad range of women. She maintained that only a complete overhaul of the nation's economic basis would truly improve the position of women. She reasoned, "If [communism, *kyōsansei*] is not established, then even if we get the vote, even if courts and universities and government offices are opened to women, only those women from the class of power will arrive there. The average woman will remain as before, excluded from these spheres."[38] In other words, without social revolution, suffrage would retain inequality by allowing women to buy into an unequal system. Fukuda's appeal for broad-based economic change was a challenge not only to conservative government officials and policymakers who sought to preserve the status quo but also to many of the women within the Seitōsha who were "from the class of power."

Other Voices

Writing in *Seitō's* 1913 New Woman supplements, these women succeeded in their personal efforts to counteract the negative image of the New Woman prevalent in the media and to broaden the debate on women. They offered a variety of definitions, ideas, paths, and solutions. They gave substance to an image that had been batted around "like a toy balloon." The impact of their efforts extended far beyond the pages of *Seitō*. Discussion of the New Woman continued actively in the press throughout 1913. Several general-interest magazines, as well as specialized journals, devoted sections or whole issues to the New Woman and the Woman Problem, creating conversations among various writers and members of Seitō. The New Woman was also discussed and debated in the pages of many popular women's magazines such as *Jogaku Sekai* (Schoolgirls' World), *Fujin no Tomo* (Ladies' Companion), and *Fujin Gahō* (Ladies' Graphic). As discussed in Chapter 6, the activities of the Seitōsha motivated the founding of a second New Woman's association and journal. This new group added to the debate by promoting a positive path for New Women that differed from the Seitōsha's. Newspaper reporters continued to focus on the lives of New Women and to look for sensational angles, but even they were providing broader, more balanced accounts than they had in the past. In June 1913, *Tokyo Nichi Nichi Shinbun* began a fifty-article series, "New Women Who Can Be Found in Japanese History," in which the reporter argued that the New Woman was not merely a foreign import but could be found throughout the ages in Japan.[39] Such accounts, by indigenizing the New Woman, encouraged wide understanding and acceptance of the phenomenon in Japanese society.

Also in June 1913, the major general-interest journal *Taiyō* (Sun) dedicated its entire issue to the Woman Problem. Most of the contributors were male, and the magazine was generally critical of the New Woman. Nonetheless, both the length and the content of the issue revealed that the New Woman was receiving serious attention. An overall bias toward reaffirming women's role within the family system was evident in articles with such titles as "Nora Will Probably Return Home," "The Solution to the Woman Problem Is Man's Responsibility," and "The New Women Who Disregard Their True Nature." Several articles on the women's movements/suffrage movements in England and the United States indicated concern about trends in the West and their possible effects on Japan. More evenhanded—though still ambivalent—accounts included "The Single Life of Women: Its Good and Evil" and "The Pros and Cons of Women as Office Workers." Even a few members of the art and literature world wrote in support of the New Woman, men like critic and stage director Shimamura Hōgetsu and naturalist writer Tayama Katai.[40]

Another major general-interest journal, *Chūō Kōron* (Central Review), produced its Woman Problem issue in July 1913. Several of the people who contributed to the *Taiyō* issue also appeared here, but in general the subject matter was more varied and more positive than in *Taiyō*. The first section contained general articles about the New Woman and the Woman Problem with contributions from a politician, a medical doctor, and several social critics. The second section, entitled "The Basic Aims of Modern Girls Education," contained articles by two high-ranking Ministry of Education officials and several girls' higher school and college principals. Another section consisted of writings by seven "accomplished women." A "Research on Women's Professions" section discussed women doctors, salesclerks, reporters, and teachers.[41] *Chūō Kōron* contributors seemed more interested in tracing the directions in which women were going than in keeping them tied to the past.

The image of the New Woman in the press was becoming varied. The changing press treatment of Hiratsuka Raichō serves as a prime example. Raichō not only provided the impetus for a serious evaluation of the New Woman but also continued to serve as a living model of the image. The New Woman debate had grown to include a broad range of issues and options, but individual lives—and especially hers—still drew attention. The previous summer Raichō had been at the center of the scandalous events swirling around Seitōsha members. Reporters had focused on the unconventional behavior of Raichō and her companions and created a trivial, negative image of the New Woman. One year later, Raichō was still being held up as a principal model of the New Woman, but this time she was viewed in a more serious—and largely more favorable—light.

Chūō Kōron's July 1913 Woman Problem issue included a series of articles grouped under the heading "Hiratsuka Raichō: A Character Review." Although established women writers like Yosano Akiko and Tamura Toshiko had been the subject of similar analyses, it was unprecedented for such a controversial person so early in her career to warrant serious attention. The ten writers who were invited to contribute to the "character review" were all supporters of the New Woman, if not specifically of Raichō. The cluster consisted of both men and women with a vested interest in seeing women advance in society. They were progressive intellectuals: writers, critics, publishers, New Women. Raichō's charismatic personality captivated them. In some cases, her status as representative of New Women caused them to demand a lot from her. Each of the writers had some form of personal connection with Raichō, yet most claimed that they did not know her well. They described an enigmatic figure, someone who was both very masculine and very feminine, both distant and engaging. For those around her, Raichō encompassed in her being the diversity of meanings that she herself desired for the New Woman.

Those who found fault with Raichō focused on the thought and actions they felt were indicative of old, and therefore inappropriate, ways for a new, modern being. Seitō member Iwano Kiyo and her husband, the literary figure Iwano Hōmei, each presented a critical view of the influence Zen had on Raichō's thought.[42] Hōmei argued that "Buddhist abstract thinking" was "outdated" and hindered the progress of New Women. He maintained, "Asserting women's awakening is new in our country, but if that awakening ends up being supported by Buddhism . . . the result can never be considered something new."[43] For Hōmei, old religions could not provide the basis for new thought. Kiyo took a more rational stance than an antireligious one in asserting that Zen had "left a little damage" on Raichō's views. She contended, "I cannot believe in a world where consciousness is detached and the self is obliterated."[44] Kiyo found the Zen deemphasizing of self counterproductive to the strengthening of women's awareness. Kiyo also conceded that "there's no denying the fact that Zen provides a good basis for training thought and intellect";[45] but both she and Hōmei considered Zen limiting and wanted Raichō to move beyond it in her efforts to improve the status of women.

Two other prominent members of the literary world, Satō Haruo and Yosano Akiko, criticized Raichō for actions they deemed unbefitting a New Woman. Satō denounced Raichō's "whimsical behavior" and declared, "It goes without saying, what truly changes the times is not principles or arguments, but personality [*jinkaku*]."[46] New Women had to be conscious of and circumspect in the image they presented to society. Yosano Akiko was even more specific than Satō. She berated Raichō for her unrestrained sexual activity. Yosano based her accusation on the scandalous stories that had circulated in the press the previous year and called on Raichō to refute or clarify the rumors. Yosano, who also served as a model for the New Woman, stressed, "I know that if women are to be free and independent, they can be so without needlessly slighting their chastity."[47] She took the gossip about Raichō at face value and likened Raichō's escapades to "the dissolute behavior of an uneducated girl."[48] According to Yosano, Raichō's thought may have been progressive but her behavior was anything but new. Apparently, the unorthodox activities of Seitō members could draw the disapproval of conservative critics and supporters alike. Even as they succeeded in being taken seriously intellectually, Seitō women could not shake the stigma of transgressive sexuality.

Raichō continued to be an elusive, contradictory figure even to these "character review" contributors who were chosen because of their associations with her. Many of them began their articles by stating some level of discomfort in commenting on Raichō. They expressed wariness at evaluating someone who was still developing as an intellectual figure, confessed that they did not know either Raichō or her writings well, or hesitated to add to the gossip surrounding her. Even fellow Seitō member Iwano Kiyo, who claimed Raichō as a good friend, concluded her article by stating, "There's no way of understanding the true [Raichō]."[49]

Another element that contributed to the enigma of Raichō was her physical appearance. Reporters often commented on Raichō's manly style of dress and deportment. Satō Haruo provided a similar description in his article, noting her choice of clothing and her distinctive strut.[50] Tamura Toshiko, another successful writer and New Woman, offered a short piece that parodied the focus on Raichō's masculine appearance by insisting that she had counted at least thirty hairs on Raichō's chin![51] Conversely, several of Raichō's advocates made note of her feminine qualities. They praised her beauty, her grace, her pleasant manner, and her gentle voice. Somehow, she managed to be both masculine and captivatingly feminine. Otake Kōkichi, the artistic personality most closely associated with Raichō and the events of the previous summer, shifted the focus to her inner feminine beauty. Otake indicated that although Raichō's mannish demeanor—referring to both her choice of clothes and her outspokenness—served her well as part of her public identity, on a personal, familiar level Raichō exhibited a kind, caring, nurturing side. Otake remarked, "She was always gentle when she came in contact with younger beings."[52] Here Otake referred both to the pet dove Raichō had raised and fretted over and to herself and others whom Raichō had mentored. This blending of masculine and feminine set Raichō apart and helped to define her as a New Woman. It seems that Raichō intentionally crafted this blending in her efforts to explore new options for women.

Behavior and appearance aside, all the "character review" writers respected Raichō's intelligence, writing ability, and maturity. Yosano Akiko praised Raichō's "rational mind" and "bold expression."[53] Iwano Kiyo applauded her ability to "write such reasonable, unified arguments." Iwano coupled the "masculine" traits of rationality, boldness, and clarity of thought with an emphasis on Raichō's lack of arrogance, her introspection, and her tolerance for others.[54] Otake Kōkichi joined Iwano in admiring Raichō's hard-working, studious nature.[55] Examining her face, Raichō's publisher Nishimura Yōkichi noted a "mature gentleness, not the immature coloring of a young person."[56] Literary man and Seitōsha supporter Baba Kōchō also commented on Raichō's maturity by noting how Raichō had grown up since the days of the Baien incident, her youthful flirtation with love and death a handful of years earlier.[57] He credited her writing now with "considerable composure and the power of common sense."[58] Although she was still held accountable for her controversial thought and actions, Raichō's efforts to expand the scope of the New Woman debate allowed for a serious and positive evaluation of her own life and thought, as well as that of other New Women.

Japan's New Woman literally and figuratively proved to have a lot more substance than the scandalous headlines of 1912 had implied. Responding to Raichō's call to action, many Seitō women rallied to assert a positive view of women in society. Their general objective was to legitimize the existence and activities of New Women like themselves. They believed that the New Woman had an integral part to play in Japan's modernizing process. They drew courage and inspiration from the West, from Japan, and from within. They did not want to create only one image of the New Woman because they did not know what a truly modern being would look like. They wanted options, alternatives, new possibilities for themselves and for Japan.

In their efforts to define and expand the Woman Problem and the image of the New Woman, the women of Seitō seemed to be addressing Seitō members themselves as often as the public. They were encouraging, criticizing, and urging each other to define a space where women could be spiritually and economically independent, where they would be recognized as individuals in their own right. They wanted to be taken seriously. And they argued for multiple and diverse meanings, not a singular definition.

By advocating spiritual, legal, and economic improvements in women's lives, many Seitō women felt they were helping society at large. Women, men, and relationships of all kinds would benefit and be strengthened. That their critics had chosen to see them as destructive and a threat to Japanese society saddened and frustrated many of the New Women, for as varied as their interpretations were they were all looking for ways to advance Japanese society, not to destroy it.

Although the Seitō women did not convince all their critics that the New Woman was a social asset, they did succeed in generating a serious examination of women's role in society. In 1913, media coverage of the New Woman and the Woman Problem increased in quantity and in content. Sensationalized accounts of New Women still flourished, but alongside them were earnest articles that explored women's existing roles and debated their future potential. The discourse on the New Woman became linked with ongoing discussions of women's educational, occupational, economic, and social issues, which all fell under the rubric of the Woman Problem. The New Woman would remain a controversial figure, but her sensationalized aspect was now coupled with a strong backbone and intellect.

CHAPTER 6

Rivalry

"TRUE NEW WOMEN" EMERGE

*A*ttempts by Seitō women to create a serious and positive image of the New Woman not only stimulated a broad discussion of women's issues but also prompted the emergence of another Tokyo-based women's group. Founded by Nishikawa Fumiko, Miyazaki Mitsuko, and Kimura Komako in early 1913, the Shinshinfujinkai (True New Woman's Association) sought to provide a wholesome, instructive alternative to the degenerate, disruptive image of the New Woman generally associated with the Seitōsha.[1] Calling themselves True New Women, these three women and their supporters adopted an oppositional and superior stance to the Seitō-style New Women. They based their authority to serve as leaders of women on their experiences as wives and mothers and asserted that women would advance by embracing these roles, not discarding them as many Seitōsha women did.

Nishikawa, Miyazaki, and Kimura differed from most Seitōsha women in that they were married and had children, as well as in their family, educational, and vocational backgrounds. The core of women who had gathered to launch Seitō were from upper-middle-class families and had graduated from Japan Women's College or similar higher schools for women. The True New Women were not so privileged. In addition, unlike most Seitōsha members, all three Shinshinfujinkai founders were born and raised outside the Tokyo area. These True New Women combined unconventional pasts and pursuits with a seemingly conventional emphasis on women's roles as wives and mothers to create yet another model for women. A brief sketch of these three women will help provide a foundation for their ideas and for their treatment in the press.[2]

Of the three, Nishikawa Fumiko had an upbringing and education most resembling that of the Seitōsha founders. However, she also had a penchant for socialist ideas and socialist men.[3] When her first husband died at an early age, she entered a second free-love marriage with another socialist man. Using socialist organizations and journals as her vehicle, Nishikawa championed the cause of improving the status of women. She also played an important role in the unsuccessful 1905 campaign to revise Article 5 of the Public Peace Police Law, the article that prohibited women from attending political meetings.[4] Miyazaki Mitsuko, in contrast, had received only an elementary education and by the age of eleven had lost both her parents. Several years later she married Miyazaki Toranosuke, the founder of a religious sect that combined elements of Christianity and Buddhism. The two traveled together spreading their faith before going to Tokyo to set up a religious center. Kimura Komako's early years were also unusual. As a child, Komako helped support her family by performing with a traveling theater group. A wealthy patron provided for a solid education but cut her off when Komako fell in love with and married his nephew, Kimura Hideo. The three women's paths crossed in Tokyo, and they decided to collaborate on the Shinshinfujinkai.

Nishikawa, Miyazaki, and Kimura launched their magazine *Shinshinfujin* (True New Woman) in May 1913. They announced their objectives in the "Declarations" of the first two issues. The first issue stated, "In the depths of each of our hearts there is a noble, true, living being. Striving to thoroughly display this infinite latent power is the lifestyle of a new, true woman. We ourselves strive towards this. We also want to encourage other women. This is the goal of undertaking to publish this magazine."[5] The same issue also mentioned "striving to broaden the narrow range of women's activity" as a goal. In the second issue the cofounders added to their list of objectives a discussion of all problems concerning women—including marriage and divorce—and a study of the Woman Problem debates in Europe and the United States and the impact they should have on Japan.[6]

The Seitōsha and the Shinshinfujinkai espoused comparable interests in promoting women's inner awareness, in uncovering women's latent power, and in cultivating new areas of activity for women. Other similarities included an emphasis on women's spiritual awakening and efforts to discuss and incorporate Western ideas. Contributions from established women writers Yosano Akiko and Tamura Toshiko helped legitimize both groups. Yet the two groups differed in their approach to the Woman Problem and in the images they offered. The Seitōsha represented women who largely opposed the assigned roles of "good wife, wise mother" and addressed themselves for the most part to young, single women. Through their unconventional behavior Seitōsha women endeavored to broaden opportunities for women. However, this same behavior earned them a reputation as unruly, indulgent young ladies. The Shinshinfujinkai women presented a more mature image than did the Seitōsha. They were proud of their status as wives and mothers and wanted to use these roles to enhance women's lives. With similar aims, but different methods, both groups worked on crafting a positive New Woman image. This chapter explores the ways in which these two groups contended with each other and expanded the definition of New Woman. It examines how and why several newspapers and magazines accentuated a sense of rivalry between the two. It will also show how the True New Women offered their own variation of what it meant to be modern.

Lecture Meetings: Claiming a Public Voice

The event that initiated the contentious relationship—both real and perceived—between the Seitōsha and the Shinshinfujinkai was in itself an example of the expansion of women's activities. Because Article 5 of the Public Peace Police Law prevented women from even attending a political meeting, women had limited opportunities to speak publicly. The Seitōsha decided to hold a public lecture meeting, at which a few of its members gave speeches. Soon after, the Shinshinfujinkai formed and countered with its own lecture meeting. Both groups desired to create a space where women could publicly join the discussion of the Woman Problem. They were claiming the right to have a public voice in determining the nature of their own futures.

On February 15, 1913, the Seitōsha held its first and only public lecture meeting. In addition to the New Woman supplements in the January, February, and March issues of *Seitō,* discussed in Chapter 5, the lecture meeting was part of the organization's attempt to reclaim and redefine the New Woman as a positive image. Seitō women wanted to be taken seriously. The five-colored-liquor and Yoshiwara incidents of the previous summer had sullied the New Woman image in general and trivialized the activities of Seitō members in particular. The speeches presented at this meeting were part of a continuing effort to defend the actions of the Seitōsha and offer alternative life-styles for young women to pursue.[7]

Unable to gather enough volunteers from its own membership, the Seitōsha had to rely on a few male supporters to help fill the list of speakers. Even though women at this time were beginning to find (and create) outlets for their writing, few had experience with public speaking. Many Seitōsha members shied away from this task. The list of speakers included three men and three women, with Hiratsuka Raichō making the closing remarks. The men—Ikuta Chōkō, Baba Kōchō, and Iwano Hōmei—were all active in literary circles. The women were Yasumochi Yoshiko, a founding member of Seitō; Itō Noe, one of Seitō's newest and youngest members; and Iwano Kiyo, one of the few members of Seitō who had previously spoken in public because of her involvement in the Article 5 revision campaign several years earlier.

Although this meeting was not overtly political, it was still uncommon for women to be speaking in public. In an effort to provide a suitable atmosphere, the Seitōsha's announcements of the lecture meeting included the stipulation that all men wishing to attend be accompanied by women. Even so, men significantly outnumbered women. According to Raichō, about two-thirds of the one thousand or so people who attended were men. Initially the audience seemed serious and attentive. Everything was progressing smoothly until one of the male speakers began expounding his unconventional views of marriage. A man from the audience became outraged and broke the decorum by charging the stage. A small scuffle ensued, but order was quickly restored and the meeting continued without further incident.[8]

The male speaker in question was Iwano Hōmei, a poet, novelist, and critic. He was also Seitōsha member Iwano Kiyo's husband. Hōmei lived an unconventional life and advocated acceptance and exploration of one's carnal nature. He did not believe marriage should hinder such activity. In his speech, Hōmei expounded on his theory that people had an animalistic aspect governed by instinct. Clearly, he was advocating sexual behavior that violated the bounds of conventional marriage. The spectator who took offense to Hōmei's speech was Miyazaki Toranosuke.[9] As previously noted, Toranosuke was the husband of Shinshinfujinkai cofounder Miyazaki Mitsuko and the self-proclaimed "Messiah-Buddha" or "Prophet" of a new religious sect.

Hōmei and Toranosuke's confrontation provided color to the newspaper coverage the following day. Reporters could now add the clash of male egos to the already controversial story of women making public addresses. One newspaper reported the incident as follows: "When [Hōmei] was about to discuss his favorite subject of the dissolution of marriage, Mr. Toranosuke Miyazaki, the self-professed savior of Marital Bliss, who happened to be in the audience, ran in a rage onto the platform and grabbing Mr. Hōmei barked at him, 'Give us your explanation of your own divorce!'"[10] Another newspaper described it as a "cockfight" and a "singular spectacle," with the audience both "cheering and heckling." This same article also printed a response from Hōmei: "I could not live in the same house with an un-awakened woman as a wife, so I divorced. In a sense, I was a male Nora."[11] Hōmei even went so far as to identify himself with the character symbolic of the New Woman! Hōmei and Toranosuke served as surrogates for what the press billed as a battle between two rival groups of women. This was not the public image either women's group had in mind. It was not the women who behaved badly, but the men.

Media accounts of the meeting also focused on physical descriptions of the women in attendance, both in the audience and on the stage. This emphasis on the appearance and behavior of the women again overshadowed the women's words and ideas. Reporters grouped the female spectators by their varying hairdos, the majority of which connoted unmarried status. Students were particularly prevalent, but there was also a smattering of married women, a few with children on their backs, and even a grandmother or two.[12] One article characterized them as "high school girls who deliberately want-ed to be thought new by wearing strange attire and wives of a new order who wished to profit as second Noras."[13] As for the female speakers, the three women presented very different images. Although Yasumochi Yoshiko's ap-pearance was described as that of a "fat schoolmistress" and Itō Noe was criticized for being young and naive, Iwano Kiyo was praised for both her appearance and her well-delivered speech. She wore a tasteful kimono and sash, and her hairstyle signified that she was a married woman. Her experi-ence in public speaking served her well; she presented a smooth, rational argument asserting women's need for ideological and economic freedom.[14] None of the reports mentioned the clothing or hairstyles of the men, who constituted two-thirds of those present.

The Seitōsha continued to publish its monthly magazine, to hold study groups, and to sponsor other activities, but it did not hold another public lecture meeting. Although Raichō and the others viewed the lecture meeting as a general success, they were disappointed about having to rely on male speakers. As Raichō acknowledged in her autobiography, "Compared with a magazine that was created solely by women's hands, that the lecture meeting was unable to be so did not make us feel like holding a second one."[15] The fight between Hōmei and Toranosuke also caused dissatisfaction by contrib-uting to the disruptive image of New Women touted in the press. In holding a public meeting, the Seitō women wanted to provide a space for women to voice their opinions. They also hoped that the rational presentation of ideas would help create a serious image of the New Woman. They did not fully succeed in reaching either goal.

Although the Seitōsha abandoned the idea of lecture meetings, this early attempt did have other meaningful consequences. The Shinshinfujinkai quickly mobilized and announced that it would sponsor its own lecture meeting the following month. The True New Women intentionally designed their meeting in contrast to the one held by the Seitōsha. They even gave it a more imposing name: on March 16, 1913, they convened the "women's oratory" meeting. Previously, Miyazaki Mitsuko had proclaimed, "We will not have the inconsistency of the recent Seitōsha lecture meeting where . . . men unashamedly gave lectures contemptuous of women. Only women will give lectures."[16] As she introduced each of the speakers, Miyazaki held her young daughter in her arms, providing a visual reminder that True New Women took pride in being mothers. The True New Women also set a Japanese tone with their choice of musical interlude. In contrast to the piano recital given at Seitō's lecture meeting, the True New Women offered a performance on the biwa, a traditional Japanese four-stringed lute. This choice reflected their emphasis on "Japaneseness" rather than on imitation of the West within attempts to be modern. The True New Women sought to create an alternate image of modern Japanese women that promoted women's awakening, rights, and access to public space while retaining an emphasis on marriage, motherhood, and tradition, an emphasis that many Japanese found comforting.

The women's oratory meeting drew a slightly smaller audience with a similar percentage of female spectators: roughly 700–800 people attended, about a third of whom were women. However, there was a noticeable difference in the audience's composition. Whereas the Seitōsha had drawn a largely youthful crowd of students, actors, and aspiring literary talents, the Shinshinfujinkai attracted a mature group of housewives, mothers, and middle-aged men.[17] Even so, Raichō, in her recollections of the gathering, noted, "The atmosphere was very different from Seitō's lecture meeting. Here the male audience's heckling was rather lively."[18] Raichō perhaps was implying that Seitōsha women were able to keep order during their meeting both before and after the single disruptive outburst of the husband of one of the True New Women, while there was a general lack of decorum throughout the True New Women's meeting. Newspaper accounts did not mention a rowdy crowd at the women's oratory meeting however.

Although the Seitōsha quickly abandoned the public-meeting strategy, the Shinshinfujinkai continued to provide a public forum for verbal expression and debate. It took the co-leaders a few months to firmly launch their association and magazine, but in June 1913 they held the first Woman Problem study group. Combining formal lectures and informal discussion, this group continued to meet almost monthly for the next several years. The True New Women conceded the point that they argued had made their first women's oratory meeting superior to the Seitōsha's public lecture meeting: they shed their women-only approach and called on both women and men to give lectures. Although open to the public, these meetings attracted a small audience, consisting largely of Shinshinfujinkai members and supporters.[19]

The Press: Creating a Sense of Competition

The media heralded the arrival of the Shinshinfujinkai by sensationalizing the drama of two women's groups locked in competition. In this way members of the press were able to avoid a serious discussion of the concerns of both groups. The New Woman was a source of amusement (and disdain), not a topic to be taken seriously. In March 1913, immediately after the Shinshinfujinkai announced its formation, the *Tokyo Nichi Nichi Shinbun* began a thirteen-article series entitled "The New Woman's New Foe." It used military terms—including *troop leader, troop headquarters,* and *battle*—to pit the two New Woman groups against each other. The opening article of the series promised the "spectacle of female combat."[20] Such coverage was patronizing and reduced the deepening discussion of women's place in society to a cat fight that would entertain male readers. The reporter interviewed Nishikawa, Miyazaki, and Kimura and provided his readers with a gossipy version of the group's formation, its antagonism toward the Seitōsha, and background information on its founders. Other newspapers and magazines joined in, adding fuel to the sense of competition. By playing up the rivalry between the Seitōsha and the Shinshinfujinkai, the media implied that there could be only one New Woman's voice. Such a restriction on women's activity ran counter to the objectives of both women's groups. Sensationalized coverage of the rivalry continued to overshadow the significant ideas of these women, even as women's issues began to be taken seriously in a handful of media outlets.

Although the media amplified the rivalry, the True New Women clearly were trying to distinguish themselves from the more notorious New Women of Seitō. One newspaper account reported that one of the Shinshinfujinkai speakers stated, "Women who got drunk on five-colored liquor and went to brothels were not New Women, but deviant women," and another, in reference to Seitō-style women, declared, "New Women are poisonous bees who sting the good national character."[21] The headline "An All-Out Attack on the Seitōsha" announced another article on the Shinshinfujinkai's oratory meeting.[22] However, the Shinshinfujinkai was not trying to eliminate the Seitōsha. Although the media declared a battle between the two groups that implied one would emerge victorious, both groups were interested in expanding women's options not limiting them. Antagonistic as the two groups were, they did not feel their differences necessitated a battle to the death. In one interview, True New Woman Nishikawa Fumiko acknowledged that it was good to have any number of New Woman associations.[23]

The initial lecture meetings hosted by the Seitōsha and the Shinshinfujinkai provided the basis for the public perception of dueling New Women groups. Seitō women, the press, and True New Women would all contribute to this perception. Years later, in her autobiography, Raichō commented, "[Our] lecture meeting unknowingly gave birth to a spin-off. Taking an anti-Seitō stance, [the Shinshinfujinkai] launched their enterprise saying, 'We are the genuine New Women.' . . . Journalism immediately jeered, 'Two New Women Associations' and 'The New Woman's New Foe,' eagerly stirring up a sense of opposition."[24]

Shinshinfujinkai cofounder Miyazaki Mitsuko at first denied any anti-Seitō feeling, declaring, "It is thought that the Shinshinfujinkai set itself up in opposition to the Seitōsha, but such was never the meaning." Miyazaki explained that she, Nishikawa, and Kimura had hoped to found the association months earlier but had been delayed, thus indicating that plans for the new group were already in motion well before the Seitōsha's controversial lecture meeting. Miyazaki even contributed an article to *Seitō*'s January 1913 New Woman supplement. In that article she expressed views the soon-to-materialize Shinshinfujinkai would come to champion. She stressed the need for social progress to be coupled with sound public morals. This linkage of the "modern" concept of progress with a conventional notion of morality would remain central to the True New Woman's self-definition. Miyazaki also called on women to voice their opinions on a variety of issues—social, political, ethical—in order to bring about change. She concluded her piece by stating, "I think it would be very timely to hold a women's lecture meeting."[25]

Clearly the lecture meeting the Seitōsha conducted that February was not what Miyazaki envisioned, although she admitted that it provided the necessary impetus to get the Shinshinfujinkai off the ground. "After attending Seitō's lecture meeting the other day," she explained, "we thought it terrible that female students and young women were poisoned by such thought and we decided to launch our Association."[26] Miyazaki continued to critique the Seitōsha's lecture meeting even months later, presenting an increasingly solid anti-Seitō stance. In her contribution to *Chūō Kōron*'s special Woman Problem issue in July 1913, she again indicated that the "theory of fleshly emancipation" and other such topics advocated at the Seitōsha's meeting prompted the immediate formation of the Shinshinfujinkai. She castigated Seitōsha members as "high-class bad girls" who had appalling taste in choosing speakers. Miyazaki also noted her conviction that the Seitō women had earned their bad reputation through "writing about and asserting the destruction of public morals."[27] By highlighting the issue of class, Miyazaki castigated the privileged, self-centered women of Seitō for not having high standards and drew attention to the fact that True New Women were interested in improving the lives of all women.

Finding the True New Woman

Although the press was interested in playing up the spectacle of female rivalry, the True New Women used that same press to argue for respectable status. Various reports aimed to clarify the difference between the two groups. One account asserted that the True New Women felt that part of their purpose was to "correct" the "harmful thought" disseminated by the Seitōsha. They were to offer a "rescue path" to impressionable young woman who were attracted to the Seitō-style New Women.[28] Other accounts reported that the True New Women wanted to differentiate between good and bad in the variety of new thought swirling around Japan and to focus on the "wholesome elements" only.[29] This focus was meant as a counterpoint to Seitō women's seemingly indiscriminate interest in anything new. Another article credited Shinshinfujinkai cofounder Kimura Komako with saying, "We must advance with a more upright ideology" than the bar-hopping, brothel-going behavior of other New Women.[30] The Shinshinfujinkai women claimed a higher ground, a more sincere purpose than the Seitō women. They considered the words and actions of the Seitō women a disgrace and imagined their own efforts would lead to women's true awakening and strength. Although the two groups shared the same vocabulary—new awakening, latent power—they provided differing images of the New Woman.

The media explicitly identified the basis for the Shinshinfujinkai's high moral ground: the three Shinshinfujinkai founders were all wives and mothers, whereas most of the Seitō women were single and childless. One reporter announced that this "splendid contrast" marked the difference between the two groups, claiming, "In short, the Shinshinfujinkai's originators all value women's essential qualities and are quite proud to be mothers and wives."[31] Nishikawa Fumiko proudly asserted, "We don't think marriage is an experience. We think it is life's most serious reality."[32] Miyazaki Mitsuko echoed her husband's sentiments by declaring, "Those who unconcernedly divorce are moral criminals."[33] However, these women did not unequivocally advocate marriage. They added the modern conditions that it should be based on love and monogamy, not familial or economic considerations and male privilege.

Miyake Setsurei, a male literary critic, focused on the marriage issue in his contribution to the June 1913 Woman Problem issue of *Taiyō*. Concerned about Raichō's refusal to marry, he compared the attitudes of the Seitōsha's New Women and the True New Women and decided the True New Women were the better alternative. Both were interested in more equal relationships based on love, but the True New Woman did not reject formal marriage. Miyake contended, "If all women without exception were to refuse marriage it would be nothing short of the downfall of society."[34] The True New Women could be praised for being womanly women, while the New Women of Seitō were vilified for rejecting Japan's existing—yet stifling—marriage and family systems. Seitō women rejected the government-endorsed roles of "good wife, wise mother," while the True New Women embraced those roles as the source of woman's power.

This difference in itself was enough to make the Shinshinfujinkai's New Woman less threatening and seemingly more deserving of public support than the New Woman of the Seitōsha. Many viewed the behavior of Seitō members as proof that excessive imitation of the West would lead to the destruction of Japan as a nation. By contrast, the True New Women (as wives and mothers) represented stability and a willingness to work within the Japanese system rather than to discard it all together. Nishikawa Fumiko remarked, "There are good reasons for Japan's old conventions and morals. Since they've been practiced for a long time, I would not dare think of overthrowing them. And since women have a social duty as women, I want to measure the development of those who unfailingly fulfill this duty. . . . I fear a radical group like Seitō will fail. I believe we will . . . advance."[35]

The *Tokyo Nichi Nichi Shinbun* series "The New Woman's New Foe" not only announced the rivalry between the Seitōsha and the Shinshinfujinkai but also provided biographical information on the three founders of the Shinshinfujinkai. Their unconventional pasts gave the press plenty of juicy material. Indeed, the True New Women's backgrounds proved to be nearly as sensational as current accounts of Seitō women's lives.[36] Even so, the True New Women were treated more favorably than the Seitōsha by the press because their ideas and activities were less objectionable. For example, the *Tokyo Nichi Nichi Shinbun* reporter underscored the fact that Nishikawa Fumiko and her husband were affiliated with the early socialist movement in Japan, a movement associated with "dangerous thought." The government effectively shut it down when in 1910, on the charge of planning to assassinate the emperor, twenty-four socialists were arrested and twelve—including female radical Kanno Suga—were executed in what became known as the "great treason incident."[37] This event sent the socialist movement underground and temporarily stifled social protest. It would take another decade for an organized movement to reemerge. As a result of both government suppression and a shift in personal beliefs, Nishikawa and her husband separated themselves from the socialist movement and turned to less radical, more acceptable activism. They now focused their energies on promoting moral cultivation.

In her youth, Miyazaki Mitsuko was drawn to the teachings of a new religious sect that combined Christian and Buddhist elements. Miyazaki defied her family when she ran off to marry the group's founder, Toranosuke, and to share in his proselytizing work. In so doing, she took the radical step of severing her family ties. Although neither the reporter nor Miyazaki ever drew the connection, this action was reminiscent of the behavior of Nora and Magda, the heroines of European plays who helped precipitate the New Woman debate in Japan. Seitō women had been castigated as Japanese Noras out to destroy the family. But there is no tone of condemnation in these articles. Mitsuko's actions seem to be more acceptable than Nora's and Magda's because—although she broke with her family—she ran into the arms of a man, married him, and set up a new household. Unlike Nora and her imitators, she did not leave for the selfish reason of "finding herself."

Kimura Komako, the third and youngest founder, spent part of her childhood roaming the countryside as an actor. Again, although the comparisons were not explicitly made, Kimura displayed similarities to the dramatic heroine Magda. Like Magda, Kimura, rejected a marriage proposal arranged by her father and entered a free-love relationship that produced a child. Kimura and her love went to Tokyo, where he opened a treatment center that offered healing through hypnosis. Kimura assisted him and pursued formal training to become an actor, a modern but dubious career path newly available to women. After four years, Kimura finally received permission from her father to enter her partner's family registry, thus making their marriage official. Unlike Magda, Kimura got married and succeeded in providing a legitimate home for her child.

These Shinshinfujinkai women all had unusual backgrounds. Did they compare favorably with the other New Women because they pulled themselves up from questionable circumstances to become respectable women, while the Seitō women had respectable backgrounds but lived disreputable adult lives? Was the Shinshinfujinkai women's way the "true" path to women's awakening? Both the press and the True New Woman seemed to answer in the affirmative. The True New Women gained their "newness" through their involvement with Western formulations of socialism, Christianity, and the theater. They came in contact with the modern and yet remained true to their mission in life as wives and mothers. They pursued radical life-styles but settled down again. The True New Women and their supporters in the press offered the public an image that incorporated Western influences into a Japanese spirit. Their experiences gave them the strength, conviction, and ability to organize and assert their ideas. The "New Woman's New Foe" series succeeded in presenting the Shinshinfujinkai as a reasonable alternative to the Seitōsha. In so doing it tacitly acknowledged that there could be a comparatively good New Woman.

After the women's oratory meeting in March, the three founders continued to spread the word about the True New Woman's Association and its objectives. Together they published the book *Atarashiki Onna no Iku Beki Michi* (The Path the New Woman Should Take), which mapped out their approach to women's awakening. The first issue of their magazine *Shinshinfujin* (True New Woman) came out in May 1913, and they contributed articles to other journals as well. In all these places they continued to define and defend the True New Woman. They were still reacting to the Seitōsha and the media coverage, but they were reacting in their own words.

Nishikawa, Miyazaki, and Kimura insisted that True New Women were not interested in imitating men or standing in opposition to them. They believed neither activity would result in women's awakening or male appreciation. With this declaration they distanced themselves from the behavior of Seitō-style New Women and in general sounded less threatening than the Seitōsha to men. Yet their emphasis on awakening resonated with the Seitōsha's purpose as well, and both groups placed the need for women's awakening ahead of the need for political and social rights. Miyazaki asserted, "Our thought for Japanese women is that something truly new and meaningful lies not in external connections with men and society, but rather in their own internal connections."[38] All three True New Woman founders believed that women would advance their cause and gain respect from men by focusing on developing their own personalities (*jinkaku*) and sense of self.[39]

These three women stressed the need for spiritual awakening before economic rights as well. Here their argument was flavored by Nishikawa's past involvement with the socialist movement. They agreed that economic independence was important for women but that happiness came from the ability to "stand as unique individuals" and not simply from material goods. Miyazaki contended, "Economic growth unaccompanied by true awakening invites nothing but extravagance and gaudiness."[40] The True New Woman was to concentrate on developing spiritually, tapping into her natural abilities, and using these abilities to benefit society.[41]

Determination and perseverance were essential qualities for True New Women. Nishikawa, Miyazaki, and Kimura admitted that both men and women were "trapped by long-standing custom," "governed by conservative sentiments," and had "stubborn spirits." As a rule, people were slow to adapt to change. Men were not the only ones who stifled women's development; women, too, were guilty of confining themselves to the world of household duties. Nishikawa and company lamented the "daily deterioration" of women who became so absorbed in housework that they forgot to nurture their souls. They argued that women should set a little time aside in their daily routines to read, study, and nurture their individuality. True New Women needed to be persistent in pursuing awakening, for such awakening would motivate other women and encourage respect from men.[42]

Although Nishikawa continued to reproach women who were complicit in their own subjugation, she also made it clear that being a New Woman and being a "good wife, wise mother" were "not at all at odds." Nishikawa identified two kinds of excessive behavior: "We cannot dismiss women's depravity as only drinking and high spirits. If a woman shuts oneself in the house and idly does nothing, she is spiritually depraved. If the former is active depravity, the latter is passive depravity."[43] However, women could and should be good wives, wise mothers, and fulfilled individuals. Nishikawa believed women enriched society through their efforts to cultivate their families and themselves. Women could cook, clean, and raise children, and at the same time write, paint, preach, or pursue other productive vocations. She cited Yosano Akiko—the famous poet, writer, and mother of eight children—as a prime example of a True New Woman.[44] Nishikawa contended that women could expand their world and maintain their family ties. In fact, she argued that suppressing women's talents was what led to "Nora-like tragedies."[45] Both Nora's existence as an unawakened wife and mother and her decision to leave home and family could be considered tragedies. In an earlier interview Nishikawa had held up the three Shinshinfujinkai founders as examples of women who were both wives and mothers and New Women. She claimed that none of them had abandoned their households or taken on maids, and even so they were able to form the association.[46]

Not only was it imperative for women to awaken, but it was the duty of those who did to guide others. True New Women had to be leaders in two senses: they had to help men adapt to a dynamic, meaningful role for women in society, and they had to help women realize their full potential. Nishikawa underscored the need for awakened women to express themselves publicly, just as she and a handful of others had done at the women's oratory meeting. True New Women needed to address other women and provide a voice for their shared experiences and perspectives. The Shinshinfujinkai was founded as a forum for such activities. Nishikawa linked the association with the long-standing female activity of exchanging knowledge and information. She declared, "This group will make well-side gossip a little more orderly and research-like, nothing other than civilized well-side gossip [*bunmei no idobata kaigi*]."[47] In other words, Nishikawa reclaimed time-honored female communication skills and aligned them with the modern traits of organization and civilization to make a space for women in the modern world. By adding this modern twist to the traditional practice of "well-side gossip," she positioned True New Women as leaders who preserve beneficial customs of the past even as they strive to advance in a new age.

The founders of the Shinshinfujinkai encouraged the existence of other women's groups as well, even that of their "rival," the Seitōsha. They continued to demonstrate a vision for women that extended beyond a concern for the present when they proclaimed, "Having various women's groups is very necessary for a future large women's movement."[48] They were interested in providing a basis from which women could build, and they realized one group could not accomplish this task alone. Nishikawa drew an analogy to the spread of women's education as an element in Japan's modernizing process: "Just as there are girls' schools in every district, we need lots of women's associations."[49] She backed up this conviction by defending some of the Seitōsha's notorious behavior, even though she did not necessarily agree with their methods. She stated, "Although it is true that some [New Women] visited brothels and drank five-colored liquor, they were only trying to take a first step in destroying perverse, old customs."[50] Clearly, not all traditional practices or attitudes were advisable in a modern society. Both Seitō women and True New Women endeavored to break down conventions they felt restricted women. Any steps that helped women progress to an awakened state were to be acknowledged. Any action was preferable to passive submission.

The True New Women believed, however, that some steps were more enlightened than others and were quick to point out how they differed from the Seitōsha women. They felt they clearly offered a superior path for women. They emphasized many of the same distinguishing features the media had highlighted in setting the two groups up as "foes." Miyazaki used age and social status as the basis of the True New Woman's authority and wisdom. She noted that most of the Seitōsha women were barely out of school, and "there are very few of them who have had the experience of having a household."[51] The True New Women based their right to serve as guides to women's awakening on their life experience as wives and mothers.

Although the main goals of the Shinshinfujinkai had been stated in the "Declarations" of the first two issues, Nishikawa continued her efforts to define the "central points of the Woman Problem" in an article by the same name in the third issue of *Shinshinfujin*. She indicated the breadth of the issues involved by enumerating five problems subsumed under the umbrella of the Woman Problem, namely those related to employment, education, rights, marriage, and prostitution. Each of these problems was multifaceted and in many ways linked to the others. They each were fueled by, and in turn fueled, societal changes and women's personal development. Nishikawa believed there was a solution to the Woman Problem as a whole and delineated both a beginning and an end. She declared, "The central point of the Woman Problem must be to cultivate women's awakening and real ability."[52] However, she also felt men were a necessary element in the resolution of these issues. Specifically, Nishikawa called for a complete revision of the confining male attitude toward women. She felt men opposed women's awakening and progress in society because they misunderstood the goals of the women's movement and feared women wanted to oppress men as men had for so long oppressed women. In fact, Nishikawa maintained that the women's movement was seeking equal opportunity and respect for women. Women wanted to stand side by side with men in society. However, men's fears and misconceptions were firmly entrenched. Men, too, needed to be encouraged to embrace new thought. Women's awakening marked the first step in resolving the Woman Problem, and men's acceptance of women's equality would mark the last.[53]

The Seitōsha and the Shinshinfujinkai would both continue for the next several years, each offering women encouragement, information, and options, and even sharing a few members.[54] The Shinshinfujinkai engaged in a variety of activities including publishing its monthly magazine, holding regular study groups and lecture meetings, and even establishing a dorm for working women. The Shinshinfujinkai was also the first group in Japan to openly discuss birth control. However, because only scattered issues of *Shinshinfujin* after 1916 remain, it is difficult to track the trajectory of the group and its ideas. Publication would cease in 1923, seven years after the demise of *Seitō*.[55]

True New Women and New Women contributed to women's awareness and empowerment by offering different images and methods for enlarging women's roles in society. The Seitōsha, as discussed in Chapter 5, expanded the definition of the New Woman by countering the negative press with visions of its own. The Shinshinfujinkai succeeded in broadening the definition even further. Their True New Women were wives and mothers who tapped into the strength and knowledge gained from their experiences to become awakened individuals actively contributing to society.

True New Women embraced the accepted roles of wife and mother, upheld traditional morality, and emphasized their Japanese spirit. However, they also linked these qualities with a modern persona and, in so doing, opened up the possibility of a less threatening, more positive New Woman than did the Seitōsha version. They came in contact with the modern concepts of socialism, New Theater, and Christianity (connected with the modernizing process in Japan), and they advocated modern practices such as marriages based on love, monogamy, and birth control. They wanted to create less confining, more public roles for women. They encouraged women to express themselves openly, and they wanted both women and men to be receptive to new ideas. True New Women were to serve as leaders and help Japan progress in the modern world.

In general, the media set up the Shinshinfujinkai and the Seitōsha as rivals and continued to sensationalize the New Woman. In many cases, these reports reinforced the image of New Women as trivial and frivolous, perhaps mildly entertaining, but definitely not to be taken seriously. However, many reporters, critics, and supporters also found that their coverage was enriched by the comparison. The True New Women played up the rivalry as well. They used it to distinguish themselves from the negative image of degenerate and destructive New Women and to legitimate their positive image of True New Women. They noted the decadent behavior of Seitō-style New Women and emphasized their own higher morality as wives and mothers. In contrast to the Seitōsha, True New Women also revealed more concern for women of all classes both in their words and in their actions. This concern set them apart from the generally upper-middle-class point of view of the Seitōsha.

Although the press and the women themselves tended to focus on their differences, True New Women and Seitō women shared some common goals and offered each other support as well. They were, after all, part of a relatively limited circle of women activists. They stressed the need for women's awakening and recognized that multiple paths to achieving it were desirable. After the two groups folded, Nishikawa Fumiko, Hiratsuka Raichō, and others would join forces to organize a women's relief group following the devastating 1923 Great Tokyo Earthquake. The Seitōsha has received more attention both from the contemporary press and from historians, but the Shinshinfujinkai also clearly played an important role in shaping the New Woman/Woman Problem debate, promoting awareness, and expanding options for women in Taishō Japan.

CHAPTER 7

New Women and Beyond

Japan was not the only nation to produce and contend with the New Woman. As both an object of gender discourse and a social reality, the New Woman emerged in numerous countries around the world. Nation-state formation and its accompanying ideology of nationalism, along with industrialization, technological and scientific advances, and increased access to education provided the necessary conditions for her appearance. In the last decades of the nineteenth century, the New Woman established her presence in Europe and the United States. By the opening decades of the twentieth century, she would appear on every inhabited continent. In all her incarnations, she signified a break with the past, a rejection of the ideology of separate spheres that locked women in a subordinate position in the home, and an overturning of restrictions on women's lives. Socially, economically, institutionally, and politically, the New Woman claimed a space for women in the public sphere.

This chapter examines the New Woman as an international phenomenon. Starting with her Euro-American manifestations in the late nineteenth century, I explore the general characteristics of the New Woman as she emerged in the discourses and public spaces of her day. Some common features span time and place, but the term *New Woman* encompasses a spectrum of ideas, behaviors, and attitudes with distinct variations across generations and national boundaries. A brief consideration of the New Woman in Egypt, China, and Korea highlights this diversity and provides interesting comparisons with her Euro-American and Japanese counterparts. The chapter concludes with a concise account of the legacy Japan's New Women left and the directions Japanese women and their organizations explored in the 1920s and 1930s.

New Women on the International Stage

In Europe and the United States, the term *New Woman* referred largely to well-educated, middle-class women who were moving beyond the confines of their domestic sphere.[1] These New Women included professional women, clubwomen, social reformers, rational homemakers, and suffragists. However, working-class women and women from various ethnic groups also contributed to the diversity of the New Woman image through their efforts on behalf of union organizing and civil rights and by forming women's groups that addressed their specific needs and concerns. Through their numerous college, club, reform, and suffrage organizations New Women gained a new sense of community and became actively engaged in the public sphere.[2]

The New Woman's most distinguishing features included her independence, her open sexuality, and her rejection of marriage as the only viable option for women. Many of her critics in the government, press, and intellectual circles found these same characteristics the most threatening to social and national order. Less restrictive clothing and a general increase in physical mobility helped to create an active, athletic image. The visual image of the Euro-American New Woman on a bicycle symbolized her newfound freedom. The theories of Sigmund Freud, Havelock Ellis, and others paved the way for an exploration of women's sexuality that Victorian sensibilities had not previously allowed. New Women exercised their freedom by taking control over their own bodies. They determined who their partners would be, if and when they would marry, and how many children they would have. They explored alternatives to marriage that included female friendships and communities, lesbianism, and free-love relationships. Although many women rejoiced in the new opportunities and areas of influence inherent in the New Woman discourse, many of the New Woman's contemporaries feared her self-reliant nature and her determination to make her own choices about marriage, family, and career.[3]

The New Woman as a cultural symbol and as an object of discourse circulated in fictional form in Europe and the United States in the 1880s and 1890s. A representative of fin-de-siècle social upheaval, the New Woman became a common feature in novels, plays, and the press. She embodied both liberating ideals for women and dangerous moral decay for society. Heroines who resisted the Victorian feminine ideal, pursued careers, and sought alternatives to the accepted roles of wife and mother figured prominently in the novels of Sarah Grand, Mona Caird, George Gissing, Grant Allen, Olive

Schreiner, and others.[4] Henrik Ibsen, August Strindberg, and George Bernard Shaw took the lead in creating roles for New Women in their plays. As in the Japanese example, these plays and their female protagonists became an integral part of the New Woman discourse. They also helped promote acting as a viable career for women.[5] Although the figure of the New Woman received some serious attention in newspapers and magazines, it was also frequently maligned through parody and caricature.[6] These various fictionalized approaches to the New Woman helped spread the discourse beyond Euro-American borders.

Alongside her discursive forms, the New Woman could be seen in the public sphere bicycling through town, attending colleges and universities, entering new professions, leading women's associations, campaigning for women's suffrage, and experimenting with new ideas, styles, and relationships. In the United States, in particular, historians have separated the New Woman into distinct generations.[7] The first generation materialized in the closing years of the nineteenth century. This New Woman was college-educated and self-sufficient. She aligned herself with the Progressive movement and engaged in careers in social work, education, and moral reform. She frequently opted to postpone or forgo marriage and instead sought female friendships in settlement houses, women's clubs, or other organizations.[8] In the 1910s, the second generation of New Women emerged. In contrast with women in the first generation, these New Women pursued more radical and bohemian life-styles and were often associated with Greenwich Village. They experimented with free love and lesbianism. Their ideals were more socialist than progressive.[9] By the 1920s, American women had gained the vote. Paradoxically, in this new era of political freedom the New Woman was no longer the dynamic creature she had been in previous decades. This third generation of New Women shifted from being producers of new social and cultural trends to being consumers of goods. Across the generations, the great variety of New Women worked at broadening women's sphere and expanding women's influence and opportunities.[10]

New Woman thus was an umbrella term that could be applied to any woman venturing beyond prescribed womanly roles. However, it also could imply a more narrowly-construed image. For example, social and moral reformers and rational homemakers, who would have fallen under the rubric of the first generation New Woman in Europe and the United States, were not so labeled in Japan. In Japanese society, these women's efforts were viewed as an extension of acceptable womanly roles and as contributions to national strength and well-being. The New Woman appellation was reserved for those Japanese women whose open sexuality, self-assertion, and unconventional behavior were considered a threat to national stability. In this way, Japan's New Woman resembled the second generation of Euro-American New Women.

Although Euro-American intellectuals, writers, reformers, and feminists in many respects set the standards for the New Woman discourse, the New Woman phenomenon was clearly not confined to the West. There were New Women elsewhere, in a variety of social and political contexts.[11] In her non-Western manifestations, the New Woman was explicitly connected with the emergence of modern nation-states and the accompanying reevaluation of gender and family roles.[12] These nationalist struggles were usually a direct or indirect response to Western aggression. Japan, for example, was eager to maintain its independence and to be treated as an equal by Western nations. The three case studies offered below examine the convergence of nationalism and the New Woman under conditions of some degree of foreign rule: Egypt was subject to British colonization; China's national sovereignty was compromised by the semicolonial intrusions of several foreign nations; Korea faced occupation by Japan, a non-Western imperialist nation.

A new discourse on women appeared in Egypt in the 1890s. A combination of Orientalist, imperialist, nationalist, and feminist concerns brought discussion of women's roles in society to the forefront. British colonial officials and Christian missionaries used the inferior position of Egyptian women—as evidenced in Islamic law and through the customs of veiling and seclusion—to help justify their intervention in Egyptian society. Egyptian nationalists and feminists were divided in their approach to Western intrusions. One course of action was to emulate European customs as a means of promoting national and personal freedoms. Another course was to preserve and revitalize the Islamic and regional heritage as the basis of independence. In each of these approaches, the need to reform the condition of women became a central issue. In reality, the Egyptian modernizing process required a complex negotiation of both indigenous and Western ideas, as it did in Japan and elsewhere.[13]

Qasim Amin is the figure most frequently associated with women's rights in Egypt during this period. A male Egyptian judge, he recognized the need for major societal changes in order to transform Egypt into a modern nation, and he favored following the European model. He addressed the status of women in two of his books: *The Liberation of Women* (1899) and *The New Woman* (1900). He believed that "the new woman is one of the fruits of modern civilization."[14] Amin was opposed to restrictions placed on women's mobility and continued to connect women with modernity by claiming that if "Egyptians wish to be a vital, advanced, and civilized nation," they need "to free . . . women from the shackles of ignorance and seclusion."[15] Although he believed every woman should aspire to be a wife and mother, he was aware that this ideal was not always a possibility. Whether women were managing the household or supporting themselves outside the home, they needed a solid education to develop a healthy mind, body, and morality. Amin acknowledged that women were well-suited for careers in teaching, women's medicine, commerce, and the arts, but he clearly felt most women should be satisfied pursuing a respected position within the family and home when circumstances allowed. Although Amin supported the need for women's education and career opportunities, he could also be accused of substituting Western visions of patriarchy for Islamic ones.[16]

Concurrent with the stirrings of a nationalist movement, the development of a male discourse on women, and advances in female education was the emergence of an Egyptian women's press. A steady flow of women's magazines began to be published (by both women and men) in the 1890s, providing a medium through which a women's movement would arise. Egyptian New Women—much like Japanese New Women—joined in the debates over changing gender and familial roles using the pages of these magazines to discuss topics that included marriage, divorce, the confinement of women to the domestic sphere, education, and career options. Contributors to these magazines offered household advice as well as literary diversions. Descriptions of the New Woman in the press highlighted her improved roles as wife, mother, and household manager, calling to mind the "good wife, wise mother" of Japan. However, one must consider Egypt's historical, cultural, and religious contexts in evaluating how "new" and radical these roles were.[17]

Egyptian New Women, like their male counterparts and other non-Western New Women, varied in whether they pursued their freedoms according to Western models or native ones. They sought to improve women's status in society through pursuing education, adding their voices to gender debates, and even expanding their role as consumers.[18] Their fight against subordinate status resonated with the nationalist struggle against colonialism. The writings and actions of Egypt's New Women laid the groundwork for social, educational, and legislative advances women would gain in the 1920s, as Egypt was gaining independence.

China's New Women were a product mainly of the May Fourth movement in the late 1910s and early 1920s.[19] However, a re-visioning of the roles of women in society had begun in the late nineteenth century as China strove to establish a modern identity. Military and diplomatic losses and an increasing foreign debt placed China in a semicolonized state. Several Western powers, as well as Japan, impinged on Chinese territory and claimed "spheres of influence." An already besieged imperial system was faced with internal unrest as well. Attempts at reform and a growing nationalist agenda allowed for a reconsideration of women's social rights and responsibilities. Many reformers, revolutionaries, and even conservative members of the Qing government equated their women's subjugated position with China's national humiliation and weakness. The need to educate women and improve their status in society, therefore, became intrinsically tied to China's modernizing project.

Chinese women were active in various reform and revolutionary activities in the first decade of the twentieth century. They demonstrated their commitment to national and social changes they believed would create an independent, revitalized China. The 1911 revolution brought down the Qing government and signaled the end of dynastic rule in China. The Republic established in its wake proved to be ineffective and corrupt, not strong and liberating. China remained fragmented and unstable as warlords seized control of various regions. Hopes for women's increased political rights were quelled, and China's modernizing process temporarily stalled.[20]

Various intellectuals, reformers, revolutionaries, and students soon mobilized to champion a radical vision for a strong, independent, and modern China. The continuing decline in China's national prestige prompted participants in the May Fourth movement (broadly spanning the years 1915–1924) to call for a complete social and cultural transformation. They aligned themselves with the "new" and the "modern" and repudiated outmoded "traditions," all the while looking to the West for models and inspiration. The discourse they created denounced Confucianism as an oppressive philosophy, rejected foot-binding and arranged marriages, advocated free love, and advanced women's rights, among other goals. Women's emancipation became inextricably linked to the national good. The inferior position of women in traditional Chinese society was considered a national disgrace. The May Fourth advocates believed that strong, independent women were an essential element in China's quest to shed its backward image and regain its national sovereignty. In their writings, May Fourth reformers urged women to awaken to their true nature and reject their traditional subordinate status.[21]

The Chinese New Woman was created to a great extent through works of (male) fiction. She was an urban figure with a Western-style education.

She was independent, a career woman, a revolutionary, a patriot, a dangerous sexual predator, a symbol of a promising modern future but also of the alienation modernity induced. Although the May Fourth movement generated a largely male discourse, women contributed through their writings and actions as well. Chinese New Women expressed their views on marriage, sexuality, free love, and women's emancipation and published magazines and newspapers of their own. They demonstrated against foreign intervention, campaigned for improved women's education and women's suffrage, and joined the women's sections of the Nationalist and Communist parties. The Chinese nation envisioned by May Fourth reformers—male and female alike—demanded that women's status improve and become more equal than it was to that of men. As the Nationalist and Communist parties headed toward civil war in the 1920s, however, women and their concerns lost much of the prominence they had enjoyed during the May Fourth movement. Many would continue to push for social and political rights, but the need for a unified and free China took precedence in the 1930s and 1940s as Nationalists and Communists battled each other while simultaneously trying to fend off Japanese invasion.[22]

Korea provides yet another example of the convergence of colonialism, nationalism, and feminism. As in China, late-nineteenth-century nationalist reformers in Korea were attempting to construct a modern national identity in the face of dynastic decline and challenges from imperialist nations. Once again, women became a focal point in a predominantly male discourse concerned with modernization and nationalism. In connection with these goals, male reformers offered a critique of Confucianism and its subordination of women and promoted the need for women's education. Once Japan annexed Korea in 1910, the nationalist discourse became focused on overthrowing Japanese colonialism.[23]

In Korea, as in the other countries examined, the nationalist reevaluation of the role of women in society stimulated the emergence of New Women. Also, as in the other countries examined, Christianity played an influential role in the development of an educated feminist elite. Korea's New Women often attended women's schools and colleges established by Christian missionaries and drew strength from the concept that men and women were equal before God. Because Korea was colonized by Japan and not a Western nation, Christianity was not as strongly linked with the imperialist mission as it was in Egypt and other countries. Instead, many Korean women turned to Christianity as a way to maintain a link to the (female) world of religion, to shed negative premodern associations with shamanism and superstition, and to benefit from a new, modern, rational education. Some of these women even traveled and studied abroad. With these increases in education and travel came exposure to the activities, writings, and debates surrounding New Women in the West and especially in Japan.[24]

The first decade of colonial rule was marked by harsh measures aimed at controlling and censoring the Korean people and shaping them into submissive subjects of the Japanese empire. A shift in Japanese colonial policy following the 1919 independence demonstrations, known as the March First movement, eased some of the repression and allowed for some cultural expression. By the 1920s, Korean New Women had developed a small but visible movement of their own. Clearly influenced by Western and Japanese New Woman discourses, Korean New Women favored free love, new marriage laws, and the overthrow of female chastity as an ideal. They especially viewed the limitations imposed by chastity as their major impediment to freedom and equality. They emphasized the need for self-awareness and encouraged women to pursue financial independence. Similar to their New Women sisters already discussed, they expressed their ideas in newly established women's magazines as well as in existing media outlets.

Although these New Women established successful careers as artists, writers, publishers, and reformers, they were best known for the way they boldly lived out their convictions. Many of them underscored their rejection of chastity by pursuing free-love relationships and marriages, divorcing and remarrying, and engaging in affairs. Reminiscent of the treatment of Seitō women and the five-colored-liquor and Yoshiwara incidents in Japan, the press in Korea focused on the scandalous behavior of New Women and trivialized their demands for women's rights. By the mid-1920s, many of the same reformers who had encouraged women to break free of confining traditions and become productive modern citizens were embracing those very traditions as the basis of a strong, independent Korean identity.[25]

The Korean New Woman's challenge to male dominance met with both internal and external opposition. During the 1930s the New Woman movement in Korea was suppressed by nationalist reformers who were reasserting the value of Confucian patriarchy as a stabilizing basis for Korean nationhood. They called on women to sacrifice their own selfish interests and to nurture Korean culture and identity through their role as mothers. In addition, Japanese colonial policy shifted again to one of brutal cultural assimilation. Japanese measures were aimed at eradicating Korean culture, language, and history in order to integrate Koreans (as second-class subjects) into the patriarchal and hierarchical Japanese empire. Rights were not a consideration, and especially not women's rights. The self-sacrificing mother, rooted though she was in patriotic ideals, seemed far less threatening than the independent New Woman to colonial authorities.[26]

Across these nations, the New Woman demanded improved conditions, rights, and opportunities for women as individuals and as valuable (and valued) citizens. In each example the emergence of New Women was facilitated by access to a modern education and the development of a women's press. An integral part of the New Woman discourse, regardless of country, was a rejection of women's inferior domestic status, whether imposed by a separate-spheres ideology, Islamic injunctions, Confucian ethics, or other patriarchal constraints. Support for improving the status of women came from a variety of groups, especially when this advance was associated with national well-being and independence. Consequently, the New Woman was linked—both positively and negatively—with her nation's modernizing process. Her independent and often sexually-charged image was a fitting symbol of the social and political upheaval that surrounded her. Nonetheless, across her numerous worldwide incarnations, as well as within specific national boundaries, the New Woman defied any singular definition. National, religious, ethnic, cultural, and class differences produced shadings and variations. New Women presented a united front in their search for awareness and freedoms, but not necessarily in the paths to follow. As noted, one of the main goals of Japanese New Women—represented by both Seitō women and True New Women—was to combat a monolithic, negative perception and argue for multiple meanings, images, and options that would allow women to advance in society.

One of the interesting differences to emerge from this cursory comparison of Western and non-Western New Women is their connection with demands for women's suffrage. In the United States and Great Britain, true universal suffrage seemed to be central to the demands of the New Woman. For the non-Western New Women we examined, increased political participation and even attaining the right to vote was part of their agenda, but often these goals were eclipsed by pressing social, economic, and national concerns. It was hard to launch an effective women's suffrage movement in countries where the majority of men were still disenfranchised. Many New Women in Egypt, China, and Korea (Japan is discussed below) believed that increasing access to education, advocating changes in the family and social systems, and expanding women's opportunities for paid employment were more immediate ways than through the ballot box to improve the position of women in their societies. They also realized, or were forced to realize, that any real progress in political rights would be deferred until national sovereignty was secured.[27]

Additional comparative work on the various manifestations of New Women around the world is necessary to provide new insights into the multifaceted, and often overlooked, role gender played in the development and pursuit of modernization, democracy, nationalism, and national sovereignty in the late nineteenth and early twentieth centuries. Many fine works on New Women in specific national contexts have already been cited, but many avenues of research remain. We need more translations than we now have of works written by and about New Women in order to deepen our understanding of the hopes, anxieties, frustrations, victories, and setbacks experienced during this time of tremendous upheaval and change. We also need additional accounts of actual New Women and how they lived their lives; such work would serve as a counterpoint to the emphasis on the New Woman as a constructed, fictional image. The similarities and differences that emerge from cross-cultural and cross-national examinations of New Women will enhance and complicate the usefulness of gender as an analytical tool. They will also remind us that gender cannot be considered apart from other factors influencing a particular historical moment and its actors. Perceptions of New Women varied from positive modern role models to selfish and destructive temptresses depending on the political, social, economic, and religious inclinations (among others) of an individual or group and the condition (independent, semicolonized, colonized) of a nation.

The Legacy of Japan's New Woman

Japan's New Women did not emerge under colonialism. The fear of being colonized by Western powers in the nineteenth century had motivated a period of rapid modernization and industrialization, and by the beginning of the twentieth century Japan had secured its place as a modern, independent nation respected by the West. The New Woman was an inevitable product of this modernizing process. Similar to her international counterparts, the Japanese New Woman benefited from increased educational opportunities and expanding public media. However, her contributions to national strength were more contested in Japan than elsewhere, most likely because Japan was concerned about maintaining independence, not securing it. The New Woman debate revealed some of the tensions and insecurities inherent in the modernizing project as the Japanese were trying to create a modern identity while preserving a Japanese essence. At a time when women were barred from any political activity, Japan's New Women battled the negative press, promoted women's awareness, and sought to create new spaces for women in modern society.

Japan's Woman Problem debate, and its discussion of the New Woman, neither began nor ended with *Seitō*. However, *Seitō*'s brief existence helped to pave the way for future efforts on behalf of women and provided a legacy for later feminist movements in Japan. Although publication of *Seitō* was suspended in 1916—largely as a result of government censorship and financial difficulties—the Seitōsha did indeed succeed in instilling a broad vision of women's place in society. The unconventional behavior associated with New Women set the precedent for additional variations and explorations by women in the 1920s. The media attention surrounding the New Women contributed to widespread and serious considerations of women's issues well into the 1930s. Many of the women who had contributed to *Seitō* and others who were inspired by their writings continued to pursue women's awakening and rights through a variety of organizations and activities. The Seitōsha had provided the link between self-awareness and concrete action. After *Seitō* folded, the Woman Problem debate shifted in emphasis, becoming increasingly political.

Hiratsuka Raichō had a long and varied career as a feminist activist that continued until her death in 1971.[28] In the years immediately following the dissolution of the Seitōsha, Raichō began advocating direct political involvement for women in order to change the male-dominated society that oppressed them. In 1918–1919 she was a major participant in the "motherhood-protection" debate, which was heatedly waged in the press. Heavily influenced by the works of Swedish feminist Ellen Key, Raichō argued for state protection of mothers and children as valuable assets to society. Three other feminist activists opposed her: Yosano Akiko, who favored women's economic independence; Yamakawa Kikue, who argued that women's rights were best attained through socialism; and Yamada Waka, who supported the "good wife, wise mother" framework. These four stances encapsulated the main arguments for women's rights for decades to come. The motherhood-protection debate remained one of words and ended without any specific actions being taken.[29]

The conditions Raichō witnessed during her visits to several textile mills during the summer of 1919 opened her eyes even further to women's need for political influence and rights. In 1919, Raichō joined forces with Ichikawa Fusae, the person who would become most associated with women's suffrage in Japan. Together they founded the New Woman's Association

(Shinfujin Kyōkai). Their main goal was to promote women's political rights, and their association was instrumental in the 1922 repeal of Article 5, Clause 2, of the Public Peace Police Law, which forbade women from attending political meetings. Two decades earlier, Fukuda Hideko, Iwano Kiyo, and Nishikawa Fumiko had tried unsuccessfully to contest this article. A shift in the political environment following World War I resulted in reduced limitations on male suffrage and proved conducive to improvements in women's political rights as well. Raichō and the New Woman's Association also used maternalist arguments to press for women's right to vote and to support controversial eugenics legislation in an effort to protect women from venereal disease. Neither of these efforts came to fruition, but they did succeed in stimulating the women's suffrage movement and in continuing to spread awareness about women's issues.[30]

The New Woman's Association dissolved in December 1922, and the momentum for political change was picked up by several emerging women's suffrage organizations. The Great Kantō Earthquake in September 1923 brought these organizations and a variety of other women's groups together as they coordinated relief efforts. This cooperation continued in a variety of ways and led to the creation of the Women's Suffrage League (Fusen Kakutoku Dōmei) in December 1924. This group would head the women's suffrage movement in the prewar years. Ichikawa Fusae, who had resigned from the New Women's Association in July 1921 and had spent two and a half years in the United States traveling and studying the women's movement, returned to Japan and became the league's leader. Petitions were submitted, politicians were lobbied, and hopes were high as universal manhood suffrage was granted in 1925. This change in the political environment allowed for increased support for women's suffrage. But just as women seemed to be on the verge of attaining at least local suffrage, this promising atmosphere vanished in the face of increased Japanese militarism following the 1931 Manchurian Incident. The Women's Suffrage League continued to hold national conventions throughout most of the 1930s but increasingly tempered its demands for suffrage and finally disbanded under pressure in 1940. Japanese women gained the right to vote in the postwar constitution.[31]

Campaigning for suffrage was not the only concrete action aimed at improving women's lives. The reemergence of women's socialist groups as well as women's involvement in labor unions and proletarian political parties were further indications of the politicized nature of the 1920s. These organizations dealt with issues of class as well as gender as they fought for an equal and democratic society. The True New Women were among the first to broach the topic of birth control in the 1910s, and Katō Shidzue spear-headed the birth-control movement in Japan from the 1920s through most of the rest of the twentieth century. In addition, a variety of women writers kept women's issues alive in their fiction and nonfiction works.[32]

Another image of women emerged in the 1920s that was mainly me-dia sensation and partially lived reality, namely the Modern Girl, or *moga*. The Modern Girl, often considered the direct heir of the New Woman, took unconventional behavior to different extremes, but to some degree the ear-lier actions of Seitō members had softened her shock value. As a symbol of modern mass consumption, the moga crossed gender, sexual, and cultural boundaries in her attire, behavior, and attitudes. In this sense, she offers com-parisons with the third generation of U.S. New Women, who also emerged in the 1920s. Historian Barbara Sato discusses the Modern Girl alongside informed housewives and professional working women in her analysis of ordinary women in the 1920s who questioned existing gender roles and ex-perimented with other possibilities.[33]

Although the 1920s ushered in new opportunities for women, they also presented new limitations. The independent spirit of Seitō and the New Women was often compromised in the 1920s and 1930s. Many female ac-tivists, suffragists, and labor leaders tried conventional channels to advance the position of women. They made accommodations with the government bureaucracy and became involved in large national women's organizations. Such collaboration proved to have dire consequences as the Japanese state moved toward fascism in the 1930s. However, the energy and activities of a variety of women and organizations in the early twentieth century laid the groundwork for increased women's rights in the immediate postwar years.

By the 1920s, the expression *New Woman* (*atarashii onna*), which had been used so negatively by the press and so proudly by Seitō women, had largely dropped out of use. The True New Women had tried to distance themselves from Seitō's scandalous image by adopting a neutral and formal configuration of characters—*shin fujin*—in describing themselves as New Women. Raichō followed suit by using *shin fujin* in naming the 1919 New Woman's Association (Shinfujin Kyōkai). The contested figure of the New Woman in the 1910s gave way in the 1920s to a number of controversial female images, including the suffragist, the socialist, a revised "good wife, wise mother," and the Modern Girl.

As a discursive phenomenon, the New Woman provided a site for discussing the impact of rapid modernization on Japanese society and the ramifications for women in the early Taishō period. The New Woman was a symbol of the modern, the West, and change itself. She was also the symbol of the destruction of Japanese ways, the family system, and Confucian ethics. She was exciting and dangerous, admired and castigated. She embodied the evils of excessive borrowing from the West and the potential of a modernity that was not necessarily Western. The New Woman represented change, but she also inspired it. And in all these ways, she helped a nation through some of its growing pains. In the end the sides were not so clearly drawn between East and West, men and women. The image of the Japanese New Woman as simply a dangerous sexual being had fractured, leaving a field of possibility. The actual New Women of the 1910s—members of the Seitōsha, the Shinshinfujinkai, and others who defied convention and sought to improve women's lives—set a precedent through their contributions to the New Woman debate. Their bold actions encouraged others in the decades to follow to question the patriarchal order, experiment with alternative visions, and pursue women's rights in a variety of forms.

NOTES

CHAPTER 1 *New Women, Gender, and Modernizing Japan*

1. Yosano Akiko, "Sozorogoto," *Seitō* 1, no. 1 (September 1911): 1–2, as translated by Dina Lowy.
2. The group as a whole is called the Seitōsha or simply Seitō. When referring specifically to the magazine, *Seitō* is italicized.
3. The New Woman and her international variations are discussed at length in Chapter 7. For general background on the New Woman in the United States, see Nancy Woloch, "The Rise of the New Woman, 1860–1920," in *Women and the American Experience,* 2d ed. (New York: McGraw-Hill, 1994), 269–307; for Europe, see Bonnie G. Smith, "The New Woman," in *Changing Lives: Women in European History since 1700* (Lexington, MA: Heath, 1989), 317–363.
4. I discuss the controversial term *modernization* in depth later in this chapter.
5. The sense of Japan as a unified entity had its roots in the sixteenth century, when Oda Nobunaga, Toyotomi Hideyoshi, and Tokugawa Ieyasu succeeded in establishing a form of centralized feudalism over a country full of independent domains. This nascent form of nationalism would reach maturity in the crisis following Japan's opening to the West in the mid-nineteenth century. See John W. Hall and Marius B. Jansen, eds., *Studies in the Institutional History of Early Modern Japan* (Princeton, NJ: Princeton University Press, 1968).
6. See Sharon L. Sievers, *Flowers in Salt: The Beginnings of Feminist Consciousness in Modern Japan* (Stanford, CA: Stanford University Press, 1983), 10–25.
7. On the Enlightenment movement, see William R. Braisted, trans., *Meiroku Zasshi: Journal of the Japanese Enlightenment* (Cambridge, MA: Harvard University Press, 1976); Fukuzawa Yukichi, *The Autobiography of Fukuzawa Yukichi,* trans. Eiichi Kiyooka (New York: Columbia University Press, 1960); and Fukuzawa Yukichi, *Fukuzawa Yukichi on Japanese Women: Selected Works,* trans. Eiichi Kiyooka (Tokyo: University of Tokyo Press, 1988). On women's involvement in the Freedom and People's Rights movement, see Sievers, *Flowers in Salt,* 26–53, and Mikiso Hane, trans., *Reflections on the Way to the Gallows: Rebel Women in Prewar Japan* (Berkeley and Los Angeles: University of California Press, 1988), 51–74.

8. On the conservative backlash, see Kenneth B. Pyle, "Meiji Conservatism," in *Modern Japanese Thought,* ed. Bob Tadashi Wakabayashi (Cambridge: Cambridge University Press, 1998), 98–146. For more on "invented traditions," see Stephen Vlastos, ed., *Mirror of Modernity: Invented Traditions of Modern Japan* (Berkeley and Los Angeles: University of California Press, 1999).

9. See Sharon H. Nolte and Sally Ann Hastings, "The Meiji State's Policy toward Women, 1890–1910," in *Recreating Japanese Women, 1600–1945,* ed. Gail Lee Bernstein (Berkeley and Los Angeles: University of California Press, 1991), 154–157.

10. Sievers, *Flowers in Salt,* 111. For more on women's status under the Meiji Civil Code, see Wakita Haruko, Hayashi Reiko, and Nagahara Kazuko, eds., *Nihon joseishi* (Tokyo: Yoshikawa Kōbunkan, 1987), 199–202. On the creation of the Civil Code, see Hirakawa Sukehiro, "Japan's Turn to the West," in *Modern Japanese Thought,* ed. Bob Tadashi Wakabayashi (Cambridge: Cambridge University Press, 1998), 71–77. Women in Western nations lived under many of the same political, economic, and familial restrictions. On changes to these restrictions in the United States through the nineteenth century, see Norma Basch, *In the Eyes of the Law: Women, Marriage, and Property in Nineteenth Century New York* (Ithaca, NY: Cornell University Press, 1982).

11. On late Meiji politics and ideology, see Carol Gluck, *Japan's Modern Myths: Ideology in the Late Meiji Period* (Princeton, NJ: Princeton University Press, 1985), 17–72.

12. However, companionate marriage was not part of the ideal in Japan as it was in the United States. On Republican Mothers and Wives, see Linda K. Kerber, "The Republican Mother: Women and Enlightenment—An American Perspective," *American Quarterly* 28 (Summer 1976): 187–205, and Jan Lewis, "Republican Wife: Virtue and Seduction in the Early Republic," *William and Mary Quarterly* 44 (October 1987): 689–721.

13. Margit Maria Nagy, "How Shall We Live?: Social Change, the Family Institution and Feminism in Prewar Japan" (PhD diss., University of Washington, 1981), 43.

14. Nolte and Hastings, "The Meiji State's Policy toward Women," 171–173.

15. Kathleen S. Uno, *The Origins of 'Good Wife, Wise Mother' in Modern Japan,* Occasional Paper 15 (Marburg, Germany: Philipps-Universität Marburg, 1994), and Kathleen S. Uno, "The Death of 'Good Wife, Wise Mother'?" in *Postwar Japan as History,* ed. Andrew Gordon (Berkeley and Los Angeles: University of California Press, 1993), 293–322. Uno discusses "good wife, wise mother" as an evolving and somewhat elastic concept in "Womanhood, War, and Empire: Transmutations of 'Good Wife, Wise Mother' before 1931," in *Gendering Modern Japanese History,* ed. Barbara Molony and Kathleen S. Uno (Cambridge, MA, and London: Harvard University Asia Center, 2005), 493–519.

16. See Sally A. Hastings, "Hatoyama Haruko: Ambitious Woman," in *The Human Tradition on Modern Japan,* ed. Anne Walthall (Wilmington, DE: Scholarly Resources, 2002), 81–98; Koyama Shizuko, "The 'Good Wife and Wise Mother' Ideology in Post–World War I Japan," *U.S.-Japan Women's Journal* 7 (1994): 31–52; Barbara Molony, "Activism among Women in the Taishō Cotton Textile Industry," in *Recreating Japanese Women, 1600–1945,* ed. Gail Lee Bernstein

(Berkeley and Los Angeles: University of California Press, 1991), 211–238; Yoshiko Miyake, "Doubling Expectations: Motherhood and Women's Factory Work under State Management in Japan in the 1930s and 1940s," in *Recreating Japanese Women, 1600–1945,* ed. Gail Lee Bernstein (Berkeley and Los Angeles: University of California Press, 1991), 267–295; and Uno, "Death of 'Good Wife, Wise Mother'?"

17. The Taishō period itself, marking the reign of Japan's second modern emperor, lasted from 1912 to 1926. The broader periodization recognizes shifts in policies and attitudes from the end of the Russo-Japanese War in 1905 to the end of party cabinets in 1932.

18. H. D. Harootunian, "Introduction: A Sense of an Ending and the Problem of Taishō," in *Japan in Crisis: Essays on Taishō Democracy,* ed. Bernard S. Silberman and H. D. Harootunian (Princeton, NJ: Princeton University Press, 1974), 11, 21, 22.

19. For additional information on the development of naturalism and individualism in Japan, see Janet A. Walker, *The Japanese Novel of the Meiji Period and the Ideal of Individualism* (Princeton, NJ: Princeton University Press, 1979), especially 93–106.

20. Janice Bridges Bardsley, "Writing for the New Woman of Taishō Japan: Hiratsuka Raichō and the Seitō Journal, 1911–1916" (PhD diss., University of California, Los Angeles, 1989), 3.

21. I use the term *feminist activity* in its broadest sense to include any activity that aims at improving women's status in society. For the Freedom and People's Rights movement and the women involved, see Sievers, *Flowers in Salt,* 26–53; Sharon L. Sievers, "Feminist Criticism in Japanese Politics in the 1880s: The Experience of Kishida Toshiko," *Signs* 6, no. 4 (Summer 1981): 602–616; Hane, *Reflections,* 29–50; and Sharlie C. Ushioda, "Fukuda Hideko and the Woman's World of Meiji Japan," in *Japan in Transition: Thought and Action in the Meiji Era, 1868–1912,* ed. Hilary Conroy, Sandra T. W. Davis, and Wayne Patterson (Rutherford, NJ: Fairleigh Dickinson University Press, 1984), 276–293.

22. Rebecca L. Copeland, *Lost Leaves: Women Writers of Meiji Japan* (Honolulu: University of Hawai'i Press, 2000), 10. See also Michael C. Brownstein, "Jogaku Zasshi and the Founding of Bungakukai," *Monumenta Nipponica* 35, no. 3 (1980): 319–336.

23. For additional information on the New Woman's literary predecessors, see Copeland, *Lost Leaves,* and Yukiko Tanaka, *Women Writers of Meiji and Taishō Japan* (Jefferson, NC: McFarland, 2000).

24. On the Women's Reform Society, see Sievers, *Flowers in Salt,* 87–113, and Rumi Yasutake, *Transnational Women's Activism: The United States, Japan, and Japanese Immigrant Communities in California, 1859–1920* (New York: New York University Press, 2004). For additional information on female educators, see Hastings, "Hatoyama Haruko"; Furuki Yoshiko, *The White Plum, a Biography of Umeko Tsuda: Pioneer in the Higher Education of Japanese Women* (New York: Weatherhill, 1991); Barbara Rose, *Tsuda Umeko and Women's Education in Japan* (New Haven, CT: Yale University Press, 1992); Winston Kahn, "Hani Motoko and the Education of Japanese Women," *Historian* 59, no. 2 (Winter 1997): 381–401; Chieko Irie Mulhern, "Hani Motoko: The Journalist-Educator,"

in *Heroic with Grace: Legendary Women of Japan* (Armonk, NY: Sharpe, 1991), 208–235; and Janine Beichman, *Embracing the Firebird: Yosano Akiko and the Birth of the Female Voice in Modern Japanese Poetry* (Honolulu: University of Hawai'i Press, 2002).

25. Sievers, *Flowers in Salt,* 114–162; and Vera Mackie, *Creating Socialist Women in Japan* (Cambridge: Cambridge University Press, 1997); Hane, *Reflections,* 51–74; and Helene Bowen Raddeker, *Treacherous Women of Imperial Japan: Patriarchal Fictions, Patricidal Fantasies* (New York: Routledge, 1997).

26. Barbara Molony, "The Quest for Women's Rights in Turn-of-the-Century Japan," in *Gendering Modern Japanese History,* ed. Barbara Molony and Kathleen Uno (Cambridge, MA: Harvard University Asia Center, 2005), 463–492.

27. Muta Kazue, "The New Woman In Japan: Radicalism and Ambivalence towards Love and Sex," in *New Woman Hybridities: Femininity, Feminism, and International Consumer Culture, 1880–1930,* ed. Ann Heilmann and Margaret Beetham (London and New York: Routledge, 2004), 205–207; Hiroko Tomida, "Hiratsuka Raichō, the Seitō Society, and the Emergence of the New Woman in Japan," in *Japanese Women: Emerging from Subservience, 1868–1945,* ed. Hiroko Tomida and Gordon Daniels (Kent, OH: Global Oriental, 2005), 196–199; and Barbara Sato, *The New Japanese Woman: Modernity, Media, and Women in Interwar Japan* (Durham, NC: Duke University Press, 2003), 13–23.

28. Hiratsuka Raichō would remain a prominent feminist figure for several decades, until her death in 1971. Following Japanese convention, family names are listed first followed by given names. Although her given name was Haruko, she chose Raichō as a pen name early in her long career. Because she is most widely and famously known by this pen name, I will refer to her as Raichō throughout the book. Unless otherwise noted, I will use family names in all other cases.

29. This incident is discussed in detail in Chapter 4.

30. Ide Fumiko, *Hiratsuka Raichō: Kindai to shinpi* (Tokyo: Shinchōsha, 1987), 65–68.

31. For an in-depth look at England's Bluestockings, see Sylvia Harcstark Myers, *The Bluestocking Circle: Women, Friendship, and the Life of the Mind in Eighteenth-Century England* (Oxford: Oxford University Press, 1990).

32. Ide Fumiko, *Seitō: Kaisetsu, sōmokuji, sakuin* (Tokyo: Fuji Shuppan, 1983), 8.

33. Ide, *Hiratsuka,* 71.

34. Fortunately *Seitō* is easily accessible in Japanese through a complete set of reprints issued by the publishing house Fuji Shuppan in 1983. Unfortunately, only a handful of articles and excerpts have been translated into English.

35. Hiratsuka Raichō, "Genshi, josei wa taiyō de atta," *Seitō* 1, no. 1 (September 1911): 37.

36. Ibid.

37. Ibid.

38. For examples, see "Iwayuru atarashii onna," *Kokumin Shinbun,* 12 July 1912, and "Atarashigaru onna," *Tokyo Nichi Nichi Shinbun,* 29 October 1912.

39. See Bardsley, "Writing for the New Woman of Taishō Japan"; Sievers, *Flowers in Salt,* 163–188; Pauline C. Reich and Fukuda Atsuko, "Japan's Literary Feminists: The Seitō Group," *Signs* 2, no. 1 (Autumn 1976): 280–291; Nancy Andrew,

The Seitōsha: An Early Japanese Women's Organization, 1911–1916, Papers on Japan, vol. 6 (Cambridge, MA: East Asian Research Center, Harvard University, 1972), 45–69; Noriko Mizuta Lippit, "Seitō and the Literary Roots of Japanese Feminism," *International Journal of Women's Studies* 2, no. 2 (March-April 1979): 155–163; Ide Fumiko, *Seitō no onnatachi* (Tokyo: Kaien Shobō, 1975); and Horiba Kiyoko, *Seitō no jidai: Hiratsuka Raichō to atarashii onna* (Tokyo: Iwanami Shoten, 1988). Two recent additions to the steady stream of scholarship in Japan are Yoneda Sayoko and Ikeda Emiko, eds., *"Seitō" wo manabu hito no tame ni* (Kyoto: Sekai Shisōsha, 1999), and Shin Feminizumu Hihyō no Kai, *Seitō wo yomu* (Tokyo: Gakugei Shorin, 1998).

40. See Kobayashi Tomie, *Hiratsuka Raichō: Hito to shisō* (Tokyo: Shimizu Shoin, 1983); Ide, *Hiratsuka;* chapters on Hiratsuka Raichō and Yosano Akiko in Shimada Akiko, *Nihon no feminizumu: Genryū to shite no Akiko, Raichō, Kikue, Kanoko* (Tokyo: Hokuju Shuppan, 1996); Yoneda Sayoko, *Hiratsuka Raichō: Kindai nihon no demokurashii to jendaa* (Tokyo: Yoshikawa Kōbunkan, 2002); Hiroko Tomida, *Hiratsuka Raichō and Early Japanese Feminism* (Leiden: Brill, 2004); Laurel Rasplica Rodd, "Yosano Akiko and the Taishō Debate over the 'New Woman,'" in *Recreating Japanese Women, 1600–1945,* ed. Gail Lee Bernstein (Berkeley and Los Angeles: University of California Press, 1991), 175–198; and Ken Miyamoto, "Itō Noe and the Bluestockings," *Japan Interpreter* 10, no. 2 (Autumn 1975): 190–204.

41. See Nagy, "How Shall We Live?"; Miriam Silverberg, "The Modern Girl as Militant," in *Recreating Japanese Women, 1600–1945,* ed. Gail Lee Bernstein (Berkeley and Los Angeles: University of California Press, 1991), 239–266; Barbara Hamill Sato, "The Moga Sensation: Perceptions of the Modan Gāru in Japanese Intellectual Circles during the 1920s," *Gender and History* 5, no. 3 (1993): 363–381; and Sato, *New Japanese Woman.* The Modern Girl is discussed in Chapter 7.

42. J. Victor Koschmann, ed., *Authority and the Individual in Japan* (Tokyo: University of Tokyo Press, 1978); Andrew Barshay, *State and Intellectual in Imperial Japan: The Public Man in Crisis* (Berkeley and Los Angeles: University of California Press, 1988); Kenneth B. Pyle, *The New Generation in Meiji Japan: Problems of Cultural Identity, 1885–1895* (Stanford, CA: Stanford University Press, 1969); Gluck, *Japan's Modern Myths;* Donald Roden, *Schooldays in Imperial Japan: A Study in the Culture of a Student Elite* (Berkeley and Los Angeles: University of California Press, 1980); and Donald Roden, "Baseball and the Quest for National Dignity in Meiji Japan," *American Historical Review* 85, no. 3 (June 1980): 511–534.

43. Stefan Tanaka, *Japan's Orient: Rendering Pasts into History* (Berkeley and Los Angeles: University of California Press, 1993).

44. Takashi Fujitani, *Splendid Monarchy: Power and Pageantry in Modern Japan* (Berkeley and Los Angeles: University of California Press, 1996).

45. Jordan Sand, "At Home in the Meiji Period: Inventing Japanese Domesticity," 191–207, and Miriam Silverberg, "The Cafe Waitress Serving Modern Japan," 208–225, both in *Mirror of Modernity: Invented Traditions of Modern Japan,* ed. Stephen Vlastos (Berkeley and Los Angeles: University of California Press, 1999). See also

Sharon A. Minichiello, ed., *Japan's Competing Modernities: Issues in Culture and Democracy, 1900–1930* (Honolulu: University of Hawai'i Press, 1998).

46. A book that enriches our understanding of the links between gender and modernity in Japan is Barbara Molony and Kathleen Uno, eds., *Gendering Modern Japanese History* (Cambridge, MA: Harvard University Asia Center, 2005).

47. Miriam Silverberg, "Constructing a New Cultural History of Prewar Japan," in *Japan in the World,* ed. Masao Miyoshi and H. D. Harootunian (Durham, NC: Duke University Press, 1993), 141–142.

48. For another look at what it meant to be modern in early-twentieth-century Japan, especially in connection with artistic and leisure activities, see Elise K. Tipton and John Clark, eds., *Being Modern in Japan: Culture and Society from the 1910s to the 1930s* (Honolulu: University of Hawai'i Press, 2000).

49. Rita Felski, *The Gender of Modernity* (Cambridge, MA: Harvard University Press, 1995), 12–13.

50. John W. Dower, "E. H. Norman, Japan and the Uses of History," in *Origins of the Modern Japanese State: Selected Writings of E. H. Norman* (New York: Pantheon Books, 1975).

51. Andrew Gordon, *The Evolution of Labor Relations in Japan: Heavy Industry, 1853–1955* (Cambridge, MA: Council on East Asian Studies, Harvard University, 1985); Sheldon Garon, *The State and Labor in Modern Japan* (Berkeley and Los Angeles: University of California Press, 1987).

52. Sheldon Garon, "Rethinking Modernization and Modernity in Japanese History," *Journal of Asian Studies* 53, no. 2 (May 1994): 346–366. Also see Tetsuo Najita, "Presidential Address: Reflections on Modernity and Modernization," *Journal of Asian Studies* 52, no. 4 (1993): 845–853.

53. Sheldon Garon, "Women's Groups and the Japanese State: Contending Approaches to Political Integration, 1890–1945," *Journal of Japanese Studies* 19, no. 1 (1993): 5–41, and Sheldon Garon, *Molding Japanese Minds: The State in Everyday Life* (Princeton, NJ: Princeton University Press, 1997).

54. Michel Foucault, *The Archaeology of Knowledge and the Discourse on Language,* trans. A. M. Sheridan Smith (New York: Pantheon Books, 1972), 229.

55. Michel Foucault, "Nietzsche, Genealogy, History," in *The Foucault Reader,* ed. Paul Rabinow (New York: Pantheon Books, 1984), 88.

56. Joan Wallach Scott, "Gender: A Useful Category of Historical Analysis," in *Gender and the Politics of History* (New York: Columbia University Press, 1988), 42.

CHAPTER 2   *Ibsen's Nora: The New Woman Debate Begins*

1. For additional information on Tsubouchi Shōyō's lectures, see "Kinseigeki ni mietaru atarashiki onna," *Osaka Asahi,* 28 July–4 August 1910; "Kinseigeki ni mietaru atarashiki onna," *Osaka Mainichi,* 28 July–8 August 1910; Toshiko Nakamura, "Ibsen in Japan: Tsubouchi Shōyō and His Lecture on New Women," *Edda* 5 (1982): 261–272.

2. Although many know the play as *A Doll's House,* Ibsen translator Rolf Fjelde, scholar Ayako Kano, and others use the more accurate translation *A Doll House.* I have followed suit, preferring the emphasis on artifice rather than possession.

3. For the connection between *A Doll House* and discussions of the New Woman, see Ayako Kano, *Acting Like a Woman in Modern Japan: Theater, Gender, and Nationalism* (New York: Palgrave, 2001), 184–199, and Sharon H. Nolte, *Liberalism in Modern Japan: Ishibashi Tanzan and His Teachers, 1905–1960* (Berkeley and Los Angeles: University of California Press, 1987), chs. 2 and 3.

4. For additional information on *Seitō,* see references in note 39 in Chapter 1.

5. On the "good wife, wise mother," see Margit Maria Nagy, "How Shall We Live?: Social Change, the Family Institution and Feminism in Prewar Japan" (PhD diss., University of Washington, 1981); Kathleen S. Uno, *The Origins of 'Good Wife, Wise Mother' in Modern Japan,* Occasional Paper 15 (Marburg, Germany: Philipps-Universität Marburg, 1994); Kathleen S. Uno, "The Death of 'Good Wife, Wise Mother'?" in *Postwar Japan as History,* ed. Andrew Gordon (Berkeley: University of California Press, 1993), 293–322; and Niwa Akiko, "The Formation of the Myth of Motherhood in Japan," *U.S.-Japan Women's Journal* 4 (1993): 70–82.

6. See Sharon L. Sievers, *Flowers in Salt: The Beginnings of Feminist Consciousness in Modern Japan* (Stanford, CA: Stanford University Press, 1983), 10–25.

7. Not only did Seitō women discuss provocative topics, like chastity, abortion, prostitution, and socialism, but many of them also lived provocative lives. They were known for frequenting bars, visiting the pleasure quarters, exploring same-sex relationships, experimenting with free-love relationships, eschewing the marriage system, having children out of wedlock, and supporting their partners and families through their creative endeavors.

8. For additional information on Western reactions to *A Doll House* as a feminist play, see Katherine Hanson, "Ibsen's Women Characters and Their Feminist Contemporaries," *Theatre History Studies* 2 (1982): 83–91, and Joan Templeton, "The *Doll House* Backlash: Criticism, Feminism, and Ibsen," *PMLA* 104 (1989): 28–40. For an example of a genderless approach to the play, see Sandra Saari, "Female Become Human: Nora Transformed," in *Contemporary Approaches to Ibsen,* vol. 6, ed. Bjorn Hemmer and Vigdis Ystad (Oslo: Norwegian University Press, 1988), 41–55. For an in-depth evaluation of the play as a whole, see Errol Durbach, *A Doll's House: Ibsen's Myth of Transformation* (Boston: Twayne, 1991).

9. Henrik Ibsen, *Four Major Plays,* vol. 1, trans. Rolf Fjelde (New York: Signet Classic, 1965).

10. This section is based on articles in two major Tokyo newspapers—*Yomiuri Shinbun* and *Tokyo Nichi Nichi Shinbun*—and a handful of popular intellectual and women's journals.

11. This ban explains the all-male nature of traditional forms of Japanese theater such as Kabuki and Nō.

12. For a discussion of the New Theater movement, see A. Horie-Webber, "Modernisation of the Japanese Theater: The Shingeki Movement," in *Modern Japan: Aspects of History, Literature and Society,* ed. W. G. Beasley (Tokyo: Tuttle, 1976), 147–165, and Kano, *Acting Like a Woman,* 151–182. Also see Kano for information on Matsui Sumako.

13. Quoted in Brian Powell, "Matsui Sumako: Actress and Woman," in *Modern Japan: Aspects of History, Literature and Society,* ed. W. G. Beasley (Tokyo: Tuttle, 1976), 140–141.

14. Quoted in Kano, *Acting Like a Woman*, 194. For additional praise for Matsui's performance and confirmation of the need for female actors, see Satō Kōroku et al., "'Ningyō no ie' no Nora ni funshita Matsui Sumako," *Shinchō* 16, no. 1 (January 1912): 38–42.

15. "Ningyō no ie no jōjō," *Yomiuri Shinbun*, Aug. 23, 1911.

16. Ichimura Shigetoshi, "Ningyō no ie' no butaikeiko," *Waseda Bungaku* 70 (September 1911): 79–81.

17. Shimamura Hōgetsu, "Ningyō no ie to buyōgeki," *Yomiuri Shinbun*, September 6, 1911.

18. Shimamura Hōgetsu, "Fujin mondai ni okeru Ibsen to Strindberg," *Yomiuri Shinbun*, September 3, 1911.

19. Ibid. He is speaking of *Seitō*, whose first issue appeared that very month, September 1911.

20. Quoted in Shimamura, "Ningyō no ie to buyōgeki."

21. Ibid.

22. "Tsubouchitei de ningyō no ie wo shoen," *Yomiuri Shinbun*, 22 September 1911. In addition, a brief article announcing the three-day run of *A Doll House* and the actors involved appeared in the *Kokumin Shinbun*, 24 September 1911.

23. Sawada Bushō, "Kakuseiseru fujin to Ibsen no Nora," *Fujin Kurabu* 4 (October 1911): 2.

24. Ibid., 8.

25. Ibid., 9.

26. Asai Shōzō, "Nora no kokoromochi no wakaru onna wo sukunai," *Fujin Kurabu* 4 (November 1911): 44. Founded in 1901, Japan Women's College was one of the first schools of higher education for women. Many of the founding members of *Seitō* were Japan Women's College graduates.

27. Ibid., 48.

28. Ukita Kazutami (1859–1945) was a liberal Christian who taught at two prestigious private universities, Dōshisha and Waseda, and who served as editor-in-chief of the general-interest journal *Taiyō*.

29. Ukita Kazutami, "Nora to fujin mondai (2)," *Tokyo Nichi Nichi Shinbun*, 24 October 1911.

30. Ukita Kazutami, "Nora to fujin mondai (1)," *Tokyo Nichi Nichi Shinbun*, 22 October 1911.

31. Ukita Kazutami, "Nora to fujin mondai (3)," *Tokyo Nichi Nichi Shinbun*, 25 October 1911.

32. Ukita Kazutami, "Ningyō no ie to fujin mondai," *Fujin no Tomo* 5 (November 1911): 24. Ibsen himself and some of his contemporaries also argued this point. See Lou Salome, *Ibsen's Heroines* (Redding Ridge, CT: Black Swan Books, 1985), 24; and Bjorn Hemmer, "Ibsen and the Realistic Problem Drama," in *The Cambridge Companion to Ibsen*, ed. James McFarlane (Cambridge: Cambridge University Press, 1994), 82.

33. Ukita, "Ningyō no ie," 24–25.

34. For additional information on Meiji-Taishō women's magazines, see Kindai Josei Bunkashi Kenkyūkai, ed., *Fujin zasshi no yoake* (Tokyo: Ozora, 1989), and Kindai Josei Bunkashi Kenkyūkai, ed., *Taishōki no josei zasshi* (Tokyo: Ozora, 1996).

35. In addition to contributions by *Seitō* members, the supplement included translations of Western criticism by Janet Lee and Bernard Shaw.
36. It was common in Europe as well for Nora to be treated as a living person rather
than as a character in a play.
37. Hiratsuka Raichō, "Norasan ni," *Seitō* 2, no. 1 (January 1912): 133.
38. Ibid., 134.
39. Ibid., 136.
40. Ibid.
41. Ibid., 134.
42. Ibid., 138.
43. Ibid., 139. Raichō was not the only one who wanted to extinguish the old "self"
and start anew. Tamura Toshiko, a renowned woman writer at that time, also
wrote of creating a new "self" in several of her short stories.
44. Ibid., 140.
45. Katō Midori, "Ningyō no ie," *Seitō* 2, no. 1 (January 1912): 118. Katō Midori was
a working mother and future newspaper reporter.
46. Ibid., 119.
47. The September performances of *A Doll House* were abridged to save time; Acts I
and III were performed with a brief summary of Act II in between. The November performances included all three acts.
48. Katō, "Ningyō no ie," 122.
49. Ibid., 123.
50. Ueda Kimi, "Ningyō no ie wo yomu," *Seitō* 2, no. 1 (January 1912): 126–127.
Emphasis mine. Ueda was a writer of fiction and plays.
51. Ibid., 130.
52. Yasumochi Yoshi, "Ningyō no ie ni tsuite," *Seitō* 2, no. 1 (January 1912): 143.
53. Ibid., 145.
54. Ibid., 151.
55. Ibid., 152.
56. Ibid.
57. Christianity was first introduced in Japan in the sixteenth century, was banned
in the seventeenth century, and was reintroduced during the Meiji period (1868–
1912). Although its followers were small in number, its greatest influence was in
the field of education, particularly in the establishment of girls' schools.
58. Yasumochi, "Ningyō no ie ni tsuite," 154.
59. Ueno Yō, "Ningyō no ie yori josei mondai e," *Seitō* 2, no. 1 (January 1912):
100–101; translated in Kano, *Acting Like a Woman,* 196.
60. Kano, *Acting Like a Woman,* 196.
61. See Chapter 1 for a description of the restrictions on women under the Civil Code
of 1898.
62. Ibsen, *Four Major Plays,* 104.
63. Ibid., 105. Emphasis mine.
64. Ibid., 107.
65. Matsui Sumako, "Butai no ue de ichiban komatta koto," *Seitō* 2, no. 1 (January
1912): 163.
66. Katō, "Ningyō no ie," 121.

67. Yasumochi, "Ningyō no ie ni tsuite," 153.
68. Ibid.
69. Ibid.
70. In 1913 *Seitō* officially shifted from being a primarily literary vehicle to one that critically engaged a variety of women's issues.
71. As the New Woman debate progressed, some female critics, such as educators Shimoda Utako and Hatoyama Haruko, would join this side as well.

CHAPTER 3   *Sudermann's Magda: New Woman Censored*

1. For the sake of consistency, I will refer to the play as *Magda* throughout. The title in German is *Heimat;* translated into Japanese it becomes *Kokyo,* and into English, *The Home.* In Japan as in Europe and the United States it was commonly called *Magda* after the female protagonist. In a similar fashion, *A Doll House* was often referred to as *Nora.*
2. For a treatment of *Magda* that focuses on its role in the development of modern theater and the modern female actor in Japan, see Ayako Kano, *Acting Like a Woman in Modern Japan: Theater, Gender, and Nationalism* (New York: Palgrave, 2001), 277–301.
3. Hasegawa Kei examines the Nora, Magda, and New Woman/Woman Problem supplements to *Seitō* issues for the contributions they made to defining the New Woman in Japan. Hasegawa Kei, "'Atarashii onna' no tankyū," in *Seitō wo yomu,* ed. Shin Feminizumu Hihyō no Kai (Tokyo: Gakugei Shorin, 1998), 285–304.
4. Hermann Sudermann, *Magda: A Play in Four Acts,* trans. Charles Edward Amory Winslow (Amsterdam, NY: Fredonia Books, 2003); reprinted from the 1899 edition. For a discussion of the radical nature of the play, see ch. 10 of Karl Leydecker's *Marriage and Divorce in the Plays of Hermann Sudermann* (New York: Lang, 1996).
5. Shimamura Hōgetsu, "Sudermann no 'kokyō' ni kakaretaru shisōmondai," *Shin Nihon* 2, no. 5 (May 1912): 120–125.
6. See "'Kokyō' gappyō," *Yomiuri Shinbun,* 5, 7–11 May 1912. One critic expressed relief when the performance was over because he felt the play was dull and out-of-date, and it left him with the "feeling that you haven't learned anything or had to consider any problem." *Yomiuri Shinbun,* 10 May 1912. Another critic wrote, "I think Sudermann is less skilled than Ibsen." "Bungei kyokai no koen," *Kokumin Shinbun,* 5 May 1912. Seitō member Naganuma Chie kept her comments on the play short and to the point: "I saw it only once and thought it disappointing as I found it weak and lacking in depth." "Magda ni tsuite," *Seitō* 2, no. 6 (June 1912): 14. See also "Yurakuza de 'Magda' wo koen," *Jiji Shinbun,* 4 May 1912, and "'Magda' no insho," *Kokumin Shinbun,* 10 May 1912.
7. "'Kokyō' gappyō," *Yomiuri Shinbun,* 7 May 1912.
8. Ibid.; and Kusuyama Masao, "'Kokyō' no inshō," *Kokumin Shinbun,* 10 May 1912.
9. "'Kokyō' gappyō," *Yomiuri Shinbun,* 8 May 1912.
10. Hasegawa Shigure, "Bungei kyōkai no Magda," *Seitō* 2, no. 6 (June 1912).
11. Otake Kōkichi, "Magda ni tsuite," *Seitō* 2, no. 6 (June 1912).

12. "Magda no jōjō kinshi," *Yomiuri Shinbun,* 19 May 1912.
13. Ibid.
14. "'Magda' kōdōmushi de kōgyōkinshi ni," *Osaka Mainichi,* 21 May 1912.
15. Quoted in "Magda no jōjō kinshi," *Yomiuri Shinbun,* 19 May 1912.
16. Ueno Chizuko, "Modern Patriarchy and the Formation of the Japanese Nation State," in *Multicultural Japan: Palaeolithic to Postmodern,* ed. Donald Denoon and Gavan McCormack (New York: Cambridge University Press, 1996), 213–223.
17. Kiuchi Tei, "Magda ni tsuite," *Seitō* 2, no. 6 (June 1912): 17.
18. For a detailed account of censorship in Meiji-Taishō Japan and the ways various writers responded to it, see Jay Rubin, *Injurious to Public Morals: Writers and the Meiji State* (Seattle: University of Washington Press, 1984). Ch. 1 of Richard H. Mitchell's *Thought Control in Prewar Japan* (Ithaca, NY, and London: Cornell University Press, 1976) also provides good background on how and why censorship was instituted in imperial Japan.
19. Araki Ikuko's short story "The Letter," an account of an affair between a married women and her lover, was the cause of *Seitō*'s first ban on publication. This breach of law and morality is discussed in Chapter 4.
20. Quoted in "Magda no jōjō kinshi," *Yomiuri Shinbun,* 19 May 1912.
21. Ibid.
22. Shimamura Hōgetsu, "Magda no kinshi mondai," *Yomiuri Shinbun,* 21 May 1912.
23. "Magda no jōjō kinshi," *Yomiuri Shinbun,* 19 May 1912.
24. Ibid.
25. Ibid.
26. Anesaki Masaharu, "'Magda' no kinshimondai," *Yomiuri Shinbun,* 22 May 1912.
27. Anesaki Masaharu, "'Magda' no kinshimondai," *Yomiuri Shinbun,* 23 May 1912.
28. "'Kokyō' no jōjō kinshi," *Fujo Shinbun,* 24 May 1912.
29. "'Kokyō' yomigaeru," *Miyako,* 24 May 1912, and "Honenuki no Magdakin wo wakaru," *Kyoto Hinode,* 27 May 1912, respectively.
30. "Magda no kinshi mondai," *Yomiuri Shinbun,* 21 May 1912.
31. "Dattaisaretaru 'Magda,'" *Miyako,* 26 May 1912.
32. "Bungei kyōkai e onegai," *Miyako,* 4 June 1912.
33. Higuchi Hideo, "Nora to Magda," *Shin Nihon* 2, no. 6 (June 1912): 26.
34. "'Kokyō' gappyō," *Yomiuri Shinbun,* 9 May 1912.
35. Sōma Gyokaze, "'Kokyō' no Magda," *Shukujo Gahō* 1, no. 3 (June 1912): 22.
36. T. Shirai, "Iwayuru atarashiki onna," *Meiji no Joshi* 9, no. 6 (June 1912): 12. This magazine was the "Official Organ of the National Committee of Young Women's Christian Associations of Japan."
37. Ikuta Chōnosuke, "Wakaki otoko no me ni eijitaru gendai josei 'Magda,'" *Jogaku Sekai* 12, no. 8 (June 1912): 51.
38. Tsutsumi Kito, "Fujin no kakusei ni tsuite (2)," *Fujo Shinbun,* 23 August 1912. Emphasis mine.
39. Miyake Yujirō, "Gendaishiki no josei," *Fujin no Tomo* 6, no. 6 (June 1912): 12.
40. Higuchi, "Nora to Magda," 27.
41. Tsutsumi Kito, "Fujin no kakusei ni tsuite (1)," *Fujo Shinbun,* 16 August 1912.

42. Tsutsumi Kito, "Fujin no kakusei ni tsuite (2)," *Fujo Shinbun,* 23 August 1912. Her stance is similar to the one Ukita Kazutami took on *A Doll House.*
43. Shirai, "Iwayuru atarashiki onna," 13.
44. Miyake, "Gendaishiki no josei," 13.
45. Shirai, "Iwayuru atarashiki onna," 14.
46. Ibid., 13.
47. "'Kokyō no jōjōkinshi," *Fujo Shinbun,* 24 May 1912.
48. Ikuta, "Wakaki otoko no me ni"; Shirai, "Iwayuru atarashiki onna," 13.
49. Hasegawa Shigure, "Bungei kyōkai no Magda," *Seitō* 2, no. 6 (June 1912): 1–5.
50. Hiratsuka Raichō, "Yonda 'Magda,'" *Seitō* 2, no. 6 (June 1912): 12.
51. Raichō, like Magda, did not reject the concept of marriage as a whole. In the fall of 1912 she would encounter the works of Swedish feminist Ellen Key for the first time. Key's ideas greatly influenced Raichō as she articulated a vision of marriage based on love, equality, and free choice. See Dina Lowy, "Love and Marriage: Ellen Key and Hiratsuka Raichō Explore Alternatives," *Women's Studies* 33, no. 4 (June 2004): 361–380.
52. It would be another six months before *Seitō* would officially change from being a literary magazine to being one that confronted women's issues.
53. Hasegawa, "Bungei kyōkai no Magda," 1.
54. Hiratsuka, "Yonda 'Magda,'" 8.
55. Ibid., 8–9.
56. Ibid., 9.
57. Ibid.
58. Ibid., 11.
59. Several years later, as a key figure in the motherhood-protection debates, Raichō would argue for state support of mothers and children. For a brief summary of these debates, see Laurel Rasplica Rodd, "Yosano Akiko and the Taishō Debate over the 'New Woman,'" in *Recreating Japanese Women, 1600–1945,* ed. Gail Lee Bernstein (Berkeley and Los Angeles: University of California Press, 1991), 175–198, and Barbara Molony, "Equality versus Difference: The Japanese Debate over 'Motherhood Protection,' 1915–50," in *Japanese Women Working,* ed. Janet Hunter (London: Routledge, 1993), 122–148.
60. See Higuchi, "Nora to Magda," 26.
61. Even in *Seitō,* it would be another two and a half years before articles discussing chastity appeared.
62. This was a standard reason for censorship; Rubin, *Injurious to Public Morals.*
63. For a discussion of the exclusion of women from succession to the imperial throne during the Meiji period, see Wakakuwa Midori, "The Gender System of the Imperial State," *U.S.-Japan Women's Journal* 20–21 (2001): 17–82.

CHAPTER 4   *Sexuality: New Women Behaving Badly*

1. The Yoshiwara was the name for the pleasure quarters, or red-light district, in Tokyo, where licensed prostitution was practiced.
2. "Good wife, wise mother" ideology is discussed in Chapter 1.

3. For more on female factory workers, see Sharon L. Sievers, *Flowers in Salt: The Beginnings of Feminist Consciousness in Modern Japan* (Stanford, CA: Stanford University Press, 1983), 54–86, and Patricia Tsurumi, *Factory Girls: Women in the Thread Mills of Meiji Japan* (Princeton, NJ: Princeton University Press, 1990).
4. See Sievers, *Flowers in Salt,* 87–113.
5. See Mikiso Hane, "Poverty and Prostitution," in *Peasants, Rebels, and Outcastes* (New York: Pantheon Books, 1982), 206–225, and Sheldon Garon, "The World's Oldest Debate?: Prostitution and the State in Imperial Japan, 1900–1945," *American Historical Review* 97, no. 3 (June 1993): 710–732.
6. These same views of male and female sexuality would be used to help justify the system of military sex slaves (or Comfort Women) instituted during World War II. See George Hicks, *The Comfort Women: Japan's Brutal Regime of Enforced Prostitution in the Second World War* (New York: Norton, 1994), and Yoshimi Yoshiaki, *Comfort Women: Sexual Slavery in the Japanese Military during World War II,* trans. Suzanne O'Brien (New York: Columbia University Press, 2000).

   However, not all forms of male sexuality were socially or legally sanctioned. See Furukawa Makoto, "The Changing Nature of Sexuality: The Three Codes Framing Homosexuality in Modern Japan," *U.S.-Japan Women's Journal* 7 (1994): 98–127, and Gregory M. Pflugfelder, *Cartographies of Desire: Male-Male Sexuality in Japanese Discourse, 1600–1950* (Berkeley and Los Angeles: University of California Press, 1999).
7. For a discussion of nationalism and feminism in Imperial Japan, see Noriyo Hayakawa, "Feminism and Nationalism in Japan, 1868–1945," *Journal of Women's History* 7, no. 4 (Winter 1995): 108–119.
8. For a discussion of this transitional period, see H. D. Harootunian, "Introduction: A Sense of an Ending and the Problem of Taishō," in *Japan in Crisis: Essays on Taishō Democracy,* ed. Bernard S. Silberman and H. D. Harootunian (Princeton, NJ: Princeton University Press, 1974), 3–28.
9. Hiratsuka Raichō, *Sakusha no Jiden 8: Hiratsuka Raichō* (Tokyo: Nihon Tosho Sentaa, 1994), 117.
10. "Iwayuru atarashii onna," *Kokumin Shinbun,* 12 July 1912.
11. "Iwayuru atarashii onna," *Kokumin Shinbun,* 13 July 1912.
12. The following background information on Otake Kōkichi is drawn primarily from the biography written with her daughter's assistance, Takai Yō and Orii Miyako, *Azami no hana* (Tokyo: Domesu Shuppan, 1985), and Hiratsuka Raichō's autobiography, *Genshi, josei wa taiyō de atta,* vol. 2 (Tokyo: Otsuki Shoten, 1992), 23–32. Otake's given name was Kazue, but she went by the pen name Kōkichi during her brief tenure with the Seitōsha. I refer to her as Kōkichi because it was during this time that she was most closely associated with the New Woman.
13. Hiratsuka, *Genshi,* vol. 2, 29. A haori is a short coat, and a *hakama* is a divided skirt. Both are worn over a kimono and are considered formal wear.
14. Takai and Orii, *Azami no hana,* 60.
15. Five-colored liquor was "a drink in which several liqueurs of different colors and densities are poured into a cup with the heaviest on the bottom. For example,

strawberry liqueur [red], peppermint [blue], cherry [white], vanilla [green], and cognac [brown]." Hiratsuka, *Sakusha no Jiden,* 115.

16. Accounts of the five-colored liquor incident can be found in Hiratsuka, *Genshi,* vol. 2, 36–37; Hiratsuka, *Sakusha no jiden,* 114–115; Sievers, *Flowers in Salt,* 173; Hiroko Tomida, *Hiratsuka Raichō and Early Japanese Feminism* (Leiden: Brill, 2004), 171–177; and Janice Bridges Bardsley, "Writing for the New Woman of Taishō Japan: Hiratsuka Raichō and the Seitō Journal, 1911–1916" (PhD diss., University of California, Los Angeles, 1989), 145–146. Raichō wrote, "She [Kōkichi] writes as if she were heavily involved in drinking, but the ones who could really drink were Araki [Ikuko] and me. Kōkichi felt triumphant simply having a beautiful bottle of Western liquor placed near her." *Genshi,* vol. 2, 30–31.

17. See "Cafe, Yoshiwara e kurikomu 'atarashii onna,'" *Tokyo Nichi Nichi Shinbun,* 4 October 1912.

18. Hiratsuka, *Genshi,* vol. 2, 38–39; Hiratsuka, *Sakusha no Jiden,* 113–114; Takai and Orii, *Azami no hana,* 69.

19. "Iwayuru atarashii onna," *Kokumin Shinbun,* 12 July 1912; "Atarashigaru onna," *Tokyo Nichi Nichi Shinbun,* 26 October 1912.

20. Social and moral reform was an acceptable extension of the "good wife, wise mother" role. Through reform societies, middle-class women were able to speak out against alcohol and prostitution, the very things with which Seitō women were increasingly associated. See Sievers, *Flowers in Salt,* 87–113.

21. "Atarashigaru onna," *Tokyo Nichi Nichi Shinbun,* 26 October 1912.

22. "Nazo no shojo," *Osaka Mainichi Shinbun,* 17 November 1912.

23. "Iwayru atarashii onna," *Kokumin Shinbun,* 12, 14 July 1912; "Atarashigaru onna," *Tokyo Nichi Nichi Shinbun,* 26 October 1912.

24. This biographical information on Araki Ikuko is taken largely from Hiratsuka, *Genshi,* vol. 2, 15–20.

25. It is important to remember that according to the Meiji Civil Code of 1898 adultery was a crime when committed by a woman.

26. Araki Ikuko, "Tegami," *Seito* 2, no. 4 (April 1912): 102–106. Translation in Bardsley, "Writing for the New Woman of Taishō Japan," 406–407.

27. Bardsley, "Writing for the New Woman of Taishō Japan," 407.

28. Ibid., 409.

29. Ibid.

30. Hiratsuka, *Genshi,* vol. 2, 20. See Jay Rubin, *Injurious to Public Morals: Writers and the Meiji State* (Seattle: University of Washington Press, 1984), for details about the process of censorship in Japan at this time.

31. Hiratsuka Raichō would follow in this pattern as she embarked on a lifelong relationship with Okumura Hiroshi, who was five years younger.

32. "Iwayuru atarashii onna," *Kokumin Shinbun,* 11 July 1912.

33. "Iwayuru atarashii onna," *Kokumin Shinbun,* 11–14 July 1912.

34. "Iwayuru atarashii onna," *Kokumin Shinbun,* 14 July 1912.

35. "Myō na koi," *Tokyo Nichi Nichi Shinbun,* 29 November 1912. For more on same-sex love during this time, see Gregory M. Pflugfelder, "'S' is for Sister: Schoolgirl Intimacy and 'Same-Sex Love' in Early Twentieth-Century Japan,"

in *Gendering Modern Japanese History,* ed. Barbara Molony and Kathleen Uno (Cambridge, MA: Harvard University Asia Center, 2005), 133–190.

36. In other words, it was accepted that women could and should be educated to fulfill their roles as wives and mothers but not to pursue their individual agendas.

37. "Myō na koi," *Tokyo Nichi Nichi Shinbun,* 29 November 1912. Although girls' schools were increasing in number and enrollment, access to a college education was still not common. The focus of female education remained "good wife, wise mother" training. Raichō insisted on pursuing subjects outside the accepted field of domestic sciences as well as Zen meditation, a religious practice that stressed individual effort and achievement and had strong links to Japan's samurai past.

38. "Myō na koi," *Tokyo Nichi Nichi Shinbun,* 30 November 1912. Emphasis mine. Shimoda Utako was a renowned, conservative, female educator of the day.

39. For a detailed account of the Shiobara incident, see Hiratsuka, *Genshi,* vol. 2, 235–310. For a summary and analysis in English, see Bardsley, "Writing for the New Woman of Taishō Japan," 72–92, and Tomida, *Hiratsuka Raichō,* 115–137.

40. Raichō claimed in her autobiography that she was neither in love with Morita nor sexually active at that time.

41. Naturalism was a literary movement very much in vogue in Japan at this time. The works this movement produced were closely scrutinized by the government because the emphases on the individual and on sexuality were deemed injurious to public morals.

42. For other examples of dangerous women in literature, see Nina Cornyetz, *Dangerous Women, Deadly Words: Phallic Fantasy and Modernity in Three Japanese Writers* (Stanford, CA: Stanford University Press, 1999).

43. "Myō na koi," *Tokyo Nichi Nichi Shinbun,* 30 November 1912. Throughout the series the reporter referred to Morita and Raichō by their given names of Sōhei and Haruko.

44. Note that in this account the "suicide" becomes Raichō's idea.

45. "Myō na koi," *Tokyo Nichi Nichi Shinbun,* 1–2 December 1912.

46. "Myō na koi," *Tokyo Nichi Nichi Shinbun,* 7 December 1912. Although Raichō agreed that she pursued the affair out of curiosity, she clearly did not view her actions as sinister. See Bardsley, "Writing for the New Woman of Taishō Japan," 86.

47. "Myō na koi," *Tokyo Nichi Nichi Shinbun,* 3 December 1912.

48. "Atarashigaru onna," *Tokyo Nichi Nichi Shinbun,* 26 October 1912.

49. "Myō na koi," *Tokyo Nichi Nichi Shinbun,* 3 December 1912.

50. "Myō na koi," *Tokyo Nichi Nichi Shinbun,* 5 December 1912.

51. "Myō na koi," *Tokyo Nichi Nichi Shinbun,* 6 December 1912.

52. Takai and Orii, *Azami no hana,* 66–67; Otake Kōkichi, "Aru yoru to aru asa," *Seitō* 2, no. 6 (June 1912): 114–116.

53. Otake Kōkichi, "'Anesama' to 'uchiwa e' no tenrankai," *Seitō* 2, no. 7 (July 1912): 107–109. This is an example of Kōkichi incorporating five-colored liquor into her writing. One reporter failed to discern Kōkichi's true intent and instead denigrated Raichō as a pedophile by declaring that the handsome youth "is really a cute, cap-wearing schoolboy of 12 or 13." "Iwayuru atarashii onna," *Kokumin Shinbun,* 12 July 1912.

54. It is important to keep in mind that Raichō wrote her autobiography many decades later and may have chosen to overlook or reinterpret her feelings.
55. Hiratsuka, *Genshi,* vol. 2, 31–32. Raichō wrote about Kōkichi joining the Seitōsha on pp. 23–32.
56. Ibid., 32.
57. Raichō gives an account of her close relationship with Kōkichi at this time, including letters Kōkichi wrote her, in Hiratsuka Raichō, "Marumado yori: Chigasaki e, Chigasaki e," *Seitō* 2, no. 8 (August 1912): 76–108.
58. Raichō, Kōkichi, and the others were so involved in their personal activities that summer in Chigasaki that the death of the Meiji Emperor on July 31—a pivotal event in modern Japanese history—went virtually unnoticed in the pages of *Seitō.* See Hiratsuka, *Genshi,* vol. 2, 54.
59. Ibid., 52–53.
60. Ibid., 53.
61. "Myō na koi," *Tokyo Nichi Nichi Shinbun,* 7 December 1912.
62. Ibid.
63. "Myō na koi," *Tokyo Nichi Nichi Shinbun,* 8 December 1912.
64. "Myō na koi," *Tokyo Nichi Nichi Shinbun,* 2 December 1912.
65. Sheldon Garon, *The State and Labor in Modern Japan* (Berkeley and Los Angeles: University of California Press, 1987), 25–26.
66. Information on and quotes from the Social Policy Association in this paragraph are from "Atarashii onna," *Tokyo Nichi Nichi Shinbun,* 23 October 1912.
67. Quoted in ibid.
68. Sharon H. Nolte and Sally Ann Hastings, "The Meiji State's Policy toward Women," 1890–1910," in *Recreating Japanese Women, 1600–1945,* ed. Gail Lee Bernstein (Berkeley and Los Angeles: University of California Press, 1991), 173.
69. Satō Kōroku, "Atarashiki onna sunawachi kusaki onna," *Shinchō* 17, no. 3 (September 1912): 21.
70. Ibid., 22.
71. Mizuno Yōshū, "Gainen wo haikei to shita guzō," *Shinchō* 17, no. 3 (September 1912): 32.
72. Satō, "Atarashiki onna," 22. Emphasis mine.
73. Ibid.
74. Ibid., 24.
75. Although for different reasons, Raichō also opposed Nora's decision to leave home and did not consider her a New Woman. See Chapter 2.
76. Satō, "Atarashiki onna," 24.
77. Ibid., 25. Although Satō was opposed to the behavior and activities of New Women, he seemed to support the advancement of women within separate spheres. His ideas fit with discussions of women's rights that emphasized respect, morality, and woman's essential nature. See Barbara Molony, "Women and the State in Modern Japan: Feminist Discourses in the Meiji and Taishō Eras," in *Japan: State and People in the Twentieth Century,* ed. Janet Hunter (London: Suntory and Toyota International Centres for Economics and Related Disciplines, 1999), 23–67.
78. Uchida Roan, "Iwayuru atarashiki onna no kaishaku," *Shinchō* 17, no. 3 (September 1912): 18.

79. Ibid., 19.
80. Baba Kōchō, "Atarashiki onna wo kangeisu," *Shinchō* 17, no. 3 (September 1912): 26.
81. Ibid.
82. Ibid., 27.
83. Ibid., 28.
84. Yamaji Aizan, "Shin ni atarashiki onna nashi," *Shinchō* 17, no. 3 (September 1912): 35.
85. Ibid., 35–36.
86. Ibid., 37.
87. Baba, "Atarashiki onna wo kangeisu," 29.
88. "Atarashigaru onna," *Tokyo Nichi Nichi Shinbun,* 25, 26, 27, 29, 30, 31 October 1912.
89. "Atarashigaru onna," *Tokyo Nichi Nichi Shinbun,* 25 October 1912.
90. "Atarashigaru onna," *Tokyo Nichi Nichi Shinbun,* 26–27 October 1912.
91. "Atarashigaru onna," *Tokyo Nichi Nichi Shinbun,* 29 October 1912.
92. "Atarashigaru onna," *Tokyo Nichi Nichi Shinbun,* 31 October 1912.
93. Hiratsuka, *Sakusha no Jiden,* 117–119.

CHAPTER 5   *Discourse: "I Am a New Woman"*

1. Hiratsuka Raichō, "Henshū shitsu yori," *Seitō* 2, no. 12 (December 1912): 124.
2. This group, the Shinshinfujinkai, and its relationship to the Seitōsha are discussed in Chapter 6.
3. Hiratsuka Raichō, *Genshi, josei wa taiyō de atta,* vol. 2 (Tokyo: Otsuki Shoten, 1992), 136.
4. Other women featured in this section included *Seitō* contributors Yosano Akiko, Tamura Toshiko, Hasegawa Shigure, and Otake Kōkichi. Conservative female educators Hatoyama Haruko and Shimoda Utako were also represented.
5. See Chapter 1 for a discussion of this important essay.
6. Translation and emphases are mine. Hiratsuka Raichō, "Atarashii onna," *Chūō Kōron* (January 1913): 193–194; reprinted in Hiratsuka Raichō, *Hiratsuka Raichō chōsakushū,* vol. 1 (Tokyo: Otsuki Shoten, 1983), 257–259.
7. Ellen Key espoused essentialist views of women's biological superiority. Like Key, over the next few years Raichō would become (and remain) a strong advocate for state-supported protection for mothers and children. For a brief overview of Key's maternalist feminism, see Molly Ladd-Taylor, *Mother-Work: Women, Child Welfare, and the State, 1890–1930* (Urbana: University of Illinois Press, 1994), 106–112. For Key's influence on Raichō, see Dina Lowy, "Love and Marriage: Ellen Key and Hiratsuka Raichō Explore Alternatives," *Women's Studies* 33, no. 4 (June 2004): 361–380.
8. Hiratsuka Raichō, "Ren'ai to kekkon—Ellen Key chō (hon'yaku to shōkai)," *Seitō* 3, no. 1 (January 1913): 2.
9. Ibid., 8. Raichō seems to have been following in the footsteps of feminists from the 1880s and 1890s who connected personhood with women's identity and women's rights. See Barbara Molony, "Women and the State in Modern Japan:

Feminist Discourses in the Meiji and Taisho Eras," in *Japan: State and People in the Twentieth Century,* ed. Janet Hunter (London: Suntory and Toyota International Centres for Economics and Related Disciplines, 1999).

10. Katō Midori, "'Atarashii onna' ni tsuite," *Seitō* 3, no. 1 (January 1913): 29.
11. Ibid., 30.
12. Iwano Kiyo, "Shisō no dokuritsu to keizaijō no dokuritsu," *Seitō* 3, no. 3 (March 1913): 2.
13. Iwano Kiyo, "Ningen to shite dansei to josei wa byōdō de aru," *Seitō* 3, no. 1 (January 1913): 23.
14. Ibid., 23–24.
15. Ibid., 25.
16. Ibid. Similar arguments about women's intellect were made a few decades earlier in the male-edited *Jogaku zasshi* (Women's Education Magazine). See ch. 2 of Rebecca L. Copeland, *Lost Leaves: Women Writers of Meiji Japan* (Honolulu: University of Hawai'i Press, 2000).
17. Hori had been romantically linked with Osugi for years. Their "free-love marriage" would continue until late 1916, when Osugi's affairs drove her to leave him. He was involved with two other Seitōsha women, Kamichika Ichiko and Itō Noe, at the same time. For an account of this love quadrangle, see Stephen S. Large, "The Romance of Revolution in Japanese Anarchism and Communism during the Taishō Period," *Modern Asian Studies* 11, no. 3 (1977): 441–467.
18. Hori Yasuko, "Watashi wa furui onna desu," *Seitō* 3, no. 1 (January 1913): 61.
19. Although many Buddhist sects promoted a negative view of women, Zen—with its emphasis on meditation and individual enlightenment—was a path open to anyone. Raichō, in particular, was drawn to Zen's search for meaning and for freedom, and she encouraged other women to look inward for strength as well. For a brief introduction to Zen, see ch. 1 in Daisetz T. Suzuki, *Zen and Japanese Culture* (Princeton, NJ: Princeton University Press, 1959).
20. On Japanese naturalism, see Chapter 1.
21. Itō had two children with Tsuji and was entered in his family registry but left him to be with Osugi. Itō had five children with Osugi. Like many other New Women, she was unconventional not just in her writings but in her life-style. For additional information on Itō Noe, see Ken Miyamoto, "Itō Noe and the Bluestockings," *Japan Interpreter* 10, no. 2 (Autumn 1975): 190–204; Stephen S. Large, "The Romance of Revolution," 443–451; and Setouchi Harumi, *Beauty in Disarray,* trans. Sanford Goldstein and Kazuji Ninomiya (Rutland, VT: Tuttle, 1993).
22. Itō Noe, "Atarashiki onna no michi," *Seitō* 3, no. 1 (January 1913): 21.
23. Ibid., 22.
24. On Fukuda Hideko, see note 37 of this chapter.
25. See Katō, "'Atarashii onna' ni tsuite."
26. Nishizaki (Ikuta) Hanayo, "Atarashii onna no kaisetsu," *Seitō* 3, no. 1 (January 1913): 38–39.
27. Ibid., 43.
28. Hiratsuka Raichō, "Yo no fujintachi ni," *Seitō* 3, no. 4 (April 1913): 157. The translations of this essay presented here are my own; for a complete translation,

see Pauline C. Reich and Fukuda Atsuko, "Japan's Literary Feminists: The Seitō Group," *Signs* 2, no. 1 (Autumn 1976): 288–291.
29. Hiratsuka Raichō, "Yo no fujintachi ni," 163.
30. Ibid., 164.
31. Katō, "'Atarashii onna' ni tsuite," 34–35.
32. Hori, "Watashi wa furui onna desu," 63.
33. Ibid., 64.
34. Katō, "'Atarashii onna' ni tsuite," 33.
35. Iwano, "Shisō no dokuritsu to keizaijō no dokuritsu," 5–6. This article was a summary of the speech she gave at the Seitōsha's Woman Problem lecture meeting in February 1913. The lecture meeting is discussed in Chapter 6.
36. Fukuda Hideko, "Fujin mondai no kaisetsu," *Seitō* 3, no. 2 (February 1913): 5.
37. On Fukuda Hideko's prior activism, see Mikiso Hane, trans., *Reflections on the Way to the Gallows: Rebel Women in Prewar Japan* (Berkeley and Los Angeles: University of California Press, 1988), 29–50, and Sharlie C. Ushioda, "Fukuda Hideko and the Woman's World of Meiji Japan," in *Japan in Transition: Thought and Action in the Meiji Era, 1868–1912,* ed. Hilary Conroy, Sandra T. W. Davis, and Wayne Patterson (Rutherford, NJ: Fairleigh Dickinson University Press, 1984), 276–293.
38. Fukuda Hideko, "Fujin mondai no kaisetsu," 6.
39. This series began on 22 June 1913 and continued almost daily until 21 August 1913.
40. *Taiyō* 19, no. 9 (15 June 1913).
41. *Chūō Kōron Rinji Sōkan Fujin Mondai Go* 28, no. 9 (15 July 1913).
42. Their given names are used here to avoid confusion.
43. Iwano Hōmei, "Hiratsuka joshi," *Chūō Kōron* 28, no. 9 (15 July 1913): 170.
44. Iwano Kiyo, "Watashi no mitaru Hiratsuka Harukoshi," *Chūō Kōron* 28, no. 9 (15 July 1913): 172.
45. Ibid., 172.
46. Satō Haruo, "Woman, All Too Woman," *Chūō Kōron* 28, no. 9 (15 July 1913): 155.
47. Yosano Akiko, "Jibun wa mayotte imasu," *Chūō Kōron* 28, no. 9 (15 July 1913): 166.
48. Ibid., 168.
49. Iwano, "Watashi no mitaru Hiratsuka Harukoshi," 173.
50. Satō, "Woman, All Too Woman," 152. Raichō, like most of the Seitōsha women, wore Japanese-style, not Western-style, clothing. However, her choice of patterns and the manner in which she wore her obi, or sash, were more casual and more masculine than was typical for women at the time.
51. Tamura Toshiko, "Hiratsukasan," *Chūō Kōron* 28, no. 9 (15 July 1913): 159.
52. Otake Kōkichi, "Jijoden wo yonde Hiratsuka-san ni itaru," *Chūō Kōron* 28, no. 9 (15 July 1913): 179.
53. Yosano, "Jibun wa mayotte imasu," 164.
54. Iwano Kiyo, "Watashi no mitaru Hiratsuka Harukoshi," 172.
55. Okake, "Jijoden wo yonde," 180.
56. Nishimura Yōkichi, "Watashi no shitte iru no Hiratsukasan," *Chūō Kōron* 28, no. 9 (15 July 1913): 157.

57. See Chapter 4.
58. Baba Kōchō, "Hiratsuka Harukokun," *Chūō Kōron* 28, no. 9 (15 July 1913): 160.

CHAPTER 6   *Rivalry: "True New Women" Emerge*

1. For additional information on the Shinshinfujinkai, see Ulrike Wöhr's "Mo hitotsu no 'Seitō,'" in *Onna to otoko no jikū: Nihon joseishi saikō*, vol. 5, ed. Okuda Akiko (Tokyo: Fujiwara Shoten, 1995), 312–334, and Okano Yukie's *Shinshinfujin: Kaisetsu, sōmokuji, sakuin* (Tokyo: Fuji Shuppan, 1994).
2. For general background information on the Shinshinfujinkai cofounders, see Ulrike Wöhr's "Between Revolution and Reaction: The Japanese Women's Movement in the Taishō Era," in *War, Revolution and Japan*, ed. Ian Neary (Sandgate: Japan Library, 1993), 53–58, and Okano's *Shinshinfujin*, 5–8. For detailed accounts, see Amano Shigeru, ed., *Heiminsha no onna: Nishikawa Fumiko jiden* (Tokyo: Aoyamakan, 1984); Ishihara Michiko, *Kumamoto hyōron no onna* (Tokyo/Kumamoto: Kazokushi Kenkyūkai, 1989); and Ishihara Michiko, "Nishikawa Fumiko, Kimura Komako, and Miyazaki Mitsuko chō 'Atarashiki onna no iku beki michi' kaisetsu," in *Atarashiki onna no iku beki michi* (Tokyo: Fuji Shuppan, 1986).
3. For information on women's involvement in Japan's socialist movement in the early twentieth century, see Sharon L. Sievers, *Flowers in Salt: The Beginnings of Feminist Consciousness in Modern Japan* (Stanford, CA: Stanford University Press, 1983), 114–138, and Vera Mackie, *Creating Socialist Women in Japan* (Cambridge: Cambridge University Press, 1997).
4. As mentioned in Chapter 5, Seitōsha member Iwano Kiyo also participated in this campaign.
5. "Sengen," *Shinshinfujin* 1 (May 1913).
6. "Sengen," *Shinshinfujin* 2 (June 1913). These goals bore a striking resemblance to those of the Seitōsha. Article 1 of the Seitōsha's initial bylaws declared, "This society aims to promote the development of women's literature, to give scope to the innate characteristics of each individual, and to give birth to the female genius of tomorrow." "Seitōsha gaisoku," *Seitō* 1, no. 1 (September 1911): 132–133, translated in Janice Bridges Bardsley, "Writing for the New Woman of Taishō Japan" (PhD diss., University of California, Los Angeles, 1989), 401. Two years later the Seitōsha officially revised its bylaws to reflect the direction the group had taken. The emphasis on literature was replaced by an emphasis on women's awakening and women's issues.
7. Hiratsuka Raichō, *Genshi, josei wa taiyō de atta*, vol. 2 (Tokyo: Otsuki Shoten, 1992), 111–114.
8. Ibid., 111–114.
9. For this section I use their given names—Kiyo/Homei and Mitsuko/Toranosuke—to avoid confusion.
10. "Gathering of New Women," *Asahi Shinbun*, 16 February 1913, as quoted in Setouchi Harumi's *Beauty in Disarray*, trans. Sanford Goldstein and Kazuji Ninomiya (Rutland, VT: Tuttle, 1993), 178. Mitsuko later wrote an article in which she belittled Hōmei's "philosophy of momentary pleasures" by equating it with the

babbling of small children. She also claimed it was a philosophy practiced not by "thinking human beings" but by animals. Miyazaki Mitsuko, "Seitōsha wo ronzu," *Chūō Kōron* 28, no. 9 (15 July 1913): 98. .

11. "Atarashii onna no ensetsukai," *Yomiuri Shinbun,* 16 February 1913, in Hiratsuka, *Genshi,* vol. 2, 113. Nora remained an important symbol of the New Woman and here is appropriated by an "awakened" man.

12. "Atarashii onna no ensetsukai," *Yomiuri Shinbun,* 16 February 1913, in Hiratsuka, *Genshi,* vol. 2, 112.

13. "Gathering of New Women," *Asahi Shinbun,* 16 February 1913, as quoted in Setouchi's *Beauty in Disarray,* 177.

14. "Gathering of New Women," *Asahi Shinbun,* 16 February 1913, as quoted in Setouchi's *Beauty in Disarray,* 177–178. Kiyo's hairstyle was called a *marumage.* Her marriage to Iwano Hōmei would end in a bitter divorce the following year. Although newspaper articles only hinted at the content of the speeches, three of them—including both Hōmei's and Kiyo's—were published in *Seitō*'s March supplement. The only time writing by men appeared in *Seitō* was in the February and March 1913 issues, and then only in the supplements devoted to the New Woman and the Woman Problem.

15. Hiratsuka, *Genshi,* vol. 2, 114.

16. "Shinshinfujin towa (4)," *Miyako,* 10 March 1913.

17. "Atarashii onna no okabu arasoi," *Tokyo Asahi Shinbun,* 17 March 1913; "Chōshūseki de kaachan: kinō no shinshinfujin ensetsukai," *Miyako,* 17 March 1913.

18. Hiratsuka, *Genshi,* vol. 2, 115–116.

19. "Fujin mondai kenkyūkai," *Shinshinfujin* 3 (July 1913), and "Fujin mondai kenkyūkai," *Shinshinfujin* 4 (August 1913). According to these reports about thirty-five people attended the first meeting and about thirty attended the second.

20. "Atarashii onna no atarashii teki (1)," *Tokyo Nichi Nichi Shinbun,* 1 March 1913.

21. "Chōshūseki de kaachan: Kinō no shinshinfujin ensetsukai," *Miyako,* 17 March 1913.

22. "Seitōsha sōkōgeki," *Yomiuri Shinbun,* 17 March 1913.

23. "Shinshinfujin towa (4)," *Miyako,* 10 March 1913.

24. Hiratsuka, *Genshi,* vol. 2, 115.

25. Miyazaki Mitsuko, "Shoshi ni nozomu," *Seitō* 3, no. 1 (January 1913): 60. Although Mitsuko claimed credit for suggesting the idea of a lecture meeting, Raichō indicated that Ikuta Chōkō, the male literary critic and strong supporter of the Seitōsha, had been pressing for one as well. Hiratsuka, *Genshi,* vol. 2, 91.

26. "Atarashii onna no atarashii teki (3)," *Tokyo Nichi Nichi Shinbun,* 7 March 1913.

27. Miyazaki, "Seitōsha wo ronzu." She was clearly referring to the speech by Iwano Hōmei that had so outraged her husband, Toranosuke.

28. "Atarashii onna no atarashii teki (1)," *Tokyo Nichi Nichi Shinbun,* 1 March 1913.

29. "Atarashii onna no atarashii teki (2)," *Tokyo Nichi Nichi Shinbun,* 6 March 1913, and "Sannin no shinshinfujin," *Yomiuri Shinbun,* 7 March 1913.

30. "Shinshinfujin towa (3)," *Miyako,* 9 March 1913.

31. "Atarashii onna no atarashii teki (3)," *Tokyo Nichi Nichi Shinbun,* 7 March 1913.

32. Quoted in "Shinshinfujin towa (2)," *Miyako,* 8 March 1913. This view clearly ran counter to Raichō's opposition to marriage under the existing system.

33. Quoted in "Shinshinfujin towa (3)," *Miyako,* 9 March 1913.
34. Miyake Setsurei, "Mondai no teikyōsha to shite no atarashii onna," *Taiyō* 19, no. 9 (June 1913: 50.
35. Quoted in "Atarashii onna no atarashii teki (6)," *Tokyo Nichi Nichi Shinbun,* 12 March 1913.
36. The biographical information that follows is drawn from "Atarashii onna no atarashii teki," *Tokyo Nichi Nichi Shinbun,* 10–20 March 1913.
37. For additional information on Kanno Suga, see Sievers, *Flowers in Salt,* 139–162; Mikiso Hane, *Reflections on the Way to the Gallows: Rebel Women in Prewar Japan* (Berkeley and Los Angeles: University of California Press, 1988), 51–74; and Helene Bowen Raddeker, *Treacherous Women of Imperial Japan: Patriarchal Fictions, Patricidal Fantasies* (New York: Routledge, 1997).
38. Miyazaki Mitsuko, "Shinshinfujin," *Shin Jokai* 5, no. 4 (April 1913): 54. Women were still strictly excluded from politics at this time. That both the Seitōsha and the Shinshinfujinkai leaders advocated awakening over political rights can be seen as a strategic move and a means of survival. They wanted their organizations to provide a space for women to discover themselves and grow strong. Overtly political discussions would have led to government suppression.
39. Nishikawa Fumiko, Miyazaki Mitsuko, Kimura Komako, "Shinshinfujinkai no mokuteki," in *Atarashiki onna no yukubeki michi* (Tokyo: Fuji Shuppan, 1986); reprinted in Suzuki Yūko, ed., *Nihon josei undō shiryō shūsei,* vol. 2 *(Tokyo: Fuji Shuppan, 1993*–1998). For a discussion of the shift in emphasis from "character" in the Meiji period to "personality" in the Taishō period, see Donald Roden, "Taishō Culture and the Problem of Gender Ambivalence," in *Culture and Identity: Japanese Intellectuals during the Interwar Years,* ed. J. Thomas Rimer (Princeton, NJ: Princeton University Press, 1990), 37–55.
40. Miyazaki, "Shinshinfujin," 55.
41. Nishikawa et al., "Shinshinfujinkai no mokuteki."
42. Ibid.
43. Nishikawa Fumiko, "Shinshinfujinkai to ryōsai kenbo," *Jogaku Sekai* 13, no. 6 (May 1913): 38.
44. Yosano Akiko would give birth to three more children in the next few years. For additional information on her life and status as a New Woman, see Laurel Rasplica Rodd's "Yosano Akiko and the Taishō Debate over the 'New Woman,'" in *Recreating Japanese Women, 1600–1945,* ed. Gail Lee Bernstein (Berkeley and Los Angeles: University of California Press, 1991), 175–198.
45. Nishikawa, "Shinshinfujinkai to ryōsai kenbo," 38.
46. "Shinshinfujin towa (4)," *Miyako,* 9 March 1913.
47. Nishikawa et al., "Shinshinfujinkai no mokuteki," 363.
48. Ibid.
49. Nishikawa, "Shinshinfujinkai to ryōsai kenbo," 34.
50. Ibid., 36.
51. Miyazaki, "Shinshinfujin," 56.
52. Nishikawa Fumiko, "Fujin mondai no chūshinten," *Shinshinfujin* 3 (July 1913); reprinted in Suzuki Yūko, ed., *Nihon josei undō shiryō shūsei,* vol. 2 *(Tokyo: Fuji Shuppan, 1993*–1998), 365.

53. Ibid. Recall that in their critique of *A Doll House,* some Seitō members pointed out that Helmer, Nora's husband, needed to awaken too. See Chapter 2.

54. *Seitō* and *Shinshinfujin* were similar in that they were both founded and run by women. However, men regularly contributed to the pages of *Shinshinfujin,* whereas *Seitō* retained its uniqueness as an outlet for women's writing only. (The one exception was a few male contributions to *Seitō*'s 1913 New Woman supplements.) For a brief comparison of the Seitōsha and the Shinshinfujinkai, see Hiroko Tomida, *Hiratsuka Raichō and Early Japanese Feminism* (Leiden: Brill, 2004), 213–219.

55. From the handful of post-1916 issues that remain, it appears that the magazine gave up its focus on women's issues and became a more conventional women's household magazine. For general background information on *Shinshinfujin,* see Okano, *Shinshinfujin,* 5–14.

CHAPTER 7   *New Women and Beyond*

1. On separate spheres, see Linda K. Kerber, "Separate Spheres, Female Worlds, Woman's Place: The Rhetoric of Women's History," *Journal of American History* 75, no. 1 (1988): 9–39.

2. On the New Woman in the United States and Europe, see Nancy Woloch, "The Rise of the New Woman, 1860–1920," in *Women and the American Experience,* 2d ed. (New York: McGraw-Hill, 1994), 269–307; Adele Heller and Lois Rudnick, "Introduction," in *1915, the Cultural Moment: The New Politics, the New Woman, the New Psychology, the New Art and the New Theatre in America,* ed. Adele Heller and Lois Rudnick (New Brunswick, NJ: Rutgers University Press, 1991), 1–13; Bonnie G. Smith, "The New Woman," in *Changing Lives: Women in European History since 1700* (Lexington, MA: Heath, 1989), 317–363; Barbara Caine, *English Feminism 1780–1980* (Oxford: Oxford University Press, 1997), 131–172; Angelique Richardson and Chris Willis, eds., *The New Woman in Fiction and in Fact* (New York: Palgrave, 2001); and Jill Bergman, "'Natural' Divisions/National Divisions: Whiteness and the American New Woman in the General Federation of Women's Clubs," in *New Woman Hybridities,* ed. Ann Heilmann and Margaret Beetham (London: Routledge, 2004), 223–239. For an in-depth look at the women's club movement, see Janice C. Steinschneider, *An Improved Woman: The Wisconsin Federation of Women's Clubs, 1895–1920* (Brooklyn: Carlson, 1994).

3. See Patricia Marks, *Bicycles, Bangs, and Bloomers: The New Woman in the Popular Press* (Lexington: University Press of Kentucky, 1990), 1–23; Elaine Showalter, *Sexual Anarchy: Gender and Culture at the Fin de Siècle* (New York: Penguin Books, 1990), 38–58; Carroll Smith-Rosenberg, "The Female World of Love and Ritual: Relations between Women in Nineteenth-Century America," *Signs* 1 (1975): 1–30; and Ellen Kay Trimberger, "The New Woman and the New Sexuality," in *1915, the Cultural Moment: The New Politics, the New Woman, the New Psychology, the New Art and the New Theatre in America,* ed. Adele Heller and Lois Rudnick (New Brunswick, NJ: Rutgers University Press, 1991), 98–115.

4. See Gail Cunningham, *The New Woman and the Victorian Novel* (London: Macmillan, 1978); Elizabeth Ammons, "The New Woman as Cultural Symbol and Social Reality," in *1915, the Cultural Moment: The New Politics, the New Woman, the New Psychology, the New Art and the New Theatre in America,* ed. Adele Heller and Lois Rudnick (New Brunswick, NJ: Rutgers University Press, 1991), 82–97; and Ann Heilmann, *New Woman Fiction: Women Writing First-Wave Feminism* (New York: St. Martin's Press, 2000).

5. See Lou Salome, *Ibsen's Heroines,* ed. Siegfried Mandel (Redding Ridge, CT: Black Swan Books, 1985), and Vivien Gardner and Susan Rutherford, eds., *The New Woman and Her Sisters: Feminism and Theatre 1850–1914* (Ann Arbor: University of Michigan Press, 1992).

6. See Marks, *Bicycles, Bangs, and Bloomers,* and Angelika Köhler, "Charged with Ambiguity: The Image of the New Woman in American Cartoons," in *New Woman Hybridities,* ed. Ann Heilmann and Margaret Beetham (London: Routledge, 2004), 158–178.

7. See Lois Rudnick, "The New Woman," in *1915, the Cultural Moment: The New Politics, the New Woman, the New Psychology, the New Art and the New Theatre in America,* ed. Adele Heller and Lois Rudnick (New Brunswick, NJ: Rutgers University Press, 1991), 69–81; Carroll Smith-Rosenberg, "The New Woman as Androgyne: Social Disorder and Gender Crisis, 1870–1936," in *Disorderly Conduct: Visions of Gender in Victorian America* (New York: Knopf, 1985), 245–296; and Martha Vicinus, *Independent Women: Work and Community for Single Women, 1850–1920* (Chicago: University of Chicago Press, 1985).

8. See Smith-Rosenberg, "The Female World of Love and Ritual"; Kathryn Kish Sklar, "Hull House in the 1890s: A Community of Women Reformers," *Signs* 10, no. 4 (1985): 658–677; and Estelle Freedman, "Separatism as Strategy: Female Institution Building and American Feminism, 1870–1930," *Feminist Studies* 5, no. 3 (1979): 512–529.

9. See June Sochen, *The New Woman: Feminism in Greenwich Village, 1910–1920* (New York: Quadrangle Books, 1972).

10. See Nancy Cott, "The Modern Woman of the 1920s, American Style," in *A History of Women in the West,* V: *Toward a Cultural Identity in the Twentieth Century,* ed. Francoise Thebaud (Cambridge, MA: Belknap Press, 1994), 76–91.

11. There are numerous variants of the New Woman—both in Europe and around the world—that are not discussed in this work. To provide just a few examples, see chapters on Irish, German, and Hungarian New Women in Ann Heilmann and Margaret Beetham, eds., *New Woman Hybridities* (London: Routledge, 2004). Danish New Women are the central topic of Birgitte Søland's *Becoming Modern: Young Women and the Reconstruction of Womanhood in the 1920s* (Princeton, NJ: Princeton University Press, 2000). There are several sources on the Russian New Woman including Lynne Atwood's *Creating the New Soviet Woman: Woman's Magazines as Engineers of Female Identity, 1922–53* (New York: St. Martin's Press, 1999). For New Women and women's movements in Australia, New Zealand, Vietnam, Indonesia, and India, see chapters in Louise Edwards and Mina Roces, eds., *Women's Suffrage in Asia: Gender, Nationalism and Democracy* (London and New York: RoutledgeCurzon, 2004), and Caroline Daley and

Melanie Nolan, eds., *Suffrage and Beyond: International Feminist Perspectives* (New York: New York University Press, 1994).

12. This argument can be made for many of her Euro-American manifestations as well, although England and the United States provide alternative models.

13. Leila Ahmed, *Women and Gender in Islam: Historical Roots of a Modern Debate* (New Haven, CT: Yale University Press, 1992), 148–152. The negotiated combination of old and new, Western and Egyptian is a theme woven throughout Mona L. Russell, *Creating the New Egyptian Woman: Consumerism, Education, and National Identity, 1863–1922* (New York: Palgrave Macmillan, 2004).

14. Qasim Amin, *The New Woman: A Document in the Early Debate on Egyptian Feminism,* 1900, trans. Samiha Sidhom Peterson (Cairo: American University in Cairo Press, 1995), 1.

15. Ibid., 92.

16. Ahmed, *Women and Gender in Islam,* 162.

17. See Beth Baron, *The Women's Awakening in Egypt: Culture, Society, and the Press* (New Haven, CT: Yale University Press, 1994); Ahmed, *Women and Gender in Islam,* ch. 9; and Russell, *Creating the New Egyptian Woman,* 80–87.

18. For more on New Women and consumerism, see Russell, *Creating the New Egyptian Woman,* chs. 3 and 4.

19. In China, Japan, and Korea, similar combinations of characters—for "new" and for "woman"—were used to express the term *New Woman.*

20. Ray Huang, *China: A Macro History* (Armonk, NY: Sharpe, 1997), 242–264. Also see Barbara N. Ramusack and Sharon Sievers, *Women in Asia: Restoring Women to History* (Bloomington: Indiana University Press, 1999), 202–207. For additional information on the emergence of New Women in China, see Hu Ying, *Tales of Translation: Composing the New Woman in China, 1898–1918* (Stanford, CA: Stanford University Press, 2000), and Hu Ying, "Naming the First New Woman," *Nan Nü* 3, no. 2 (2001): 196–231. For a brief chronology of the Chinese women's movement from the 1898 Reforms through the May Fourth movement, see Lu Meiyi, "The Awakening of Chinese Women and the Women's Movement in the Early Twentieth Century," in *Holding Up Half the Sky: Chinese Women Past, Present, and Future,* ed. Tao Jie, Zheng Bijun, and Shirley L. Mow (New York: Feminist Press, 2004), 55–70.

21. Christina Kelley Gilmartin, "Introduction: May Fourth and Women's Emancipation," in *Women in Republican China: A Sourcebook,* ed. Hua R. Lan and Vanessa L. Fong (Armonk, NY: Sharpe, 1999), ix-xxv. This book includes translations of forty-three essays about women's issues written during the May Fourth movement. Only thirteen of these essays were written by women.

22. Ibid. Also see Ramusack and Sievers, *Women in Asia,* 209–218, and Charlotte L. Beahan, "In the Public Eye: Women in Early Twentieth-Century China," in *Women in China: Current Directions in Historical Scholarship,* ed. Richard W. Guisso and Stanley Johannesen (Youngstown, NY: Philo Press, 1981), 215–238. For narratives of several Chinese New Women's lives see Wang Zheng, *Women in the Chinese Enlightenment: Oral and Textual Histories* (Berkeley: University of California Press, 1999). For representations of Chinese New Women in fiction and the press, see Jin Feng, *The New Woman in Early Twentieth-Century*

Chinese Fiction (West Lafayette, IN: Purdue University Press, 2004); Sarah E. Stevens, "Figuring Modernity: The New Woman and the Modern Girl in Republican China," *NWSA Journal* 15, no. 3 (Fall 2003): 82–103; and Bryna Goodman, "The New Woman Commits Suicide: The Press, Cultural Memory, and the New Republic," *Journal of Asian Studies* 64, no. 1 (February 2005): 67–101. For an account of women's activism within the Communist Party, see Lily Xiao Hong Lee, "The Chinese Women's Movement before and after the Long March," in *Holding Up Half the Sky: Chinese Women Past, Present, and Future,* ed. Tao Jie, Zheng Bijun, and Shirley L. Mow (New York: Feminist Press, 2004), 71–91.

23. Insook Kwon, "'The New Women's Movement' in 1920s Korea: Rethinking the Relationship between Imperialism and Women," *Gender and History* 10, no. 3 (1998): 381–405, and Ramusack and Sievers, *Women in Asia,* 204–206.

24. For additional information on the connection between religion and education, see Kenneth M. Wells, "Expanding Their Realm: Women and Public Agency in Colonial Korea," in *Women's Suffrage in Asia: Gender, Nationalism and Democracy,* ed. Louise Edwards and Mina Roces (London and New York: RoutledgeCurzon, 2004), 156–160. For a comparison of Japanese New Women and Korean New Women, see Kwon, "'The New Women's Movement' in 1920s Korea," 388–390.

25. Kwon, "'The New Women's Movement' in 1920s Korea," 392–395.

26. Jiweon Shin, "Social Construction of Idealized Images of Women in Colonial Korea: The 'New Woman' versus 'Motherhood,'" in *Decolonization: Perspectives from Now and Then,* ed. Prasenjit Duara (London and New York: Routledge, 2004), 239–252. For additional information on how women's issues lost out to nationalist concerns, see Kenneth M. Wells, "The Price of Legitimacy: Women and the Kŭnuhoe Movement, 1927–1931," in *Colonial Modernity in Korea,* ed. Gi-Wook Shin and Michael Robinson (Cambridge, MA: Harvard University Asia Center, 1999), 191–220. For an examination of what being a New Woman meant to ordinary Koreans, see Kyeong-Hee Choi's literary analysis, "Neither Colonial nor National: The Making of the 'New Woman' in Pak Wansŏ's 'Mother's Stake 1,'" in *Colonial Modernity in Korea,* ed. Gi-Wook Shin and Michael Robinson (Cambridge, MA: Harvard University Asia Center, 1999), 221–247.

27. See Louise Edwards and Mina Roces, "Introduction: Orienting the Global Women's Suffrage Movement," in *Women's Suffrage in Asia: Gender, Nationalism and Democracy, ed. Louise Edwards and Mina Roces* (London and New York: RoutledgeCurzon, 2004), 1–23; Louise Edwards, "Chinese Women's Campaigns for Suffrage: Nationalism, Confucianism and Political Agency," in *Women's Suffrage in Asia: Gender, Nationalism and Democracy,* ed. Louise Edwards and Mina Roces (London and New York: RoutledgeCurzon, 2004), 59–78; and Wells, "Expanding Their Realm."

28. For more on Raichō's post-Seitō activities, see chs. 5–7 of Hiroko Tomida, *Hiratsuka Raichō and Early Japanese Feminism* (Leiden: Brill, 2004), and vols. 3 and 4 of Hiratsuka, *Genshi.*

29. For the motherhood-protection debate, see Laurel Rasplica Rodd, "Yosano Akiko and the Taishō Debate over the 'New Woman,'" in *Recreating Japanese Women, 1600–1945,* ed. Gail Lee Bernstein (Berkeley and Los Angeles: University of California Press, 1991), 175–198; Barbara Molony, "Equality versus Difference:

The Japanese Debate over 'Motherhood Protection,' 1915–50," in *Japanese Women Working*, ed. Janet Hunter (London: Routledge, 1993), 122–148; and Tomida, *Hiratsuka Raicho*, 221–262.

30. Tomida, *Hiratsuka Raichō*, 263–330; Miyako Orii and Hiroko Tomida, *"Shin Fujin Kyōkai* (The Association for New Women) and the Women Who Aimed to Change Society," in *Japanese Women: Emerging from Subservience, 1868–1945*, ed. Hiroko Tomida and Gordon Daniels (Kent, OH: Global Oriental, 2005), 232–257; and Akiko Tokuza, *The Rise of the Feminist Movement in Japan* (Tokyo: Keio University Press, 1999), 107–191. For additional information on the eugenics campaign, see Sumiko Otsubo, "Engendering Eugenics: Feminists and Marriage Restriction Legislation in the 1920s," in *Gendering Modern Japanese History*, ed. Barbara Molony and Kathleen Uno (Cambridge, MA: Harvard University Asia Center, 2005), 225–256.

31. For the suffrage movement in Japan, see Barbara Molony, "Citizenship and Suffrage in Interwar Japan," in *Women's Suffrage in Asia: Gender, Nationalism and Democracy,,* ed. Louise Edwards and Mina Roces (London and New York: RoutledgeCurzon, 2004), 127–151; Yukiko Matsukawa and Kaoru Tachi, "Women's Suffrage and Gender Politics in Japan," in *Suffrage and Beyond: International Feminist Perspectives,* ed. Caroline Daley and Melanie Nolan (New York: New York University Press, 1994), 171–183; and Sharon Nolte, "Women's Rights and Society's Needs: Japan's 1931 Suffrage Bill," *Comparative Studies in Society and History* (1986): 690–714. For additional information on Ichikawa Fusae, see Barbara Molony, "Ichikawa Fusae and Japan's Pre-war Women's Suffrage Movement," in *Japanese Women: Emerging from Subservience, 1868–1945*, ed. Hiroko Tomida and Gordon Daniels (Kent, OH: Global Oriental, 2005), 57–92, and Dee Ann Vavich, "The Japanese Women's Movement: Ichikawa Fusae, a Pioneer in Woman's Suffrage," in *Women and Women's Issues in Post World War II Japan,* ed. Edward R. Beauchamp (New York: Garland, 1998), 30–64.

32. Mikiso Hane, *Reflections on the Way to the Gallows: Rebel Women in Prewar Japan* (Berkeley and Los Angeles: University of California Press, 1988), 125–174; Vera Mackie, *Creating Socialist Women in Japan* (Cambridge: Cambridge University Press, 1997), 95–153; Vera Mackie, *Feminism in Modern Japan* (Cambridge: Cambridge University Press, 2003), 73–98; Helen M. Hopper, *A New Woman of Japan: A Political Biography of Katō Shidzue* (Boulder, CO: Westview Press, 1996); Baroness Shidzue Ishimoto, *Facing Two Ways: The Story of My Life* (Stanford, CA: Stanford University Press, 1984); and Ronald P. Loftus, ed., *Telling Lives: Women's Self-Writing in Modern Japan* (Honolulu: University of Hawai'i Press, 2004).

33. Barbara Sato, *The New Japanese Woman: Modernity, Media, and Women in Interwar Japan* (Durham, NC: Duke University Press, 2003). See also Barbara Hamill Sato, "The Moga Sensation: Perceptions of the Modan Gāru in Japanese Intellectual Circles during the 1920s," *Gender and History* 5, no. 3 (1993): 361–381; Miriam Silverberg, "The Modern Girl as Militant," in *Recreating Japanese Women, 1600–1945*, ed. Gail Lee Bernstein (Berkeley and Los Angeles: University of California Press, 1991), 239–266; and Koyama Shizuko, "The 'Good Wife and Wise Mother' Ideology in Post-World War I Japan," *U.S.-Japan Women's*

Journal 7 (1994): 31–52. Other examples of transgressing existing gender roles are discussed in Donald Roden, "Taishō Culture and the Problem of Gender Ambivalence," in *Culture and Identity: Japanese Intellectuals during the Interwar Years,* ed. J. Thomas Rimer (Princeton, NJ: Princeton University Press, 1990), 37–55, and Jennifer Robertson, "Gender-Bending in Paradise: Doing 'Female' and 'Male' in Japan," *Genders* 5 (Summer 1989): 50–69.

BIBLIOGRAPHY

Ahmed, Leila. *Women and Gender in Islam: Historical Roots of a Modern Debate.* New Haven, CT: Yale University Press, 1992.

Amano Shigeru, ed. *Heiminsha no onna: Nishikawa Fumiko jiden.* Tokyo: Aoyamakan, 1984.

Amin, Qasim. *The New Woman: A Document in the Early Debate on Egyptian Feminism.* 1900. Translated by Samiha Sidhom Peterson. Cairo: American University in Cairo Press, 1995.

Ammons, Elizabeth. "The New Woman as Cultural Symbol and Social Reality." In *1915, the Cultural Moment: The New Politics, the New Woman, the New Psychology, the New Art and the New Theatre in America,* edited by Adele Heller and Lois Rudnick. New Brunswick, NJ: Rutgers University Press, 1991.

Andrew, Nancy. *The Seitōsha: An Early Japanese Women's Organization, 1911–1916.* Papers on Japan, vol. 6. Cambridge, MA: East Asian Research Center, Harvard University, 1972.

Araki Ikuko. "Tegami." *Seitō* 2, no. 4 (April 1912): 102–106.

Asai Shōzō. "Nora no kokoromochi no wakaru onna wo sukunai." *Fujin Kurabu* 4 (November 1911): 44–48.

Atwood, Lynne. *Creating the New Soviet Woman: Woman's Magazines as Engineers of Female Identity, 1922–53.* New York: St. Martin's Press, 1999.

Baba Kōchō. "Atarashiki onna wo kangeisu." *Shinchō* 17, no. 3 (September 1912): 25–30.

———. "Hiratsuka Harukokun." *Chūō Kōron* 28, no. 9 (15 July 1913): 159–162.

Bardsley, Janice Bridges. "Writing for the New Woman of Taishō Japan: Hiratsuka Raichō and the Seitō Journal, 1911–1916." PhD diss., University of California, Los Angeles, 1989.

Baron, Beth. *The Women's Awakening in Egypt: Culture, Society, and the Press.* New Haven, CT: Yale University Press, 1994.

Barshay, Andrew. *State and Intellectual in Imperial Japan: The Public Man in Crisis.* Berkeley and Los Angeles: University of California Press, 1988.

Basch, Norma. *In the Eyes of the Law: Women, Marriage, and Property in Nineteenth Century New York.* Ithaca, NY: Cornell University Press, 1982.

Beahan, Charlotte L. "In the Public Eye: Women in Early Twentieth-Century China." In *Women in China: Current Directions in Historical Scholarship,* edited by Richard W. Guisso and Stanley Johannesen. Youngstown, NY: Philo Press, 1981.

Beichman, Janine. *Embracing the Firebird: Yosano Akiko and the Birth of the Female Voice in Modern Japanese Poetry.* Honolulu: University of Hawai'i Press, 2002.

Bergman, Jill. "'Natural' Divisions/National Divisions: Whiteness and the American New Woman in the General Federation of Women's Clubs." In *New Women Hybridities,* edited by Ann Heilmann and Margaret Beetham. London: Routledge, 2004.

Braisted, William R., trans. *Meiroku Zasshi: Journal of the Japanese Enlightenment.* Cambridge, MA: Harvard University Press, 1976.

Brownstein, Michael C. "Jogaku Zasshi and the Founding of the Bungakukai." *Monumenta Nipponica* 35, no. 3 (1980): 319–336.

Caine, Barbara. *English Feminism 1780–1980.* Oxford: Oxford University Press, 1997.

Choi, Kyeong-Hee. "Neither Colonial nor National: The Making of the 'New Woman' in Pak Wansŏ's 'Mother's Stake 1.'" In *Colonial Modernity in Korea,* edited by Gi-Wook Shin and Michael Robinson. Cambridge, MA: Harvard University Asia Center, 1999.

Copeland, Rebecca L. *Lost Leaves: Women Writers of Meiji Japan.* Honolulu: University of Hawai'i Press, 2000.

Cornyetz, Nina. *Dangerous Women, Deadly Words: Phallic Fantasy and Modernity in Three Japanese Writers.* Stanford, CA: Stanford University Press, 1999.

Cott, Nancy. "The Modern Woman of the 1920s, American Style." In *A History of Women in the West, V: Toward a Cultural Identity in the Twentieth Century,* edited by Francoise Thebaud. Cambridge, MA: Belknap Press, 1994.

Cunningham, Gail. *The New Woman and the Victorian Novel.* London: Macmillan, 1978.

Daley, Caroline, and Melanie Nolan, eds. *Suffrage and Beyond: International Feminist Perspectives.* New York: New York University Press, 1994.

Dower, John W. "E. H. Norman, Japan and the Uses of History." In *Origins of the Modern Japanese State: Selected Writings of E. H. Norman.* New York: Pantheon Books, 1975.

Durbach, Errol. *A Doll's House: Ibsen's Myth of Transformation.* Boston: Twayne, 1991.

Edwards, Louise. "Chinese Women's Campaigns for Suffrage: Nationalism, Confucianism and Political Agency." In *Women's Suffrage in Asia: Gender, Nationalism and Democracy,* edited by Louise Edwards and Mina Roces. London and New York: RoutledgeCurzon, 2004.

Edwards, Louise, and Mina Roces. "Introduction: Orienting the Global Women's Suffrage Movement." In *Women's Suffrage in Asia: Gender, Nationalism and Democracy, edited by Louise Edwards and Mina Roces.* London and New York: RoutledgeCurzon, 2004.

———, eds. *Women's Suffrage in Asia: Gender, Nationalism and Democracy.* London and New York: RoutledgeCurzon, 2004.

Felski, Rita. *The Gender of Modernity.* Cambridge, MA: Harvard University Press, 1995.

Foucault, Michel. *The Archaeology of Knowledge and the Discourse on Language.* Translated by A. M. Sheridan Smith. New York: Pantheon Books, 1972.

―――. "Nietzsche, Genealogy, History." In *The Foucault Reader,* edited by Paul Rabinow. New York: Pantheon Books, 1984.

Freedman, Estelle. "Separatism as Strategy: Female Institution Building and American Feminism, 1870–1930." *Feminist Studies* 5, no. 3 (1979): 512–529.

Fujitani, Takashi. *Splendid Monarchy: Power and Pageantry in Modern Japan.* Berkeley and Los Angeles: University of California Press, 1996.

Fukuda Hideko. "Fujin mondai no kaisetsu." *Seitō* 3, no. 2 (February 1913): 1–7.

Fukuzawa Yukichi. *The Autobiography of Fukuzawa Yukichi.* Translated by Eiichi Kiyooka. New York: Columbia University Press, 1960.

―――. *Fukuzawa Yukichi on Japanese Women: Selected Works.* Translated by Eiichi Kiyooka. Tokyo: University of Tokyo Press, 1988.

Furukawa Makoto. "The Changing Nature of Sexuality: The Three Codes Framing Homosexuality in Modern Japan." *U.S.-Japan Women's Journal* 7 (1994): 98–127.

Furuki Yoshiko. *The White Plum, a Biography of Umeko Tsuda: Pioneer in the Higher Education of Japanese Women.* New York: Weatherhill, 1991.

Gardner, Vivien, and Susan Rutherford, eds. *The New Woman and Her Sisters: Feminism and Theatre 1850–1914.* Ann Arbor: University of Michigan Press, 1992.

Garon, Sheldon. *Molding Japanese Minds: The State in Everyday Life.* Princeton, NJ: Princeton University Press, 1997.

―――. "Rethinking Modernization and Modernity in Japanese History." *Journal of Asian Studies* 53, no. 2 (May 1994): 346–366.

―――. *The State and Labor in Modern Japan.* Berkeley and Los Angeles: University of California Press, 1987.

―――. "Women's Groups and the Japanese State: Contending Approaches to Political Integration, 1890–1945." *Journal of Japanese Studies* 19, no. 1 (1993): 5–41.

―――. "The World's Oldest Debate?: Prostitution and the State in Imperial Japan, 1900–1945." *American Historical Review* 97, no. 3 (June 1993): 710–732.

Gilmartin, Christina Kelley. "Introduction: May Fourth and Women's Emancipation." In *Women in Republican China: A Sourcebook,* edited by Hua R. Lan and Vanessa L. Fong. Armonk, NY: Sharpe, 1999.

Gluck, Carol. *Japan's Modern Myths: Ideology in the Late Meiji Period.* Princeton, NJ: Princeton University Press, 1985.

Goodman, Bryna. "The New Woman Commits Suicide: The Press, Cultural Memory, and the New Republic." *Journal of Asian Studies* 64, no. 1 (February 2005): 67–101.

Gordon, Andrew. *The Evolution of Labor Relations in Japan: Heavy Industry, 1853–1955.* Cambridge, MA: Council on East Asian Studies, Harvard University, 1985.

Hall, John W., and Marius B. Jansen, eds. *Studies in the Institutional History of Early Modern Japan.* Princeton, NJ: Princeton University Press, 1968.

Hane, Mikiso. *Peasants, Rebels, and Outcastes.* New York: Pantheon Books, 1982.

————, trans. *Reflections on the Way to the Gallows: Rebel Women in Prewar Japan.* Berkeley and Los Angeles: University of California Press, 1988.

Hanson, Katherine. "Ibsen's Women Characters and Their Feminist Contemporaries." *Theatre History Studies* 2 (1982): 83–91.

Harootunian, H. D. "Introduction: A Sense of an Ending and the Problem of Taishō." In *Japan in Crisis: Essays on Taishō Democracy,* edited by Bernard S. Silberman and H. D. Harootunian. Princeton, NJ: Princeton University Press, 1974.

Hasegawa Kei. "'Atarashii onna' no tankyū." In *Seitō wo yomu,* edited by Shin Feminizumu Hihyō no Kai. Tokyo: Gakugei Shorin, 1998.

Hasegawa Shigure. "Bungei kyōkai no Magda." *Seitō* 2, no. 6 (June 1912): 1–5.

Hastings, Sally A. "Hatoyama Haruko: Ambitious Woman." In *The Human Tradition on Modern Japan,* edited by Anne Walthall. Wilmington, DE: Scholarly Resources, 2002.

Hayakawa Noriyo. "Feminism and Nationalism in Japan, 1868–1945." *Journal of Women's History* 7, no. 4 (Winter 1995): 108–119.

Heilmann, Ann. *New Woman Fiction: Women Writing First-Wave Feminism.* New York: St. Martin's Press, 2000.

Heilmann, Ann, and Margaret Beetham, eds. *New Woman Hybridities.* London: Routledge, 2004.

Heller, Adele, and Lois Rudnick, "Introduction." In *1915, the Cultural Moment: The New Politics, the New Woman, the New Psychology, the New Art and the New Theatre in America,* edited by Adele Heller and Lois Rudnick. New Brunswick, NJ: Rutgers University Press, 1991.

Hemmer, Bjorn. "Ibsen and the Realistic Problem Drama." In *The Cambridge Companion to Ibsen,* edited by James McFarlane. Cambridge: Cambridge University Press, 1994.

Hicks, George. *The Comfort Women: Japan's Brutal Regime of Enforced Prostitution in the Second World War.* New York: Norton, 1994.

Higuchi Hideo. "Nora to Magda." *Shin Nihon* 2, no. 6 (June 1912): 25–30.

Hirakawa Sukehiro. "Japan's Turn to the West." In *Modern Japanese Thought,* edited by Bob Tadashi Wakabayashi. Cambridge: Cambridge University Press, 1998.

Hiratsuka Raichō. "Atarashii onna." *Chūō Kōron* (January 1913): 193–194.

————. *Genshi, josei wa taiyō de atta,* vols. 2, 3, 4. Tokyo: Otsuki Shoten, 1992.

————. "Genshi, josei wa taiyō de atta." *Seitō* 1, no. 1 (September 1911): 37–52.

————. *Hiratsuka Raichō chōsakushū.* 8 vols. Tokyo: Otsuki Shoten, 1983–1984.

————. "Marumado yori: Chigasaki e, Chigasaki e." *Seitō* 2, no. 8 (August 1912): 76–108.

————. "Norasan ni." *Seitō* 2, no. 1 (January 1912): 133–141.

————. "Ren'ai to kekkon—Ellen Key chō (hon'yaku to shōkai)." *Seitō* 3, no. 1 (January 1913): 1–19.

————. *Sakusha no Jiden 8: Hiratsuka Raichō.* Tokyo: Nihon Tosho Sentaa, 1994.

————. "Yo no fujintachi ni." *Seitō* 3, no. 4 (April 1913): 156–164.

————. "Yonda 'Magda.'" *Seitō* 2, no. 6 (June 1912): 6–13.

Hopper, Helen M. *A New Woman of Japan: A Political Biography of Katō Shidzue.* Boulder, CO: Westview Press, 1996.

Hori Yasuko. "Watashi wa furui onna desu." *Seitō* 3, no. 1 (January 1913): 61–65.

Horiba Kiyoko. *Seitō no jidai: Hiratsuka Raichō to atarashii onna.* Tokyo: Iwanami Shoten, 1988.

Horie-Webber, A. "Modernisation of the Japanese Theater: The Shingeki Movement." In *Modern Japan: Aspects of History, Literature and Society,* edited by W. G. Beasley. Tokyo: Tuttle, 1976.

Hu Ying. "Naming the First New Woman." *Nan Nü* 3, no. 2 (2001): 196–231.

———. *Tales of Translation: Composing the New Woman in China, 1898–1918.* Stanford, CA: Stanford University Press, 2000.

Huang, Ray. *China: A Macro History.* Armonk, NY: Sharpe, 1997.

Ibsen, Henrik. *Four Major Plays,* vol. 1. Translated by Rolf Fjelde. New York: Signet Classic, 1965.

Ichimura Shigetoshi. "'Ningyō no ie' no butaikeiko." *Waseda Bungaku* 70 (September 1911): 79–81.

Ide Fumiko. *Hiratsuka Raichō: Kindai to shinpi.* Tokyo: Shinchōsha, 1987.

———. *Seitō: Kaisetsu, sōmokuji, sakuin.* Tokyo: Fuji Shuppan, 1983.

———. *Seitō no onnatachi.* Tokyo: Kaien Shobō, 1975.

Ikuta Chōnosuke. "Wakaki otoko no me ni eijitaru gendai josei 'Magda.'" *Jogaku Sekai* 12, no. 8 (June 1912): 48–53.

Ishihara Michiko. *Kumamoto hyōron no onna.* Tokyo/Kumamoto: Kazokushi Kenkyūkai, 1989.

———. "Nishikawa Fumiko, Kimura Komako, and Miyazaki Mitsuko chō 'Atarashiki onna no iku beki michi' kaisetsu." In *Atarashiki onna no iku beki michi.* Tokyo: Fuji Shuppan, 1986.

Ishimoto, Baroness Shidzue. *Facing Two Ways: The Story of My Life.* Stanford, CA: Stanford University Press, 1984.

Itō Noe. "Atarashiki onna no michi." *Seitō* 3, no. 1 (January 1913): 20–22.

Iwano Hōmei. "Hiratsuka joshi." *Chūō Kōron* 28, no. 9 (15 July 1913): 168–170.

Iwano Kiyo. "Ningen to shite dansei to josei wa byōdō de aru." *Seitō* 3, no. 1 (January 1913): 23–28.

———. "Shisō no dokuritsu to keizaijō no dokuritsu." *Seitō* 3, no. 3 (March 1913): 1–7.

———. "Watashi no mitaru Hiratsuka Harukoshi." *Chūō Kōron* 28, no. 9 (15 July 1913): 171–173.

Jin Feng. *The New Woman in Early Twentieth-Century Chinese Fiction.* West Lafayette, IN: Purdue University Press, 2004.

Kahn, Winston. "Hani Motoko and the Education of Japanese Women." *Historian* 59, no. 2 (Winter 1997): 381–401.

Kano, Ayako. *Acting Like a Woman in Modern Japan: Theater, Gender, and Nationalism.* New York: Palgrave, 2001.

Katō Midori. "'Atarashii onna' ni tsuite." *Seitō* 3, no. 1 (January 1913): 29–35.

———. "Ningyō no ie." *Seitō* 2, no. 1 (January 1912): 115–125.

Kerber, Linda K. "The Republican Mother: Women and Enlightenment—An American Perspective." *American Quarterly* 28 (Summer 1976): 187–205.

———. "Separate Spheres, Female Worlds, Woman's Place: The Rhetoric of Women's History." *Journal of American History* 75, no. 1 (1988): 9–39.

Kindai Josei Bunkashi Kenkyūkai, ed. *Fujin zasshi no yoake.* Tokyo: Ozora, 1989.

————, ed. *Taishōki no josei zasshi.* Tokyo: Ozora, 1996.

Kiuchi Tei. "Magda ni tsuite." *Seitō* 2, no. 6 (June 1912): 17.

Kobayashi Tomie. *Hiratsuka Raichō: Hito to shisō.* Tokyo: Shimizu Shoin, 1983.

Köhler, Angelika. "Charged with Ambiguity: The Image of the New Woman in American Cartoons." In *New Woman Hybridities,* edited by Ann Heilmann and Margaret Beetham. London: Routledge, 2004.

Koschmann, J. Victor, ed. *Authority and the Individual in Japan.* Tokyo: University of Tokyo Press, 1978.

Koyama Shizuko. "The 'Good Wife and Wise Mother' Ideology in Post–World War I Japan." *U.S.-Japan Women's Journal* 7 (1994): 31–52.

Kwon, Insook. "'The New Women's Movement' in 1920s Korea: Rethinking the Relationship between Imperialism and Women." *Gender and History* 10, no. 3 (1998): 381–405.

Ladd-Taylor, Molly. *Mother-Work: Women, Child Welfare, and the State, 1890–1930.* Urbana: University of Illinois Press, 1994.

Large, Stephen S. "The Romance of Revolution in Japanese Anarchism and Communism during the Taisho Period." *Modern Asian Studies* 11, no. 3 (1977): 441–467.

Lee, Lily Xiao Hong. "The Chinese Women's Movement before and after the Long March." In *Holding Up Half the Sky: Chinese Women Past, Present, and Future,* edited by Tao Jie, Zheng Bijun, and Shirley L. Mow. New York: Feminist Press, 2004.

Lewis, Jan. "Republican Wife: Virtue and Seduction in the Early Republic." *William and Mary Quarterly* 44 (October 1987): 689–721.

Leydecker, Karl. *Marriage and Divorce in the Plays of Hermann Sudermann.* New York: Lang, 1996.

Lippit, Noriko Mizuta. "Seitō and the Literary Roots of Japanese Feminism." *International Journal of Women's Studies* 2, no. 2 (March-April 1979): 155–163.

Loftus, Ronald P., ed. *Telling Lives: Women's Self-Writing in Modern Japan.* Honolulu: University of Hawai'i Press, 2004.

Lowy, Dina. "Love and Marriage: Ellen Key and Hiratsuka Raichō Explore Alternatives." *Women's Studies* 33, no. 4 (June 2004): 361–380.

Lu Meiyi. "The Awakening of Chinese Women and the Women's Movement in the Early Twentieth Century." In *Holding Up Half the Sky: Chinese Women Past, Present, and Future,* edited by Tao Jie, Zheng Bijun, and Shirley L. Mow. New York: Feminist Press, 2004.

Mackie, Vera. *Creating Socialist Women in Japan.* Cambridge: Cambridge University Press, 1997.

————. *Feminism in Modern Japan.* Cambridge: Cambridge University Press, 2003.

Marks, Patricia. *Bicycles, Bangs, and Bloomers: The New Woman in the Popular Press.* Lexington: University Press of Kentucky, 1990.

Matsui Sumako. "Butai no ue de ichiban komatta koto." *Seitō* 2, no. 1 (January 1912): 162–163.

Matsukawa, Yukiko, and Kaoru Tachi. "Women's Suffrage and Gender Politics in Japan." In *Suffrage and Beyond: International Feminist Perspectives,* edited by Caroline Daley and Melanie Nolan. New York: New York University Press, 1994.

Minichiello, Sharon A., ed. *Japan's Competing Modernities: Issues in Culture and Democracy, 1900–1930.* Honolulu: University of Hawai'i Press, 1998.

Mitchell, Richard H. *Thought Control in Prewar Japan.* Ithaca, NY, and London: Cornell University Press, 1976.

Miyake Setsurei. "Mondai no teikyōsha to shite no atarashii onna." *Taiyō* (June 1913): 49–51.

Miyake, Yoshiko. "Doubling Expectations: Motherhood and Women's Factory Work under State Management in Japan in the 1930s and 1940s." In *Recreating Japanese Women, 1600–1945,* edited by Gail Lee Bernstein. Berkeley and Los Angeles: University of California Press, 1991.

Miyake Yujirō. "Gendaishiki no josei." *Fujin no Tomo* 6, no. 6 (June 1912): 11–15.

Miyamoto, Ken. "Itō Noe and the Bluestockings." *Japan Interpreter* 10, no. 2 (Autumn 1975): 190–204.

Miyazaki Mitsuko. "Seitōsha wo ronzu." *Chūō Kōron* 28, no. 9 (15 July 1913): 98.

———. "Shinshinfujin." *Shin Jokai* 5, no. 4 (April 1913): 54–56.

———. "Shoshi ni nozomu." *Seitō* 3, no. 1 (January 1913): 57–60.

Mizuno Yōshū. "Gainen wo haikei to shita guzō." *Shinchō* 17, no. 3 (September 1912): 30–34.

Molony, Barbara. "Activism among Women in the Taishō Cotton Textile Industry." In *Recreating Japanese Women, 1600–1945,* edited by Gail Lee Bernstein. Berkeley and Los Angeles: University of California Press, 1991.

———. "Citizenship and Suffrage in Interwar Japan." In *Women's Suffrage in Asia: Gender, Nationalism and Democracy,* edited by Louise Edwards and Mina Roces. London and New York: RoutledgeCurzon, 2004.

———. "Equality versus Difference: The Japanese Debate over 'Motherhood Protection,' 1915–50." In *Japanese Women Working,* edited by Janet Hunter. London: Routledge, 1993.

———. "Ichikawa Fusae and Japan's Pre-war Women's Suffrage Movement." In *Japanese Women: Emerging from Subservience, 1868–1945,* edited by Hiroko Tomida and Gordon Daniels. Kent. OH: Global Oriental, 2005.

———. "The Quest for Women's Rights in Turn-of-the-Century Japan." In *Gendering Modern Japanese History,* edited by Barbara Molony and Kathleen Uno. Cambridge, MA: Harvard University Asia Center, 2005.

———. "Women and the State in Modern Japan: Feminist Discourses in the Meiji and Taisho Eras." In *Japan: State and People in the Twentieth Century,* edited by Janet Hunter. London: Suntory and Toyota International Centres for Economics and Related Disciplines, 1999.

Molony, Barbara, and Kathleen Uno, eds. *Gendering Modern Japanese History.* Cambridge, MA: Harvard University Asia Center, 2005.

Mulhern, Chieko Irie. "Hani Motoko: The Journalist-Educator." In *Heroic with Grace: Legendary Women of Japan.* Armonk, NY: Sharpe, 1991.

Muta Kazue. "The New Woman in Japan: Radicalism and Ambivalence towards Love and Sex." In *New Woman Hybridities: Femininity, Feminism, and International Consumer Culture, 1880–1930,* edited by Ann Heilmann and Margaret Beetham. London and New York: Routledge, 2004.

Myers, Sylvia Harcstark. *The Bluestocking Circle: Women, Friendship, and the Life of the Mind in Eighteenth-Century England.* Oxford: Oxford University Press, 1990.

Naganuma Chie. "Magda ni tsuite." *Seitō* 2, no. 6 (June 1912): 14.

Nagy, Margit Maria. "How Shall We Live?: Social Change, the Family Institution and Feminism in Prewar Japan." PhD diss., University of Washington, 1981.

Najita, Tetsuo. "Presidential Address: Reflections on Modernity and Modernization." *Journal of Asian Studies* 52, no. 4 (1993): 845–853.

Nakamura, Toshiko. "Ibsen in Japan: Tsubouchi Shōyō and His Lecture on New Women." *Edda* 5 (1982): 261–272.

Nishikawa Fumiko. "Fujin mondai no chūshinten." *Shinshinfujin* 3 (July 1913).

———. "Shinshinfujinkai to ryōsai kenbo." *Jogaku Sekai* 13, no. 6 (May 1913): 33–38.

Nishikawa Fumiko, Miyazaki Mitsuko, and Kimura Komako. "Shinshinfujinkai no mokuteki." In *Atarashiki onna no yukubeki michi.* Tokyo: Fuji Shuppan, 1986.

Nishimura Yōkichi. "Watashi no shitte iru no Hiratsukasan." *Chūō Kōron* 28, no. 9 (15 July 1913): 156–158.

Nishizaki (Ikuta) Hanayo. "Atarashii onna no kaisetsu." *Seitō* 3, no. 1 (January 1913): 36–45.

Niwa Akiko. "The Formation of the Myth of Motherhood in Japan." *U.S.-Japan Women's Journal* 4 (1993): 70–82.

Nolte, Sharon H. *Liberalism in Modern Japan: Ishibashi Tanzan and His Teachers, 1905–1960.* Berkeley and Los Angeles: University of California Press, 1987.

———. "Women's Rights and Society's Needs: Japan's 1931 Suffrage Bill." *Comparative Studies in Society and History* (1986): 690–714.

Nolte, Sharon H., and Sally Ann Hastings. "The Meiji State's Policy toward Women, 1890–1910." In *Recreating Japanese Women, 1600–1945,* edited by Gail Lee Bernstein. Berkeley and Los Angeles: University of California Press, 1991.

Okano Yukie. *Shinshinfujin: Kaisetsu, sōmokuji, sakuin.* Tokyo: Fuji Shuppan, 1994.

Orii, Miyako, and Hiroko Tomida. "*Shin Fujin Kyōkai* (the Association for New Women) and the Women Who Aimed to Change Society." In *Japanese Women: Emerging from Subservience, 1868–1945,* edited by Hiroko Tomida and Gordon Daniels. Kent, OH: Global Oriental, 2005.

Otake Kōkichi. "'Anesama' to 'uchiwa e' no tenrankai." *Seitō* 2, no. 7 (July 1912): 107–109.

———. "Aru yoru to aru asa." *Seitō* 2, no. 6 (June 1912): 114–116.

———. "Jijoden wo yonde Hiratsukasan ni itaru." *Chūō Kōron* 28, no. 9 (15 July 1913): 174–181.

———. "Magda ni tsuite." *Seitō* 2, no. 6 (June 1912): 14–16.

Otsubo, Sumiko. "Engendering Eugenics: Feminists and Marriage Restriction Legislation in the 1920s." In *Gendering Modern Japanese History,* edited by Barbara Molony and Kathleen Uno. Cambridge, MA: Harvard University Asia Center, 2005.

Pflugfelder, Gregory M. *Cartographies of Desire: Male-Male Sexuality in Japanese Discourse, 1600–1950.* Berkeley and Los Angeles: University of California Press, 1999.

———. "'S' is for Sister: Schoolgirl Intimacy and 'Same-Sex Love' in Early Twentieth-Century Japan." In *Gendering Modern Japanese History,* edited by Barbara Molony and Kathleen Uno. Cambridge, MA: Harvard University Asia Center, 2005.

Powell, Brian. "Matsui Sumako: Actress and Woman." In *Modern Japan: Aspects of History, Literature and Society,* edited by W. G. Beasley. Tokyo: Tuttle, 1976.

Pyle, Kenneth B. "Meiji Conservatism." In *Modern Japanese Thought,* edited by Bob Tadashi Wakabayashi. Cambridge: Cambridge University Press, 1998.

―――. *The New Generation in Meiji Japan: Problems of Cultural Identity, 1885–1895.* Stanford, CA: Stanford University Press, 1969.

Raddeker, Helene Bowen. *Treacherous Women of Imperial Japan: Patriarchal Fictions, Patricidal Fantasies.* New York: Routledge, 1997.

Ramusack, Barbara N., and Sharon Sievers. *Women in Asia: Restoring Women to History.* Bloomington: Indiana University Press, 1999.

Reich, Pauline C., and Fukuda Atsuko. "Japan's Literary Feminist: The Seitō Group." *Signs* 2, no. 1 (Autumn 1976): 280–291.

Richardson, Angelique, and Chris Willis, eds. *The New Woman in Fiction and in Fact.* New York: Palgrave, 2001.

Robertson, Jennifer. "Gender-Bending in Paradise: Doing 'Female' and 'Male' in Japan." *Genders* 5 (Summer 1989): 50–69.

Rodd, Laurel Rasplica. "Yosano Akiko and the Taishō Debate over the 'New Woman.'" In *Recreating Japanese Women, 1600–1945,* edited by Gail Lee Bernstein. Berkeley and Los Angeles: University of California Press, 1991.

Roden, Donald. "Baseball and the Quest for National Dignity in Meiji Japan." *American Historical Review* 85, no. 3 (June 1980): 511–534.

―――. *Schooldays in Imperial Japan: A Study in the Culture of a Student Elite.* Berkeley and Los Angeles: University of California Press, 1980.

―――. "Taishō Culture and the Problem of Gender Ambivalence." In *Culture and Identity: Japanese Intellectuals during the Interwar Years,* edited by J. Thomas Rimer. Princeton, NJ: Princeton University Press, 1990.

Rose, Barbara. *Tsuda Umeko and Women's Education in Japan.* New Haven, CT: Yale University Press, 1992.

Rubin, Jay. *Injurious to Public Morals: Writers and the Meiji State.* Seattle: University of Washington Press, 1984.

Rudnick, Lois. "The New Woman." In *1915, the Cultural Moment: The New Politics, the New Woman, the New Psychology, the New Art and the New Theatre in America,* edited by Adele Heller and Lois Rudnick. New Brunswick, NJ: Rutgers University Press, 1991.

Russell, Mona L. *Creating the New Egyptian Woman: Consumerism, Education, and National Identity, 1863–1922.* New York: Palgrave Macmillan, 2004.

Saari, Sandra. "Female Become Human: Nora Transformed." In *Contemporary Approaches to Ibsen,* vol. 6, edited by Bjorn Hemmer and Vidgis Ystad. Oslo: Norwegian University Press, 1988.

Salome, Lou. *Ibsen's Heroines.* Edited by Siegfried Mandel. Redding Ridge, CT: Black Swan Books, 1985.

Sand, Jordan. "At Home in the Meiji Period: Inventing Japanese Domesticity." In *Mirror of Modernity: Invented Traditions of Modern Japan,* edited by Stephen Vlastos. Berkeley and Los Angeles: University of California Press, 1999.

Sato, Barbara Hamill. "The Moga Sensation: Perceptions of the Modan Gāru in Japanese Intellectual Circles during the 1920s." *Gender and History* 5, no. 3 (1993): 361–381.

———. *The New Japanese Woman: Modernity, Media, and Women in Interwar Japan.* Durham, NC: Duke University Press, 2003.

Satō Haruo. "Woman, All Too Woman." *Chūō Kōron* 28, no. 9 (15 July 1913): 150–156.

Satō Kōroku. "Atarashiki onna sunawachi kusaki onna." *Shinchō* 17, no. 3 (September 1912): 21–25.

Satō Kōroku, Miyake Setsurei, Hasegawa Shigure, Mori Ritsuko. "'Ningyō no ie' no Nora ni funshita Matsui Sumako." *Shinchō* 16, no. 1 (January 1912): 38–42.

Sawada Bushō. "Kakuseiseru fujin to Ibsen no Nora." *Fujin Kurabu* 4 (October 1911): 2–10.

Scott, Joan Wallach. "Gender: A Useful Category of Historical Analysis." In *Gender and the Politics of History.* New York: Columbia University Press, 1988.

Setouchi Harumi. *Beauty in Disarray.* Translated by Sanford Goldstein and Kazuji Ninomiya. Rutland, VT: Tuttle, 1993.

Shimada Akiko. *Nihon no feminizumu: Genryū to shite no Akiko, Raichō, Kikue, Kanoko.* Tokyo: Hokuju Shuppan, 1996.

Shimamura Hōgetsu. "Sudermann no 'kokyō' ni kakaretaru shisōmondai." *Shin Nihon* 2, no. 5 (May 1912): 120–125.

Shin Feminizumu Hihyō no Kai. *Seitō wo yomu.* Tokyo: Gakugei Shorin, 1998.

Shin, Jiweon. "Social Construction of Idealized Images of Women in Colonial Korea: The 'New Woman' versus 'Motherhood.'" In *Decolonization: Perspectives from Now and Then,* edited by Prasenjit Duara. London and New York: Routledge, 2004.

Shirai, T. "Iwayuru atarashiki onna." *Meiji no Joshi* 9, no. 6 (June 1912): 10–14.

Showalter, Elaine. *Sexual Anarchy: Gender and Culture at the Fin de Siècle.* New York: Penguin Books, 1990.

Sievers, Sharon L. "Feminist Criticism in Japanese Politics in the 1880s: The Experience of Kishida Toshiko." *Signs* 6, no. 4 (Summer 1981): 602–616.

———. *Flowers in Salt: The Beginnings of Feminist Consciousness in Modern Japan.* Stanford, CA: Stanford University Press, 1983.

Silverberg, Miriam. "The Cafe Waitress Serving Modern Japan." In *Mirror of Modernity: Invented Traditions of Modern Japan,* edited by Stephen Vlastos. Berkeley and Los Angeles: University of California Press, 1999.

———. "Constructing a New Cultural History of Prewar Japan." In *Japan in the World,* edited by Masao Miyoshi and H. D. Harootunian. Durham, NC: Duke University Press, 1993.

———. "The Modern Girl as Militant." In *Recreating Japanese Women, 1600–1945,* edited by Gail Lee Bernstein. Berkeley and Los Angeles: University of California Press, 1991.

Sklar, Kathryn Kish. "Hull House in the 1890s: A Community of Women Reformers." *Signs* 10, no. 4 (1985): 658–677.

Smith, Bonnie G. "The New Woman." In *Changing Lives: Women in European History since 1700.* Lexington, MA: Heath, 1989.

Smith-Rosenberg, Carroll. "The Female World of Love and Ritual: Relations between Women in Nineteenth-Century America." *Signs* 1 (1975): 1–30.

———. "The New Woman as Androgyne: Social Disorder and Gender Crisis, 1870–1936." In *Disorderly Conduct: Visions of Gender in Victorian America.* New York: Knopf, 1985.

Sochen, June. *The New Woman: Feminism in Greenwich Village, 1910–1920.* New York: Quadrangle Books, 1972.

Søland, Birgitte. *Becoming Modern: Young Women and the Reconstruction of Womanhood in the 1920s.* Princeton, NJ: Princeton University Press, 2000.

Sōma Gyokaze. "'Kokyō' no Magda." *Shukujo Gahō* 1, no. 3 (June 1912): 22–27.

Steinschneider, Janice C. *An Improved Woman: The Wisconsin Federation of Women's Clubs, 1895–1920.* Brooklyn: Carlson, 1994.

Stevens, Sarah E. "Figuring Modernity: The New Woman and the Modern Girl in Republican China." *NWSA Journal* 15, no. 3 (Fall 2003): 82–103.

Sudermann, Hermann. *Magda: A Play in Four Acts.* Translated by Charles Edward Amory Winslow. Amsterdam, NY: Fredonia Books, 2003. Reprinted from the 1899 edition.

Suzuki, Daisetz T. *Zen and Japanese Culture.* Princeton, NJ: Princeton University Press, 1959.

Suzuki Yūko, ed. *Nihon josei undō shiryō shūsei. Tokyo: Fuji Shuppan, 1993*–1998.

Takai Yō, and Orii Miyako. *Azami no hana.* Tokyo: Domesu Shuppan, 1985.

Tamura Toshiko. "Hiratsukasan." *Chūō Kōron* 28, no. 9 (15 July 1913): 158–159.

Tanaka, Stefan. *Japan's Orient: Rendering Pasts into History.* Berkeley and Los Angeles: University of California Press, 1993.

Tanaka, Yukiko. *Women Writers of Meiji and Taishō Japan.* Jefferson, NC: McFarland, 2000.

Templeton, Joan. "The *Doll House* Backlash: Criticism, Feminism, and Ibsen." *PMLA* 104 (1989): 28–40.

Tipton, Elise K., and John Clark, eds. *Being Modern in Japan: Culture and Society from the 1910s to the 1930s.* Honolulu: University of Hawai'i Press, 2000.

Tokuza, Akiko. *The Rise of the Feminist Movement in Japan.* Tokyo: Keio University Press, 1999.

Tomida, Hiroko. *Hiratsuka Raichō and Early Japanese Feminism.* Leiden: Brill, 2004.

———. "Hiratsuka Raichō, the Seitō Society, and the Emergence of the New Woman in Japan." In *Japanese Women: Emerging from Subservience, 1868–1945,* edited by Hiroko Tomida and Gordon Daniels. Kent, OH: Global Oriental, 2005.

Trimberger, Ellen Kay. "The New Woman and the New Sexuality." In *1915, the Cultural Moment: The New Politics, the New Woman, the New Psychology, the New Art and the New Theatre in America,* edited by Adele Heller and Lois Rudnick. New Brunswick, NJ: Rutgers University Press, 1991.

Tsurumi, Patricia. *Factory Girls: Women in the Thread Mills of Meiji Japan.* Princeton, NJ: Princeton University Press, 1990.

Uchida Roan. "Iwayuru atarashiki onna no kaishaku." *Shinchō* 17, no. 3 (September 1912): 18–20.

Ueda Kimi. "Ningyō no ie wo yomu." *Seitō* 2, no. 1 (January 1912): 126–132.

Ueno Chizuko. "Modern Patriarchy and the Formation of the Japanese Nation State." In *Multicultural Japan: Palaeolithic to Postmodern,* edited by Donald Denoon and Gavan McCormack. New York: Cambridge University Press, 1996.

Ueno, Yō. "Ningyō no ie yori josei mondai e." *Seitō* 2, no. 1 (January 1912): 62–114.

Ukita Kazutami. "Ningyō no ie to fujin mondai." *Fujin no Tomo* 5 (November 1911): 18–26.

Uno, Kathleen S. "The Death of 'Good Wife, Wise Mother'?" In *Postwar Japan as History,* edited by Andrew Gordon. Berkeley: University of California Press, 1993.

———. *The Origins of 'Good Wife, Wise Mother' in Modern Japan.* Occasional Paper 15. Marburg, Germany: Philipps-Universität Marburg, 1994.

———. "Womanhood, War, and Empire: Transmutations of 'Good Wife, Wise Mother' before 1931." In *Gendering Modern Japanese History,* edited by Barbara Molony and Kathleen Uno. Cambridge, MA, and London: Harvard University Asia Center, 2005.

Ushioda, Sharlie C. "Fukuda Hideko and the Woman's World of Meiji Japan." In *Japan in Transition: Thought and Action in the Meiji Era, 1868–1912,* edited by Hilary Conroy, Sandra T. W. Davis, and Wayne Patterson. Rutherford, NJ: Fairleigh Dickinson University Press, 1984.

Vavich, Dee Ann. "The Japanese Women's Movement: Ichikawa Fusae, a Pioneer in Woman's Suffrage." In *Women and Women's Issues in Post World War II Japan,* edited by Edward R. Beauchamp. New York: Garland, 1998.

Vicinus, Martha. *Independent Women: Work and Community for Single Women, 1850–1920.* Chicago: University of Chicago Press, 1985.

Vlastos, Stephen, ed. *Mirror of Modernity: Invented Traditions of Modern Japan.* Berkeley and Los Angeles: University of California Press, 1999.

Wakakuwa Midori. "The Gender System of the Imperial State." *U.S.-Japan Women's Journal* 20–21 (2001): 17–82.

Wakita Haruko, Hayashi Reiko, and Nagahara Kazuko, eds. *Nihon joseishi.* Tokyo: Yoshikawa Kōbunkan, 1987.

Walker, Janet A. *The Japanese Novel of the Meiji Period and the Ideal of Individualism.* Princeton, NJ: Princeton University Press, 1979.

Wang Zheng. *Women in the Chinese Enlightenment: Oral and Textual Histories.* Berkeley: University of California Press, 1999.

Wells, Kenneth M. "Expanding Their Realm: Women and Public Agency in Colonial Korea." In *Women's Suffrage in Asia: Gender, Nationalism and Democracy,* edited by Louise Edwards and Mina Roces. London and New York: Routledge-Curzon, 2004.

———. "The Price of Legitimacy: Women and the Kŭnuhoe Movement, 1927–1931." In *Colonial Modernity in Korea,* edited by Gi-Wook Shin and Michael Robinson. Cambridge, MA: Harvard University Asia Center, 1999.

Wöhr, Ulrike. "Between Revolution and Reaction: The Japanese Women's Movement in the Taishō Era." In *War, Revolution and Japan,* edited by Ian Neary. Sandgate, England: Japan Library, 1993.

———. "Mo hitotsu no 'Seitō.'" In *Onna to otoko no jikū: Nihon joseishi saikō,* vol. 5, edited by Okuda Akiko (Tokyo: Fujiwara Shoten, 1995).

Woloch, Nancy. "The Rise of the New Woman, 1860–1920." In *Women and the American Experience,* 2d ed. New York: McGraw-Hill, 1994.

Yamaji Aizan. "Shin ni atarashiki onna nashi." *Shinchō* 17, no. 3 (September 1912): 35–37.

Yasumochi Yoshi. "Ningyō no ie ni tsuite." *Seitō* 2, no. 1 (January 1912): 143–154.

Yasutake, Rumi. *Transnational Women's Activism: The United States, Japan, and Japanese Immigrant Communities in California, 1859–1920.* New York: New York University Press, 2004.

Yoneda Sayoko. *Hiratsuka Raichō: Kindai nihon no demokurashii to jendaa.* Tokyo: Yoshikawa Kōbunkan, 2002.

Yoneda Sayoko and Ikeda Emiko, eds. *"Seitō" wo manabu hito no tame ni.* Kyoto: Sekai Shisōsha, 1999.

Yosano Akiko. "Jibun wa mayotte imasu." *Chūō Kōron* 28, no. 9 (15 July 1913): 162–168.

———. "Sozorogoto." *Seitō* 1, no. 1 (September 1911): 1–9.

Yoshimi Yoshiaki. *Comfort Women: Sexual Slavery in the Japanese Military during World War II.* Translated by Suzanne O'Brien. New York: Columbia University Press, 2000.

INDEX

Amin, Qasim, 120–121
Araki Ikuko, 17, 62–64
Asai Shōzō, 29
atarashii onna. See New Woman
Ayako Kano, 36

Baba Kōchō, 75–77, 97–98, 103
Bluestocking. *See Seitō*

censorship, 63–64. *See also Magda:*
  banning and revision
Chūō Kōron (magazine), 81, 94–95
Civil Code of 1898, 4, 56, 58, 90
cult of domesticity, 4

Doi Shunsho, 27, 44
A Doll House (Ibsen), 18, 21–22, 40;
  controversy, 28–31, 37; implications
  of, 28; Nora as a model, 74, 109, 110,
  112; preparation for performance, 26,
  27; reactions to, 28–38; synopsis of,
  23–24

education, 5, 77; female educators, 5,
  7–8; for women, 4, 58, 95, 121, 123;
  women's schools, 7, 9, 113
Enlightenment movement, 6
family system, 4, 6–7, 14, 55, 94; marriage, 36, 90–92, 109, 124
feminism: consciousness of, 12, 76,
  84, 89, 127; and economic independence, 76, 89–93, 104, 112; relation
  to socialism, 8, 87, 93, 101, 110–111,

128; scholarship on, 7, 12, 94–95; in
  writing, 7, 65, 94–95
five-colored liquor incident. *See* scandals
Freedom and People's Rights move-
  ment, 3, 7, 51, 89, 93
Fujin Gahō (magazine), 94
Fujin Kurabu (magazine), 30–31
Fujin no Tomo (magazine), 30–31, 94
Fukuda Hideko, 7, 8, 17, 89, 93, 128.
  See also Freedom and People's Rights
  movement

gender roles: construction of, 13, 19,
  82–83; discussion of, 3, 9, 54–55,
  65–66, 85–86, 112; examples of, 4,
  46, 71–72, 97–98. *See also* "good
  wife, wise mother"; modernity; New
  Woman
"good wife, wise mother": compared
  with New Woman, 16, 36, 39, 109;
  definition of, 2, 4–5, 14, 144n20; as
  government policy, 29, 58; and True
  New Woman, 112

Hasegawa Shigure, 44, 52, 53
Hatoyama Haruko, 5, 7
Hiratsuka Raichō, 17, 55, 127–128;
  character of, 95–98; descriptions of,
  65–66, 72, 77; founding Seitōsha,
  9–11; and Otake Kōkichi, 60–62, 69;
  reactions to lecture meetings, 104,
  105, 107; redefinition of New Woman,
  79, 81–84; response to *A Doll House,*

ryōsai kenbo. *See* "good wife, wise
mother"

same-sex love, 68–71
Satō Haruo, 96–97
Satō Kōroku, 73–75
Sawada Bushō, 28
scandals: five-colored liquor incident,
60–61, 102, 124, 143n15; Shiobara
incident, 66–68; "Strange Love"
articles, 65–72; Yoshiwara incident,
61–62, 102, 124
Seitō (magazine): and censorship,
63–64; creation of, 2, 10–13; and
Hiratsuka Raichō, 31–33, 52–54,
79, 81; *Magda* supplement, 52–54;
New Woman supplements, 84–93;
Nora supplement, 31–39; and Otake
Kōkichi, 44, 61, 69–70
Seitōsha: compared with Shinshinfujinkai, 100–102, 106–109, 113–116;
creation of, 2, 10–13; lecture meeting,
102–104; legacy, 127; and scandals, 57,
59–64. *See also* New Woman; *Seitō*
sexuality: and New Women, 57–58,
61–64; and prostitution, 58, 114. *See
also* same-sex love
Shimamura Hōgetsu, 26–27, 42, 47,
49, 94
Shimoda Utako, 5, 7
Shiobara incident. *See* scandals
shin fujin. See New Woman
Shinshinfujin (magazine), 101, 111,
114–115
Shinshinfujinkai, 19, 81; compared
with Seitōsha, 100–102, 106–109,
113–116; lecture meeting, 105–106
socialism. *See under* feminism
Social Policy Association, 72–73
"Strange Love" articles. *See* scandals
Sudermann, Hermann, 17, 21, 40

"Taishō Democracy," 5, 133n17
Taiyō (magazine), 94, 109
Tamura Toshiko, 17, 97, 101
Tōgi Tetsuteki, 27, 44
Tokyo Women's Reform Society, 7
True New Woman's Association. *See*
Shinshinfujinkai
True New Women, 100–102, 104–109,
111–115, 128. *See also* New Woman
Tsubouchi Shōyō, 9, 21, 24, 26. *See also*
A Doll House
Tsuda Umeko, 8

Uchida Roan, 47, 75
Ueda Kimi, 34–35
Ueno Yō, 36
Ukita Kazutami, 29–30, 48, 138n28

Waseda Bungaku (journal), 26
Woman Problem: debate over, 1–2,
93–95, 102, 127; in Europe, 26–27,
29; and Hiratsuka Raichō, 84; in
Japan, 29–30, 50, 105, 109, 114; and
Seitō, 80, 87. *See also* gender roles;
Seitōsha; Shinshinfujinkai
women's magazines: in China, 123;
in Egypt, 121; in Japan (*see Fujin
Kurabu, Fujin no Tomo, Jogaku
Zasshi, Seitō, Shinshinfujin*); in
Korea, 123
women's suffrage, 125, 128

Yamaji Aizan, 76
Yasumochi Yoshiko, 17, 35–36, 38, 63,
103–104
Yosano Akiko, 1, 8, 17, 96–97, 101,
112, 127
Yoshiwara incident. *See* scandals

Zen Buddhism, and Hiratsuka Raichō,
9–10, 33, 66, 67, 82, 83, 96, 148n19